Loving Vampires

Loving Vampires

Our Undead Obsession

Tom Pollard

DISCARD

McFarland & Company, Inc., Publishers
Jefferson, North Carolina

LIBRARY OF CONGRESS CATALOGUING-IN-PUBLICATION DATA

Names: Pollard, Tom.
Title: Loving vampires : our undead obsession / Tom Pollard.
Description: Jefferson, North Carolina : McFarland & Company, Inc.,
Publishers, 2016. | Includes bibliographical references and index.
Identifiers: LCCN 2016006304 | ISBN 9780786497782
(softcover : acid free paper) ∞
Subjects: LCSH: Vampires. | Vampires in popular culture.
Classification: LCC GR830.V3 P66 2016 | DDC 398.21—dc23
LC record available at http://lccn.loc.gov/2016006304

BRITISH LIBRARY CATALOGUING DATA ARE AVAILABLE

ISBN (print) 978-0-7864-9778-2
ISBN (ebook) 978-1-4766-2430-3

Front cover image © 2016 Ivan Bliznetsov/iStock

Printed in the United States of America

McFarland & Company, Inc., Publishers
Box 611, Jefferson, North Carolina 28640
www.mcfarlandpub.com

To Sue Dickey
for her love and encouragement
throughout this book's creation

Table of Contents

Preface

The inspiration for this study came during my assessment of the impact of September 11, 2001, on pop culture. Interest in vampire characters spiked after 9/11, raising questions about the reasons for such a dramatic increase. Vampires represent an amazing symbolic diversity, serving as cultural metaphors for a variety of issues. *Loving Vampires* examines the socio/political roles that vampires perform in popular culture.

People often debate the relative power and influence of popular culture on the world. In his 1821 essay "A Defense of Poetry," the English poet Percy Bysshe Shelley famously proclaimed that "poets are the unacknowledged legislators of the world."[1] In Shelley's era many poets, including Shelley himself, were read widely and functioned as part of the popular culture. To what degree did they "legislate" and arbitrate popular culture? That question continues to stimulate debate, but many scholars agree with author and sociology professor Tim Delaney that pop culture both reflects and influences mass media and society.[2]

This book explores pop culture's vampires as sexual seducers, savage monsters, noble protectors, and drainers of energy. Seductive "rake" vampires first appeared during the Romantic Movement that began in Europe in the late eighteenth century, and they continue to captivate readers and audiences today. Sexy female vampires from the same time period exemplified assertiveness, power, and seduction—traits still valued today. Other vampires developed as gruesome, savage, monstrous demons plotting humanity's demise. These "monster" vampires symbolize the dark side of human behavior, and they often appear alongside special "slayer" characters gifted in the arts of vampire eradication. Finally, "psychic vampires" prey on various forms of human energy, especially sexuality.

The following chapters trace these themes from their introduction into pop culture up to the present, noting significant transformations along the way. Various sources of vampire lore are explored, from ancient mythology and the pioneering literary works of the eighteenth and nineteenth centuries up to the most recent manifestations in popular culture. The symbolic role of vampires in pop culture is discussed as seductive, sexual predators; savage, monstrous aggressors; canny, courageous vampire slayers; negative, exhausting human characters; and even unplugged electrical appliances. The diversity of these roles provides a case study of the complexity of pop culture and its ability to communicate humanity's most sensitive, taboo issues and personalities.

This study situates current vampires within both pop and elite cultural history, theorizing about the roles cultural metaphors play in language, history, psychology, economics, politics, and sociology. Their tremendous versatility and malleability make vampires excellent subjects for such a study.

The first chapter defines vampires, examines their role in history, and discusses horror and vampire iconography. Cultural metaphors are examined, and vampires are organized into metaphorical categories. Finally, the theoretical foundation of this book is articulated.

Chapter Two examines vampires as metaphors for sexuality. Vampires are the most sexual of paranormal characters, far more so than werewolves, zombies, ghosts, witches, and demons—although each of these serves as an occasional sexual metaphor. Zombies—close rivals of vampires for popularity—usually appear too dazed, slow-witted, and single-minded to evoke many sexual fantasies, despite recent attempts to make them more attractive. Their appearance and behavior render them asexual and unappealing, something that used to be true of vampires.

Gender is as an important human dimension symbolized by vampirism, and Chapter Three focuses on vampires as gender metaphors. Gay, lesbian, bisexual, transgender, and other gender manifestations often are symbolized through vampirism. Victorian England witnessed the first transgender vampire characters, descending from real-life Romantic Era rakes such as Lord Byron (1788–1824) to fictional vampire demons created by Samuel Taylor Coleridge, Sheridan Le Fanu, Bram Stoker, and Rudyard Kipling. These and other writers invented vampire characters whose gender diversity paved the way for today's fascination with gender.

Chapter Four focuses on vampires as symbols for inhumane, savage, and violent behavior. In life as in pop culture, violence and sex become closely related. Some vampire narratives focus on the aggressive, murderously cruel individuals who never seem to disappear from the human stage. They never lack in courage and strength, and they pose incredible challenges to their human and paranormal victims. In addition to the negative aspects of these violent characters, this chapter also examines the more positive warrior qualities of savage, "Nosferatu" vampires. The nexus between sexuality and aggression, love and violence is also examined.

Chapter Five looks at "psi" or energy vampires. Inhabiting a hidden universe of invisible energy sources, these characters exist exclusively to drain humans of their sexuality, life force, breath, auras, and souls. These insidious predators warrant a chapter of their own to explore the multiple meanings that have come to be associated with "energy vampires." It turns out that most people may have encountered one or more of these nefarious creatures, usually without realizing it. According to this interpretation, behavior that many attribute to psychological or sociological conditions—including borderline personality disorder (BPD), paranoia, and schizophrenia—may be the work of psychic or energy vampires. This chapter also discusses nonhuman energy "vampires" such as inefficient automobiles and electrical appliances that are left plugged in. Every wasted energy watt, it turns out, may be attributed to psi or energy vampires.

When studying vampires, it helps to understand their opposites: the slayers. Chapter Six explores the complex personalities and attributes of the individuals who possess the skills, knowledge, and characteristics to defeat these pernicious foes. Vampire slayers are some of the most fascinating and unique characters in pop culture. They inhabit a point somewhere between vampires and humans, symbolizing the solutions, hopes, and dreams of those suffering from a variety of real or imagined evils.

Vampire/slayer narratives contain metaphoric codes for taboo behavior, and the final chapter assesses the broad ramifications of vampires as cultural metaphors and "master narratives" symbolizing issues too sensitive for direct depiction. Vampires often function as stand-ins for real issues plaguing humanity—such as immigration, violence, aggression, sexual predation, financial predation, and political predation. According to medieval literature professor Morton Bloomfield, vampire narratives may symbolize corporate greed, torturous interrogation, pedophilia, governmental arrogance, obesity, penis envy, or other modern-day manifestations of the original "seven deadly sins."[3]

I gratefully acknowledge the tireless efforts of editor Phyllis Elving in helping me prepare the manuscript. I would also like to acknowledge the assistance given by National University, including a Presidential Scholars Award that provided release time to complete this project. For their support, I also appreciate the insightful comments from Dr. Michael Parenti, Dr. Carl Boggs, Nan Sandusky, and Felicity Boute-Wilson.

• One •

Vampires

Vampires—we love them, and we love to hate them. They both attract and repulse, starring as pop culture's most diverse and versatile characters. At times vampires assist and protect humanity, while at other times they prey upon humans to satisfy their biological needs. When they transform their human victims into new vampires, and the new vampires then transform other humans into still newer vampires, they threaten to extinguish all human life. At this point, "vampire slayers" often arise to save humanity from these seductive, deadly characters.

On the positive side, vampires can bequeath humans with immortality, while arming them with superpowers such as shapeshifting, hypnosis, mind-reading, x-ray vision, invisibility, super strength, and the ability to fly. Vampires often seem to be irresistibly attractive, causing humans to fall in love, have sex with them, and produce vampire/human hybrid offspring. Depending on the socio/historical context, vampires may represent the entire range of human activity. Their tremendous power as metaphors lies in their ability to evoke society's most sensitive, compelling issues and taboos.

Vampires appear in novels, films, television shows, computer games, music, art, theater, comic books, and videos, entertaining millions worldwide. Their versatility and dramatic persona account for their perennial popularity:

Comic books: *The Tomb of Dracula* (1972–1979), *Blade* (1973–1974), *Buffy the Vampire Slayer* (1998–2004), *Anita Blake: Vampire Hunter* (2006–2012), *Nosferatu* (2010), *American Vampire: The Long Road to Hell* (2013), *Li'l Vampi* (2014), *Vampire Diaries* (2014)

Video games: *Vampires: The Masquerade* (2004), *Darkwatch* (2005), *Night of the Raving Dead* (2008), *Countdown Vampires: Part 1* (2009), *Infamous: Festival of Blood* (2011), *Skyrim* (2011), *The Adventures of Shuggy* (2012), *Vampire Season* (2012), *BloodLust Vampire Shadow Hunter* (2013), *Dark* (2013)

Television: *Buffy the Vampire Slayer* (1997–2003), *True Blood* (2008–present), *The Vampire Diaries* (2009–present), *Morganville Vampires* miniseries (2014)

Movies: *Buffy the Vampire Slayer* (1992), *Twilight* series (2008–2012), *Byzantium* (2012), *Innocence* (2013), *Dracula Untold* (2014), *Vampire Academy* (2014)

Novels: *The Vampire Diaries* series (1991–present), *Twilight* series (2008–2012), *The Passage* (2010), *House of Night* series (2011–2013), *The Twelve* (2012)

Vampires form a prominent subset of paranormal characters—functioning "beyond the range of normal experience or scientific explanation," according to a dictionary definition of "paranormal."[1] Paranormals include angels, extraterrestrials, demons, devils, ghosts, hybrids, immortals, psychics, shapeshifters, superheroes, mermaids, time travelers, warlocks, werewolves, witches, and zombies. These characters evoke Romanticism and the allure of magic in an era of science, appealing to artistic young bohemians who find the world of conscious, factual reality tedious and uninspiring. Vampires exist in an imaginative world of supernatural forces and powerful, godlike beings. They invoke religious beliefs along with Christian rituals and prejudices. As creatures of Romanticism, they symbolize the primacy of nature over science, of emotions over reason. Adding to their appeal, they exude sexuality and violence—the most powerful stimuli in popular culture.

Immortal Dracula–like characters often refuse to die in readers' and viewers' memories because they resonate deep inside human imagination, where eternal life, super strength, the ability to fly, powers of hypnosis, and other extraordinary abilities thrive. Nineteenth-century German philosopher Friedrich Nietzsche extolled "overman" or "Ubermensch," an individual surpassing him or herself to overcome past experiences and achieve his or her highest potential. Doing so lets one transcend the constant timeline of past-present-future and live in eternity—in the eternal "now." In *Thus Spake Zarathustra* (1885), Nietzsche's hero asks:

> Where is the lightning to lick you with its tongue? Where is the frenzy with which you should be inoculated?
> Behold, I teach you the overman: he is that lightning, he is that frenzy.[2]

Armed with superpowers and causing tumultuous change, vampires embody Nietzsche's "overman," while ordinary humans—through their blood, energy, and souls—sustain them. Overman, like vampires, wreaks havoc on common humanity while inspiring great acts of courage and ingenuity in human victims.

To some, vampires represent a higher evolutionary stage of the humanity from which they evolved. Even real vampire bats demonstrate an advanced stage of development! Science writer Ewen Calloway reports that Latin American vampire bats represent a stage of evolution that allows them to live solely on animal blood—one of the most complete and nutritious foods in the world. Calloway notes that vampire bats possess a genetic plasminogen activator that prevents blood from coagulating, letting them feed deeply from the animals they attack. He observes that humans also have this gene, but in humans it serves a different role, preventing heart attacks by breaking up blood clots. Without it, humans would die from heart disease at an even greater rate than now occurs.[3]

The idea of vampires as highly evolved humans dates from the nineteenth century. Novelist Paul P. Jesep postulates that vampires represent an ancient evolutionary split. Two separate migrations from the African rainforest to India and the Middle East exposed the humans to more sunlight than they were accustomed to, resulting in sensitivity to light. According to Jesep, Charles Darwin suggested in an unpublished essay that because it was more difficult to extract subsistence in their new homelands, these groups evolved to prey on human blood instead of traditional prey—giving rise to vampire legends.[4]

Vampire legends present beings that, in fact, appear superior to humans in many ways, including longevity and abilities, both physical and mental. The vampire Deacon Frost, in the first *Blade* movie (1998) says to Blade, a vampire/human hybrid vampire slayer, "What difference does it make how their world ends? Plague ... war ... famine. Morality doesn't even enter into it. We're just a function of natural selection, man. The new race."

If vampires represent a series of genetic adaptations to local conditions, could some of their inherited powers be recreated in humans? That question, along with contemporary fears and anxieties, may explain much of the attraction to today's pop culture vampires. Considerable current interest exists in identifying and cultivating real human superpowers. In fact, some unique (human) individuals apparently possess super strength, the ability to generate body heat at will, the ability to affect magnetic fields, the ability to visualize completely through sonar, and many other powers previously reserved for paranormal characters. Science writer Jeff Wise observes, "When we find ourselves under intense pressure, fear unleashes reserves of energy that normally remain inaccessible. We become, in effect, superhuman."[5]

For many psychologists, vampires symbolize hidden parts of the self. Sigmund Freud (1856–1939) connected religion and psychology by describing supernatural characters as "monsters from the id." The id becomes "the devil's playground," manufacturing fantastic creatures that reflect our innermost fears and desires.[6] To Freud, monsters indeed symbolized parts of the unconscious, serving as powerful religious and psychological symbols.

Whether arising from the id, imagination, or historical events, vampire characters play major roles in religion, magic, mythology, history, literature, film, drama, music, painting, and psychology. In interactions with humans, they may become romantically involved with their mortal cousins, at which point vampire narratives become paranormal romances. Explaining their appeal, romance novelist Anne Stuart says, "At the heart of the vampire myth is a demon lover who is both elegant and deadly, a creature whose savagery is all the more shocking when taken with his beauty and style."[7]

Because of their violent feeding habits, vampires form a subset of the horror genre. Authors Ronald Tamborini and James Weaver, writing about horror films, observe that horror arises from "fear of some uncertain threat to existential nature and ... disgust over its potential aftermath." They assert that "the source of threat is [often] supernatural in its composition."[8]

Horror also plays a major role in tragedy, a closely related genre. *Prometheus Bound*, attributed to the Greek dramatist Aeschylus in the fifth century BCE, depicts the Titan Prometheus bound in chains while a giant vulture devours his heart and liver. Sophocles' *Oedipus Rex,* from the fifth century BCE, ends with an insane and bloody King Oedipus gouging out his eyes. The Chorus summarizes the play's irony: "No man shall be considered fortunate who is not dead." The Old English epic *Beowulf,* written sometime between the eighth and eleventh centuries, includes bloody scenes of the monster Grendel attacking drinkers in a mead hall, along with bloody battles with dragons and a final battle in which Beowulf is mortally wounded while slaying his last dragon.

William Shakespeare made full use of horror in his plays, especially in the tragedies. H. P. Lovecraft, considered a master of horror fiction, observed that "the oldest and strongest emotion of mankind is fear, and the oldest and strongest kind of fear is fear of the unknown."[9] Modern-day horror writer Stephen King suggests that we create fictional monsters to protect us against real ones. He says that the horror film "deliberately appeals to all that is worst in us. It is morbidity unchained, our most base instincts let free, our nastiest fantasies realized ... and it all happens, fittingly enough, in the dark."[10]

Recent cinematic vampire gore includes numerous scenes in *30 Days of Night* (2007), in which vampires hunt a dwindling supply of humans in Point Barrow, Alaska, during the winter month of complete darkness. A band of fierce, hungry vampires arrives to take advantage of the darkness and systematically hunt the humans, slaughtering them for their blood. In one scene a little girl vampire rips out one human's throat, then turns to the others and says, "I'm done playing with this one. You want to play with me now?" Later

Alaska resident Stella Oleson (Melissa George) aims at vampires attacking the town of Barrow during the annual month of no sunshine in *30 Days of Night* (2007) (Kobal Collection at Art Resource, New York).

one of the humans is bitten by a vampire and begs Sheriff Oleson (Josh Hartnett) to behead him to prevent him from turning into a vampire.

In *Abraham Lincoln: Vampire Hunter* (2012), vampires wage war against humans for ultimate domination. Lincoln swears vengeance and vows, "I shall kill them all!" Later, a pharmacist captures Lincoln and hangs him upside down, placing a bowl under his head and threatening to slit his throat with a razor. "Don't worry," he assures him. "It will only hurt for a moment. Did you eat today?"

The *Blade* film series (1998–2004) contains many scenes of Blade (Wesley Snipes) wielding swords, knives, and other weapons to dismember and kill vampires. In one scene, Blade blasts a club full of vampires with a shotgun, causing them to explode as the shots penetrate their bodies. In the *Underworld* series (2003–2012), bloody fight scenes rank among the most graphic in recent film history, including a final scene in which Selene (Kate Beckinsale) slices diagonally through the head of Viktor (Bill Nighy). Viktor appears surprised and puzzled, at which time a large slice of his head falls to the floor. Vampire lore teems with such scenes. Vampires biting, gouging, and ripping apart human flesh provide abundant opportunities for graphic horror. And slayers decapitating, burning, slicing, blasting, shooting, and burning vampires yield many more. The potential for horror scenes in vampire stories seems infinite.

Horror evokes fear and disgust—fear as readers and film audiences anticipate violent vampire attacks on human characters, followed by disgust as violence strikes. Gothic literature scholar Devendra Varma characterizes this sequence of emotions as ranging from apprehension to sickening realization.[11] These elements keep readers and audiences mesmerized. According to Aristotle in the fourth century BCE, evoking such powerful emotions brings about a profound emotional release of pity and fear, or "catharsis"—a Greek word that means "purification" or "cleansing." He theorized that theater-goers viewing tragedies experience "purging of the spirit of morbid and base ideas or emotions by witnessing the playing out of such emotions or ideas on stage."[12]

Violence forms an important element in horror. Traditionally it occurs as part of the plot, but in psychological horror it may exist only as a threat.[13] Economists Gordon Dahl and Stefano DellaVigna maintain that watching violent movies actually dampens violent behavior and that "the showing of violent films in the United States has decreased assaults by around 1,000 per weekend."[14]

Fear of violence transforms into horror and disgust after violent, horrific events occur, a common occurrence in pop culture. In the vampire horror classic *Sleepwalkers* (1992), written by Stephen King, director Mick Garris introduced an idyllic small town inspired by Norman Rockwell paintings, then horrified audiences by exposing the violence and gore lurking beneath the surface. "The movie was really Norman Rockwell goes to Hell," Garris explained.[15]

Along with horror, vampirism evokes sex. Vampires penetrate other characters' bodies, contaminating their blood. The act of sucking blood represents sexual activity. Before the science of genetics revealed the role of DNA in human reproduction, many believed that genetic material resided in blood, so mixing blood represented sexual intercourse. During the Victorian era, openly depicting sex was taboo; sexuality could be represented only through metaphor. Vampirism provided the ideal sexual metaphor, with its reliance on mixing vital fluids, with or without the victim's consent. Pop culture's vampires exude sexuality that often involves seduction and nudity as well as traditional sex. When used in combination, filmmakers and writers realize that "sex and violence sell—they attract audiences—and that translates into cash!"[16]

Mythology

Vampire-like, blood-seeking demons date from the dawn of history. Ancient Greeks called them Lamia, Empusa, or Stirge: mythological creatures feeding on human blood and sometimes engaging in sexual relations with humans. Lamia became associated with snakes, and Stirge reputedly transformed into birds. In ancient Assyria and Babylonia, doomed souls of the dead were thought to roam the earth tormenting the living and feeding off their blood. Ancient Romans named them Lemures, spirits of departed humans that exhaust their victims' life forces. Ancient bloodsuckers and similar demons also populate Druid and Indian mythology.[17] Eastern Europe also possesses a rich vampire tradition, much of it imported from the Far East by travelers on the Silk Road, and by the expansion of the Ottoman Empire. Historically, Slavic people feared vampire attacks while sleeping.[18]

Vampire myths first came on the scene in Western Europe during the eighteenth century. The word "vampire" appeared in a 1732 English translation of a German report about Arnold Paole, a farmer in Serbia who died during strenuous farm labor. After several of Paole's neighbors also died, Paole was rumored to be a reanimated vampire.[19] Like Paole, eighteenth-century vampires were considered fearful demons from hell intent on wreaking havoc on society.

Literary Sources

The Romantic Movement of the late eighteenth to mid-nineteenth centuries provided an ideal cultural environment for fictional vampires. Horace Walpole's *Castle of Otranto* (1765) foreshadowed Gothic fiction plot elements by setting the action in a gloomy castle inhabited by doomed characters, replete with an ancient prophecy. Walpole's novel features a giant and an enormous metallic helmet covered with black feathers that appears out of nowhere, slamming into a young man and crushing him to death. *Castle of Otranto* helped prepare the reading public for the even stranger, more bizarre characters to come: vampires. Interest in these supernatural beings rose in reaction to the scientific rationalism and industrial technology of the Enlightenment era. Writers John Keats, Lord Byron, Mary Shelley, Sheridan le Fanu, and Bram Stoker emphasized fantasy, the supernatural, and creations of the id over the rational mind. Their vampire characters invaded Gothic literature, making their appearance during an epic struggle of science and technology versus spirituality and emotionalism. These tensions lie at the heart of Bram

Stoker's *Dracula* (1897), contrasting Count Dracula's supernatural powers of transmigration, hypnosis, and telekinesis with vampire slayer Abraham Van Helsing's reliance on scientific blood transfusions, railroads, typewriters, and audio recording devices as well as religious icons. Allan Johnson, in his essay "Modernity and Anxiety in Bram Stoker's Dracula," observes that although Count Dracula "can transform into mist and summon bloodthirsty wolves, these powers prove to be poorly matched against the new technologies and conveniences of everyday life in England."[20]

Although relatively few Victorians read *Dracula*, interest in Stoker's novel grew until it became the most influential vampire novel in history.[21] Stoker drew inspiration from earlier sources, including the transformational novels *Carmilla* (1872) and *The Vampyre* (1819), and also from several actual historical figures: fifteenth-century Prince Vlad the Impaler, sixteenth-century Countess Elizabeth Bathory, and nineteenth-century poet Lord Byron. Long considered pulp fiction, *Dracula* is now regarded by critics as one of the most important works of Victorian literature.[22] Stoker's novel has inspired contemporary writers such as Anne Rice, Stephenie Meyer, Laurell K. Hamilton, and Stephen King, whose novels consistently appear on bestseller charts. Today the vampire genre seems poised to achieve even greater popularity.

Cinema

Motion pictures appeared at almost the exact moment that Stoker published *Dracula*. Film provided an ideal dramatic vehicle for depicting the conflicts between heart and mind, reason and emotion, science and religion. One of the earliest commercial films, George Méliès' *The Devil's Castle* (1896), anticipated vampire mythology by featuring a large flying bat that alights in a medieval castle and transforms into Mephistopheles (Satan), played by Méliès himself. From a bubbling cauldron, Mephistopheles withdraws skeletons, ghosts, and witches. Finally a menacing character appears brandishing a crucifix, and Mephistopheles vanishes in a puff of smoke. Mephistopheles, bat, castle, caldron, and skeletons provide a proto-vampire touch. Méliès' film appeared one year before the publication of Bram Stoker's *Dracula* in 1897. This film, Stoker's novel, and Rudyard Kipling's influential poem "The Vampire" (1897) all arrived at virtually the same time, inaugurating new cycles of vampire lore. During this time, vampires found their way into painting and theater as well. Today they populate all forms of culture, including ballet, music, theater, opera, painting, and video games.

Metaphors

Metaphors—imaginative linguistic comparisons—prove fascinating to scholars. To Aristotle, metaphors represented stylistic excellence when properly employed. "Metaphor especially has clarity and sweetness and strangeness, and its use cannot be learned from anyone else," he wrote in *The Rhetoric*. "One should speak both epithets and metaphors that are appropriate, and this will be from analogy."[23] Metaphor "eyes" allow one to see new meaning by comparing something unknown with a known thing. As Spanish philosopher José Ortega y Gasset observed in a 1925 essay (English translation 1948), "The metaphor is perhaps one of man's most fruitful potentialities." Its power and efficacy "verge on magic, and it seems a tool for creation which God forgot inside one of His creatures when He made him."[24] Metaphors help define reality by comparing the unknown or mysterious with something known. The comparison expands knowledge by applying information about familiar quantities to the unknown ones. We achieve new understanding, not from reason and logic but through symbolic evocations of sensitive issues.

Erin Collopy, who teaches a university class on vampires, believes that vampires owe their immense and rising popularity to their remarkable ability to symbolize society's most sensitive, taboo issues. "I think the reason vampires are so popular is because they are such an effective metaphor for our own anxieties and desires," Collopy says. Through metaphors, "we often try to work things out about ourselves."[25]

In fact, vampire metaphors prove so powerful an allure that a growing subculture of self-proclaimed "vampires" exists, consciously adopting a "vampire lifestyle" replete with implanted fangs and occasional forays into blood consumption. Practitioners adopt a brooding "Goth" persona with black period clothing, nocturnal activity, and self-mutilation. An "eccentric diversity" within Goth culture results in an "acceptance" and "openness" to gender identities, says student essayist Simon Pascal Klein.[26] A large industry supplies aspiring vampires with capes, fangs, wigs, rings, and belts. "Vampire fang" dental reshaping and inserting enlarged canine teeth earned the status of one of the hottest fads in dentistry.[27]

In an important study on the use of metaphors in our daily lives, linguist George Lakoff and philosopher Mark Johnson contend that cultural metaphors allow people to conceptualize life's complex and often vexatious issues and events. They explain that "metaphor is pervasive in life, not just in language but in thought and action." As they maintain, "Our ordinary conceptual system, in terms of which we both think and act, is fundamentally metaphorical in nature." Furthermore, "the way we think, what we experience, and what we do every day is very much a matter of metaphor."[28]

Johnson and Lakoff argue that metaphors influence public perceptions about government policies and projects as well as social and cultural issues. War is a common cultural metaphor that often goes unrecognized. Government policies quickly become "wars"—the "war on poverty," "war on drugs," "war on gangs," "gender wars," and "class warfare." This war metaphor affects public ideas about poverty, drugs, gangs, genders, and social classes, fostering aggressive thinking and leading to "campaigns," "battles," and "skirmishes."

Cultural metaphors often take the form of narratives in which characters undertake actions and experiences and learn to cope with the consequences. In Homer's epic saga *The Odyssey*, the hero Odysseus embarks on a ten-year sea voyage to return to his home of Ithaca following the Trojan War. Here Odysseus's journey symbolizes the "road of life." Since Odysseus's era, the "road of life" still transforms into a "hard road" teeming with challenges and dangers, on which individuals must endure numerous hardships and challenges.

Vampires as metaphors range from fierce monsters to gentle protectors. A harsh, abusive boss becomes a metaphorical vampire, a "bloodsucker" who "preys on" or "devours" the workers. Philosopher Stephen T. Asma observes that humans perform a "metaphorical operation" when they say, "He was a monster," or that a colleague at work "uses people" or seems to "feed" on them. "Loose" or seductive women may be described as "vamps." Such symbolism lets us understand the positive and negative actions of others.[29] Some critics acknowledge, along with author Eric Nuzum, that vampirism provides a nearly "perfect vessel" for obtaining insights about sensitive social and political issues. Maintains Nuzum, "If you want to understand any moment in time, or any cultural moment, just look at their vampires." Over time, vampires may symbolize sexuality, violence, predatory capitalism, illegal immigration, organized crime, infectious disease, addiction, or international and domestic terrorism.[30]

As metaphors, vampires illumine our most secret feelings about issues too sensitive to discuss openly. Peter Day, in his introduction to *Vampires: Myths and Metaphors of Enduring Evil* (2006), observes that "in the modern world vampires come in all forms, they can be perpetrators or victims, metaphors or monsters, scapegoats for sinfulness or mirrors of our own evil."[31] Literary scholar Nina Auerbach, in *Our Vampires: Ourselves* (1997), says that each age recasts vampire mythology according to its own needs. During the second half of the twentieth century, vampires alternatively symbolized "fears of communism, of McCarthyism, of nuclear war, of not being certified sexually normal by paternalistic Freudian authorities."[32] What began as a metaphor for sexuality during the Victorian period transforms into metaphors about a wide variety of social issues. As *Newsweek's* Jennie Yabroff noted in a 2008 article, "Depending on whom you ask, vampire stories can be read as symbols of venereal disease, capitalism, immigration, industrialization, colonialism, AIDS, homosexuality, mental illness, and anti–Semitism, technology or class warfare."[33] Vampire characters alternate between being vicious monsters or humanity's saviors, transforming into semi-divine superheroes locked in a struggle against deadly supervillains.

Fictional vampires often slay or otherwise harm innocent humans, making them ideal vehicles for depicting human aggression. Monstrous, savage "Nosferatu" vampires predate today's more attractive, nuanced, suppressed, and repressed vampires. Nosferatu monster vampires represent a wide range of anxieties, including fear of rape or incest, criminals and organized mobsters, unchecked corporate power, domestic or foreign terrorists, foreign occupation, and clandestine social and political movements.

Yet another notable metaphor type is the "energy" vampire that preys on human emotions, often specifically on sexuality or human souls, but not on human blood. "Psi" or "energy" vampires reference an array of socio/political issues and problems, from needy and demanding people to shortages in gasoline or electricity, humanity's widespread inhumanity, hostile aliens, or threatening cyborgs. In recent times, energy or "psi" vampires signify electrical appliances left in their plugged position, as well as energy-inefficient appliances, doors, windows, attics, and basements. In an age experiencing increasing energy costs, blackouts, brownouts, and energy rationing, vampirism may symbolize a variety of older, more profligate, "bad" energy choices.

Like vampires themselves, slayers sprang from the minds of Romantic Movement writers. Slayers are important elements in vampire mythology, often representing science—particularly medical science—blended with supernaturalism and esoteric lore. While vampires often symbolize dangerous or undesirable human traits, slayer characters symbolize socially desirable ones. Thus vampires and their slayers function as metaphorical dyads, adding depth to vampire mythology.

Blood

Vampires are often paired with blood, usually as their sustenance. Blood's power to shock and disgust lies in its essentialness to life, and bleeding represents a life-threatening event. The most common icon in vampire mythology, blood symbolizes bestiality, carnality, female sexuality, and sexual abuse. In Bram Stoker's *Dracula*, Count Dracula and his thrall Renfield repeat: "The blood is the life." Vampires usually seek human blood as their sole source of nutrition. They typically obtain it by puncturing the jugular vein and other arteries with powerful fangs, leaving either pinprick marks or bloody gashes. Blood may escape from these punctures or flow freely from arms, legs, thighs, or other body parts. Furthermore, blood gets smeared on vampires' faces and drips down their chins—as if they no longer can or desire to keep their faces clean while feeding.

In music, art, literature, and cinema, horror often is expressed in the form of blood. Blood serves as a familiar icon in crime, horror, and science fiction genres. It plays an important symbolic role in tragedy, melodrama, and comedy, and it shows up in hundreds of song lyrics.

Blood-drinking and bloodletting both symbolize anger and aggression—as in the expressions "The boss was so mad he was drinking blood" and "There will be blood." A person's face may become "flushed with anger" as his or her adrenaline surges, veins and arteries dilate, and blood flow accelerates. Conflicts arise when "bad blood" exists between individuals or groups, and people may "blow their tops"—implying that their blood pressure rises high enough to cause their skulls to explode. Combat narratives feature serious injuries and frequently open with horrific, bloody battle scenes.

Blood also carries abundant religious connotations. According to Aztec and other Mesoamerican mythologies, human blood was sacrificed to appease the gods, since the gods had opened their veins originally to give life to every living thing. Noted author Barbara Ehrenreich observes, "A consensus is emerging that human sacrifice, far from being an oddity, has been a widespread practice among diverse cultures, from small-scale tribes to mighty urban civilizations like the fifteenth century Aztec."[34] Blood—particularly healthy blood—represents life. Anemia, a deficiency of red blood cells, occurs as a result of bleeding, iron depletion, or other nutritional and physical disorders. Through blood exposure, infection from pathogens or viruses may occur. During the nineteenth century, Joan Gordon and Veronica Hollinger observe in *Blood Read: The Vampire as Metaphor in Contemporary Culture*, vampirism presented "a natural metaphor for the symptoms of tuberculosis."[35]

Blood functions as a powerful symbol of genetics, evoking the expression "blood is thicker than water." Blood symbolizes close friendships, and intimates sometimes refer to each other as "blood brothers" and "blood sisters." But blood may become tainted or diseased, of course. Fictional vampires may transmit their essences by means of virus-like diseases that ultimately infect humans and sometimes animals as well, referencing fears of HIV and other pandemics.

In 1902, Stanford University president David Starr Jordon identified blood as the sole vehicle for transmitting genetic information in humans. Jordan originated the notion of "race and blood" in his 1901 essay "The Blood of the Nation: a Study of the Decay of Races Through Survival of the Unfit." He emphasized a belief—widely held at that time—that human qualities, including talent and poverty, pass to future generations through *blood*.[36] Although biology has long since disproved Jordon's claims, even today the folk belief in blood's inheritance properties persists. Prior to the discovery of DNA and RNA, belief in blood-borne inheritance led to the systematic practice of segregating medical blood supplies according to the donor's race. The Red Cross didn't begin accepting Negro blood until 1942 and even then kept it segregated from white blood until 1950.[37]

Blood sacrifice serves as one of humanity's most revered religious icons. In Christianity's Sacrament of Holy Communion, participants symbolically drink the blood of Jesus, in certain denominations incanting the phrase "blood of Christ." In the Bible (John 6:53), Jesus exhorts his disciples, "I tell you the truth, unless you eat the flesh of the Son of Man and drink his blood, you have no life in you." The Doctrine of the Eucharist at Holy Communion remains one of the most dramatic Christian ceremonies. In what amounts to metaphoric cannibalism, the Catholic Doctrine of Transubstantiation maintains that communion wine actually transforms into something resembling Christ's blood, just as communion wafers transform into His body through divine intervention. Believers "consume" Jesus' blood and body each time they take part in Holy Communion. With such a strong emphasis upon blood, the fact that vampire mythology incorporates much of this symbolism should come as no surprise.

In the Biblical apocalyptic narrative of Revelation, the Second Angel pours his bowl into the oceans and they transform into blood. But instead of bequeathing eternal life, the End of Days blood proves toxic. Whereas the blood of God's son provides life, the blood of the Apocalypse arises from God's divine plan to overthrow evil and establish His kingdom on earth (Revelation 16:3).

To Christians, Jesus' blood bestows eternal life. Believers end up in heaven, a blissful paradise. In vampirism, vampire blood bestows eternal life to victims—but usually at a price. Those bitten end up on earth in a state of eternal damnation. Vampirism mocks Holy Communion with another kind of metaphoric communion that perverts Christian symbols while simultaneously and subtly reinforcing their power. By borrowing Christian icons and ceremonies, vampire lore draws on their widespread use and cultural respect.

Other Icons

Fangs are potent symbols of animalism and violence while also referencing sex. Vampire fangs penetrate the soft tissue in women's necks, making them strong phallic symbols. Although vampire fangs may produce life, the "life" of the new vampire corresponds in many ways to death and may not receive positive depiction in pop culture. Wolves, dogs, snakes, and vampire bats also possess fangs for attacking or killing their prey. Like snakes, contemporary vampire characters may have retractable fangs that—like penises—become aroused and erect. As Lorna Piatti-Farnell says in *The Vampire in Contemporary Popular Literature*, "As soon as the fangs are put on display—with their multiple layers of horror and gore—the vampire is understood for the aberration that it is: the transformed human that has lost all of its humanity, and has been left with the hunger of a predator."[38]

Vampires use their mouths and teeth as tools to obtain blood-born nutrients, perhaps symbolizing the cannibalism that was universally practiced in prehistory. Vampires supposedly represent a separate species, but since they closely resemble and often pass for humans, they remain close cousins. Therefore, preying on human blood constitutes a form of cannibalism.

Widely practiced in the ancient world, cannibalism eventually became universally taboo. Writer John Roach demonstrates from genetic evidence that humans widely engaged in cannibalism as early as 500,000 years ago in very disparate societies in Africa, Asia, and Europe, with a few cultures continuing the practice until recent times.[39] Modern human jaws continue to possess incredible power. In 2010, Australian researchers made the surprising discovery that, pound for pound, humans have bites that are 40 percent to percent stronger than those of gorillas and other great apes. Previously scholars assumed that thousands of years of evolution had rendered human jaws relatively weak. Instead, scientists learned that because of leverage and tooth enamel, modern human jaws are as powerful as those of ancient human ancestors—including the strong-jawed "Nutcracker Man."[40] Thus the mythology of carnivorous and blood-drinking people reflects both a historical reality and a physical possibility for humans as well as vampires.

Modern vampires increasingly reject cannibalism and even the consumption of human blood, opting for some form of vegetarianism or the blood of other animals. In HBO's popular television series *True Blood*, vampires purchase a synthetic version of blood called "True Blood." With no need to feed on humans, vampires become their friends and lovers. This reverses the earlier vampire trope of the monstrous predator. Other of today's vampires prefer to slaughter animals in lieu of humans for blood. In the *Twilight* novels and movies, "good" vampires like the Cullen family feed exclusively on the blood of wild animals. The Cullens use their superpowers to capture deer and other wild game, turning away from cannibalism. The substitution of animal blood for that of humans fails to satisfy animal rights advocates but represents far less violence than attacking or murdering humans, giving rise to the term "vegan vampires." Whether synthetic or animal blood is chosen, the venerable metaphor of savage monsters is transformed into one of benevolent human protectors.

Also making significant contributions to vampire metaphors are the colors red and black, which over time have became iconic for vampires. As a "hot" color—the color of blood—red appears on everything from Count Dracula's bright red collar to his ruby red lips. A prominent power color, red suggests fiery heat and danger. It symbolizes anger and lust, and it may suggest menstruation and placental bleeding during birth. Marketers often rely on red for its attention-attracting qualities.[41] Black, on the other hand, represents night, death, and obliteration, evoking the fear of dark places such as basements, empty buildings, caves, and tunnels. Vampires inhabit a world of blackness and wear black clothing, existing in darkness and night. Upon hearing howling wolves outside his castle, Count Dracula exclaims, "Listen to them, children of the night. What sweet music they make!"

Black also assumes a romantic quality, as does the color red—as we witness every Valentine's Day. Red and black both figure prominently in horror scenarios, often displayed during Halloween. Author and screenwriter John L. Flynn maintains that vampires constitute metaphors for Romanticism and the hidden powers of darkness, and vampire stories represent "the disturbing survival of romantic ideals (represented by the vampire) in an era of industrialism or scientific rationalism (contemporary society)." He links the appeal of vampires to a belief in magic in rationalistic society.[42]

Sex

Vampires seem sexy, and are associated with sex in many ways. Sex, of course, is one of humanity's most powerful drives. Vampires as seductive rakes were one of the earliest and most powerful vampire myths. This metaphor started with early nineteenth-century English poet Lord Byron, who co-created (with John Polidori) a new vampire character: a handsome, seductive rake. Byron/Polidori's antagonist turns out to be a symbolic rendering of Lord Byron himself—youthful, rich, and handsome—but answering to the name Lord Ruthven. One critic has noted that the Byron/Polidori vampire character "took a dramatic leap forward, leaving behind the shabby, stupid, blundering image of the Nosferatu savage for a more sophisticated and refined social animal, the Toreador or Byronic vampire." This Byronic vampire appears human on the outside "with no huge teeth in the front of its mouth (the canine fangs were a later invention), and no bald head or pointed ears, a creature with human emotions and human drives, a creature that can pass freely in the world of men and need not fear detection in the enlightened society through which he stalks."[43]

In her essay "Fictional conventions and sexuality in *Dracula*," Carol Fry identifies vampires such as Ruthven and Dracula as renderings of a character type that Victorian critics loved to hate—the highly sexual rake. Rakes allegedly preyed upon Victorian upper-class women, thereby threatening the entire social order. As Fry observes, the rake was the male counterpart of the female vamp, and the public strongly disapproved of both types. However, males seduced by males in that period proved far more threatening than males seduced by females. Men who seduced women left behind "fallen women," a marginalized category that included prostitutes. A female vamp—as they have come to be called—could turn professional prostitute and seduce men into becoming vampires.[44] By casting vampires as rakes and vamps, writers and filmmakers have been able to evoke sexuality with less fear of censorship than if they had used humans for the same purpose.

Gender

Gender plays a major role in vampire narratives, as in human life. Count Dracula seduces humans of both sexes, thus transforming into a symbolic bisexual. The female vampire named Carmilla in Sheridan Le Fanu's *Carmilla* (1872) seduces both males and females, especially in her more recent iterations, making her a symbolic bisexual as well. Other versions of Carmilla depict her as a lesbian/feminist, seducing young women whenever opportunity presents itself.

Within this context of bisexuality, homosexuality, and lesbianism, however, Dracula and other vampires inhabit a patriarchal universe. Count Dracula, with his "wives" and other human pets, lords over all the inhabitants of his castle and the surrounding villages and, later, over his dispirited thralls.

Dracula's many imitators, especially during the nineteenth and twentieth centuries, function as polygamous patriarchs—clan dictators with abundant opportunities for intimacy.

Vampire lore does provide strong female characters, either as vampires or as their slayers. One of the most enduringly popular is Le Fanu's Carmilla, who continues to inspire pop culture creators seeking passionate, potent female characters. Carmilla's popularity skyrocketed during the 1970s, corresponding with the rise of Second Wave Feminism. Feminists demanded assertive female characters, and novelists and filmmakers responded with a spate of psychologically realistic lesbian vampires, each an adaptation of *Carmilla*. Among them were several popular British films: *The Vampire Lovers* (1970), *Lust for a Vampire* (1971), and *Twins of Evil* (1971). These films, labeled the Karnstein Trilogy, feature vampire lesbians who practice what many 1960s and 1970s lesbian feminists strongly believed—namely, that loving themselves and other women constituted a rejection of patriarchy. In a 1970 manifesto, a group calling themselves the Radicalesbians asked, "Why is it that women have related to and through men?" Because of male hegemony, they declared, women "have internalized the male culture's definition of ourselves. That definition consigns us to sexual and family functions, and excludes us from defining and shaping the terms of our lives."[45] Feminist author Claire Johnston notes that "feminist" films of the 1960s and 1970s constitute a "counter cinema" in which previously suppressed images and narratives of women finally appear.[46]

The 1990s brought more female images, most notably Buffy, the first teenage female vampire slayer. More recently, powerful feminist vampires have appeared in the film *Byzantium* (2012), the *Twilight* novels (2005–2008) and films (2008–2012), and the *True Blood* television series (2008–2014).

The Nude Vampire (1970), *Vampire Vixens from Venus* (1995), and *Bordello of Blood* (1996) are among many films featuring young, beautiful females as sexy heterosexual vampires. *Bram Stoker's Dracula* (1992) and *From Dusk Till Dawn* (1996) both have sexy female vampire characters who slip easily to prostitute roles, including Salma Hayek's exotic dancer Satanico Pandemonium in *From Dusk Till Dawn*. Romantic films such as *The Breed* (2001), *Underworld* (2003), and *Twilight: Breaking Dawn* (2011) spice up their content with sexual relationships between vampires and humans or hybrids.

Monsters

F. W. Murnau's *Nosferatu* (1922) was the first feature film showcasing a monstrous type of vampire—an often grotesque, savage killer that terrorizes its victims and commits murder and mayhem. In the movie, Count Orlok (Max Schreck) transforms into Nosferatu, with hideous looks and animalistic behavior (eating rodents and lusting after a beautiful actress). Such frightening creatures—referred to as "Nosferatu" throughout this book—had migrated from mythology to popular culture during the Romantic Era, inspired by writers such as John Polidori and Bram Stoker. This type of vampire represents humanity's deepest fears about violence and aggression.

Many vampires encompass both metaphors—vampires as seducers and as monsters. *Twilight's* Edward Cullen and *True Blood's* Bill Compton are seductive vampires who appeal especially to female audiences, while the horrific Jan Vale in *Vampires* (1998) and Viktor in *Underworld* (2003) have a masculine appeal. Often both vampire types exist in the same novel or film, even within the same character. Contemporary vampires often symbolize the fear of violent and catastrophic events in addition to sexuality and the hope for supernatural salvation.

Often shadowy and vast in numbers, vampires form cells and strictly regulated societies in which each thrall owes obedience to the vampire that turned him or her into a vampire. Only the original vampire founder any true power or authority over the many vampires created by him or her. This organizational structure may invoke fear of criminal syndicates and terrorist organizations. The idea of clandestine cells of subordinates obliged to obey their superiors conjures up images of Nazi SS officers infiltrating communities to seize and exterminate Jews and other "undesirables," or Soviet fifth columnists dedicated to overthrowing the U.S. government.

Immigration

Vampire characters typically function as members of a threatening, dangerous, alien species. They easily become metaphors for unwanted immigration, a hot-button issue throughout history. Since vampires sprang originally from foreign—especially Eastern European—mythology, the vampire literature and films of the nineteenth and early twentieth centuries often contain unmistakable hints of anti–Semitism. Bram Stoker's Count Dracula, with his aristocratic heritage and inherited wealth, could serve as a stand-in for Baron Rothschild, whose London-based German/Jewish banking dynasty generated considerable envy during that time period. Vampires may also suggest miscegenation—a sensitive issue over the past two centuries.[47] In fact, Dracula has symbolized every immigrant and minority group that looks different or speaks English with a foreign or regional accent. In response to increasing population diversity, today's vampires spring from a dizzying array of ethnicities, religions, and genders.

Psychological Dimensions

Psychologists note a correlation between vampirism and various personality disorders, from borderline personality disorder (BPD) to criminal psychosis. Sometimes referred to as "energy," "emotional," or "psi" vampires, psychological vampires provide such a metaphor. Albert J. Bernstein, in *Emotional Vampires: Dealing with People Who Drain You Dry* (2002), observes that emotional vampires—those that feed not on blood but on heightened human emotions—display one or more of these mental illness disorders: antisocial, histrionic, narcissistic, obsessive/compulsive, paranoia.[48] Psychic vampires may also symbolize humans who have the following characteristics: constant complaining with no desire to seek true resolution, an air of negativity, blaming others for their feelings, a tendency to cope by withdrawing, self-indulgent attention-seeking, having trouble setting boundaries, being dependent on others' approval.[49]

Psychologists have developed a diagnostic test for deviancy. The "triad" of personality traits that qualify as negative or deviant includes the tendency to seek admiration and special treatment (narcissism), to be callous and insensitive (psychopathology), and to manipulate others (Machiavellianism).[50] Each of these traits easily applies to the aggressive "Nosferatu" vampires.

Pop culture includes vampires that devour not just emotions but also sexuality and "psi" or psychic energy. Notable psychic vampire films include *Captain Kronos: Vampire Hunter* (1974), *The Keep* (1983), and *Lifeforce* (1985). The vampires in these films absorb various forms of energy and omit blood sucking. Unburdened by blood sucking, psi vampires focus directly on the relationships between individuals and groups. Some researchers conclude that most individuals experience psychic vampires at one time or another without knowing it. They may feel emotionally drained after an encounter with a friend or family member, unaware that they have been victimized by a psychic vampire.[51]

Future of Vampires

Throughout history, vampires have been pop culture's the most frequently depicted villain or antihero. Count Dracula ranks first in popularity, followed by Carmilla and a variety of others, including psi vampires. These characters play an impressive number of sociological roles in pop culture, and their social meanings transform to suit the times and the circumstances. The most common narratives depict vampires seducing humans, playing metaphoric gender roles, and serving as symbols of human bestiality, violence, and other forms of predation. These stories are often filled with abundant and potent sexuality and violence.

Some have speculated recently that vampires constitute a passing fad, an old paradigm that is rapidly being supplanted by newer, more exciting characters such as zombies, witches, and wizards. However, it appears much too soon to write off vampires. They've existed in pop culture for thousands of years, and they give every indication of persevering. Because of their dramatic potential, versatility, and magnetism, vampires seem likely to continue populating stories, novels, plays, movies, television, video games, and the Internet for the foreseeable future.

• Two •

Seducers

Vampires constitute one of the most sexualized genres within pop culture. The earliest known image of a vampire—drawn on a prehistoric drinking cup—depicts a man copulating with a beheaded vampire. Like prostitutes, vampires lurk in the dark, and after penetrating their victims—often female—they depart feeling satisfied and often satiated.[1]

Today the link between vampires and sex appears most clearly in the Goth movement, which embraces vampirism as a lifestyle. Scholar and author David Keyworth observes that "eroticism has become so entwined with the contemporary vampire scene that popular vampire magazines, like *Bloodstone*, include previews of the latest vampire pornography, featuring combined acts of sex and blood-letting."[2] In addition, a growing number of fetishists eroticize blood. Blood fetishists derive "intense erotic/sexual arousal or satisfaction from the taste, sight, or feel of human blood," as one vampire-focused website explains. Fetishists say they practice bloodletting "as an expression of trust, intimacy, and bonding, apart from specifically erotic aspects."[3]

Vampire culture today places greater emphasis on sex than ever before. *Huffington Post* writer Emma Gray observes that recent movies and television series, such as *Twilight* and *True Blood*, send a clear message that "vampires are all about sex." She concludes that "the vampire trend has created a space for a more in-depth discussion of sexuality than existed before."[4]

Long before contemporary Goths, literary vampires of the Romantic era were associated with sex through seduction, rape, bisexuality, and homosexuality. The first literary vampires acted in the role of rakes: male seducers of virginal young women, or female seducers of young females. Modern male rakes are descendants of the "Merry Gang," a group of male libertines that originated with the court of Charles II in late seventeenth-century England. They included George Villiers, 2nd Duke of Buckingham; John Wilmot, 2nd Earl of Rochester; Sir Charles Sedley; Charles Sackville, 6th Earl of Dorset; and playwrights William Wycherley and George Etherege. Rakes were distinguished by binge drinking, sodomizing each other, womanizing, and witty conversation.[5] This group enjoyed gambling, fighting, dueling, and generally thumbing their noses at society. In one memorable episode, Sir Charles Sedley and the Earl of Dorset attracted a crowd beneath an alehouse balcony in Covent Garden as they pretended to preach while simulating sex with each other. Later, in typical rake style, the Duke of Buckingham killed the Earl of Shrewsbury in a duel over Shrewsbury's wife.[6]

Eighteenth-century artist William Hogarth captured the appeal of this semi-tragic yet comic character in a series of paintings called "A Rake's Progress." Reproduced by the artist as engravings, they feature a young rake—named, appropriately enough, Tom Rakewell—who inherits a fortune from his father but squanders it on luxuries and women. His "beneficiaries" repay his largess by robbing him of his fortune.[7]

With the advent of the Romantic Movement in the late eighteenth and early nineteenth centuries, rakes regained popularity. Romantics valued emotion over reason, feelings over logic, and passion over dispassion: a perfect climate for rakes. English poet Lord George Gordon Byron (1788–1824), one of the originators of modern vampire literature, was the prototype for the first "vampire" rake.[8] Critics now refer to aristocratic, handsome, and seductive vampires as "Byronic vampires." Byron earned his reputation as a rake after conducting well-publicized affairs with women and men of every social standing, including his own half-sister. In addition, Byron admitted to sexual intimacy with more than 200 women over a two-year period in Italy. With his iconic persona, sexual excesses, and popular narrative poems *Don Juan* and *Childe Harold's Pilgrimage,* Byron served as the role model for Lord Ruthven, the protagonist in John Polidori' story "The Vampyre." The real-life Lord Grey de Ruthvyn, a suitor of Byron's mother, reputedly molested the underage Byron at their Newstead Abbey manor. Supposedly a female servant also molested Byron when he was nine years old.[9] Perhaps Byron's proclivity for pedophilia and bisexuality owes something to these encounters.

After his literary career skyrocketed, Byron enjoyed a status equivalent to that of today's rock stars, and he rapidly acquired a reputation as a seducer. One lurid affair involved a young married aristocrat, Lady Caroline Lamb. Byron, then 24, and Lady Caroline, age 26, met in 1812. Though she initially spurned his advances, Byron wooed her through poetic letters and she fell helplessly in love. But he soon grew tired of her and moved on to others. After several attempts to rekindle his ardor, she famously summarized him as "mad, bad, and dangerous to know."[10] In retaliation, in 1816 Lamb published the novel *Glenarvon,* with a villain strongly resembling Byron. The novel's non-vampire seducer is called Ruthven Glenarvon, possibly a reference to the molester of the underage Lord Byron. Glenarvon seduces a married woman whose reputation is ruined by the affair, at which point he abruptly terminates their relationship and pursues others. Lamb never recovered her equilibrium after her encounter with Byron. She engaged in numerous affairs in later years and died in 1828 of complications from alcoholism and drug addiction.[11]

In 1816 Byron co-created the first seductive male vampire as the result of his challenge to friends while marooned by inclement weather in the Villa Diodati lodge near Lake Geneva. The eruption of Mt. Tambora in Indonesia and its effect on weather worldwide caused 1816 to be labeled "the year without a summer," and Byron's party were among many would-be hikers forced indoors by unseasonal weather. To relieve the monotony, Byron challenged his friends—including the poet Percy Shelley, Shelley's future wife Mary Wollstonecraft Godwin, Godwin's stepsister Claire Clairmont (who was passionately in love with Byron), and Byron's personal physician and reputed lover Dr. John Polidori—to a ghost story contest.[12] The contest was thought to be primarily between literary giants Byron and Shelley, but two of the lesser-known guests ended up writing much more influential literary works. Godwin (reputedly with assistance from her future husband) eventually penned and published the novel *Frankenstein* (1818), which continues to inspire writers and filmmakers. Polidori, following up on Byron's initial inspiration for a tale featuring an upper-class British male like himself, published "The Vampyre" in 1819—launching the first fictional vampire into popular culture.

Byron's own effort, a brief fragment dated June 1816, lays out the essence of the narrative perfected by Polidori. Byron named his vampire character Augustus Darvell, and he created a younger male character as Darvell's friend and traveling companion. The two journey to a remote cemetery in Turkey, where Darvell appears to age rapidly. With his health apparently failing, Darvell instructs his young friend to bury him in the cemetery but tell no one of his death. At this point Byron ceased writing, although he discussed this fragment with the rest of the group. Thereafter Byron grew weary of Polidori's company, made him the butt of jokes, and dismissed him from his services.[13]

Polidori completed the work begun by Byron, without informing his former friend. The finished novella appeared in the April 1819 issue of *New Monthly Magazine* under the title "The Vampyre—A Tale by Lord Byron." An outraged Byron quickly disavowed authorship, and Polidori demanded that the novella be credited to him alone. The two never reconciled, and publication of "The Vampyre" drove them even further apart.[14] Depressed and impoverished by gambling debts, Polidori died two years later, allegedly by self-administered cyanide.[15] He ended his life like many fictional vampire victims—seduced, used, and abandoned.

Byron conducted another well-documented affair with a teenage Greek boy, Nicolo Giraud. He also slept with his own half-sister, Augusta Leigh.[16] With his wealth, fame, talent, personality, and good looks, Byron had no problem sexually attracting large numbers of people. The angst-ridden libertine became the model for the popular "Byronic hero" as well as the "Byronic vampire," and Byronic literary heroes rocketed to popularity. Unlike conventional heroes possessed of heroic virtue, Byronic heroes are rendered larger than life by their dark qualities. They exhibit heightened passion, pride, and sensitivity, often becoming moody and pessimistic and at times appearing arrogant, overconfident, abnormally sensitive, and extremely self-conscious. At the same time, they usually possess superior intellectual gifts.[17] This kind of character appealed to a generation of readers enamored of nature and the supernatural, retreating from the dominant rationalism of the previous Age of Enlightenment, with its emphasis on scientific experimentation.

In Polidori's hands, Byron's original vampire Darvell is now the vampire Ruthven—rich, handsome, and gifted, yet morally despicable. As Aubrey, his youthful traveling companion, becomes acquainted with Ruthven, he notices disturbing aspects about his friend's character. Though Ruthven gravitates toward the lowest debauchees, he ignores openly licentious women and focuses instead on seducing women of the highest moral virtue, as if he could achieve greater merit by seducing the pure.

Troubled by his friend's constant philandering, Aubrey parts company with Ruthven. He falls in love with a beautiful Greek woman, but she soon dies under suspicious circumstances—as if drained of blood. The culprit turns out to be Lord Ruthven, preying on his friend's virtuous girlfriend. After Ruthven's apparent murder by robbers, he resurfaces in London as the Earl of Marsden. Aubrey, who suspects Ruthven of being a vampire, realizes that Marsden is in fact Ruthven—but he is prevented from exposing the truth because he swore to Ruthven on his supposed deathbed that he would remain silent about the death for a year and a day.

To his horror, Aubrey discovers that Ruthven/Marsden plans to marry Aubrey's beloved sister. He tries in vain to prevent the marriage, but he feels he must obey his oath of silence even at the cost of his only sibling. Without a hint of remorse, Ruthven/Marsden drains the blood from his new bride. As Polidori expresses it, "Aubrey's sister had glutted the thirst of a VAMPYRE!"

In Polidori's narrative, the ties of friendship outweigh all other considerations. The Aubrey/Ruthven relationship echoes the Romantic friendship ideal, as exemplified in the well-known professional and social relationship between Romantic poets William Wordsworth and Samuel Taylor Coleridge. To English professor Nina Auerbach, the closeness and intimacy of male friends served as a Romantic ideal in what she refers to as "the lures of Romantic vampirism."[18] The fictional Aubrey and the real-life Polidori, junior partners in their relationships, adhere to the unwritten law of subservience to their senior partners. Ruthven and Byron demand respect, without which the relationships wither and die. The intimate bond between men implies a homoerotic subtext, similar to the relationship between Lord Byron and John Polidori.

"The Vampyre" introduced the male rake vampire character to the world. Previous vampire reports had focused on crude, rural predators that gorged on the blood of anyone and anything that happened by—including, in one case from northern England, some hapless sheep allegedly attacked by a huge vampire dog in 1810.[19] In contrast, the Byron/Polidori hero comes across as intriguing, charming, and attractive. The aristocratic figure of Ruthven "mingles in high society, delighting and thrilling all with his strange mannerisms and moods," writes one critic. Thus Byron/Polidori's vampire character "took a dramatic leap forward, leaving behind the shabby, stupid, blundering image of the Nosferatu for a more sophisticated and refined social animal, the Toreador or Byronic vampire." The Byronic vampire appears human on the outside, "with no huge teeth in the front of its mouth (the canine fangs were a later addition), and no bald head or pointed ears, a creature with human emotions and human drives, a creature that can pass freely in the world of men and need not fear detection in the enlightened society through which he stalks." This was "a far cry from the lonely beast rampaging through the forest tearing out the throat of any passing creature in order to carry on his vile existence."[20]

In the Byronic vampire metaphor, females constitute prizes and prey for predatory males like Ruthven and his literary descendant, Count Dracula. In 1820 the French writer Cyprien Berard published a novel titled *Lord Ruthwin ou les Vampires* (*The Vampire Lord Ruthwen*) as a sequel to Polidori's novella. Like Polidori, Berard sends his vampire to Europe to seduce women, one of whom became the first female literary vampire. Ruthwen describes his feelings upon reanimating a female: "I felt a fire in my veins that devoured me. My eyes shone in the profound gloom, my burning lips quivered, the quaking earth opened up, and like terrifying claps of thunder, these terrible words resounded in mid-air: 'Vampire woman! Emerge from the tomb!'" Warns Berard, "Strangers to remorse and pity, vampires choose victims who are most charming in their delightful form, most interesting in their weakness, and most enchanting in their beauty."[21] Like Polidori's Ruthven, Berard's rake vampire relentlessly deflowers and destroys only the most beautiful and virtuous women.[22]

Stage plays continued to popularize the womanizing aristocrat, among them Charles Nodier's *The Vampire* (1820) and Eugene Scribe's vaudeville play *Being Lord Ruthven* (1821). Alexander Dumas published the novel *The Return of Lord Ruthven* in 1851, and Frank J. Morlock published a prequel, *Lord Ruthven Begins,* in 1868, testifying to the continuing popularity enjoyed by Polidori's creation of fifty years earlier. This popularity appeared to wane by the mid-nineteenth century, only to be revived when the seductive vampire reappeared in 1897 in Bram Stoker's novel *Dracula* and in Rudyard Kipling's poem "The Vampire."

In 1847 a gothic vampire novel appeared in England designed to appeal to a mass readership. Published as a serialized "penny dreadful" novel and attributed to Thomas Preskett Prest (sometimes to James Malcolm Rymer), *Varney the Vampyre: or the Feast of Blood* appeared in 109 installments. The serial novel at first features a demonic, twelve-foot-tall vampire named Varney who has a horrible face as well as superhuman strength and occult powers. Varney also seems to be attracted to beautiful and virtuous young ladies. Prest describes Varney's first victim, Flora Bannerworth, as follows:

> Oh, what a world of witchery was in that mouth, slightly parted, and exhibiting within the pearly teeth that glistened even in the faint light that came from that bay window. How sweetly the long silken eyelashes lay upon the cheek. Now she moves, and one shoulder is entirely visible—whiter, fairer than the spotless clothing of the bed on which she lies, is the smooth skin of that fair creature, just budding into womanhood, and in that transition state which presents to us all the charms of the girl—almost of the child, with the more matured beauty and gentleness of advancing years.

Flora's youth and beauty make her ideal vampire prey, and she need not wait long in her sleep of innocence before Varney breaks a window in her upper-story bedroom and enters her chambers. Prest provides readers with an early glimpse of a huge body and pale white, bloodless face. "The eyes look like polished tin; the lips are drawn back, and the principal feature next to those dreadful eyes is the teeth—the fearful looking teeth—projecting like those of some wild animal, hideously, glaringly white, and fang-like."

Prest pioneered two of the now-classic vampire characteristics: fangs that leave two tiny punctures in victims' necks, and superhuman strength. Furthermore, Prest combined two familiar tropes in Varney, the sophisticated, upper-class gentleman Byronic vampire and the monstrous Nosferatu. At one point Flora's lover, Charles Holland, asks, "Are there vampyres, and is this man of fashion—this courtly, talented, educated gentleman one?" Like Lord Ruthven, Sir Francis Varney possesses numerous physical, mental, and social graces; yet he, like the legendary Nosferatu vampires, also has a monstrous, powerful, and deadly side. Varney thus became the first dualistic vampire character—both rake and monster.

Bram Stoker's *Dracula* (1897), the most influential vampire novel of all time, has inspired hundreds of motion pictures and launched countless copies and critical works. Dracula displays bisexuality in his selection of both male and female victims, both of whom he bites on the neck while cradling their heads in his arms. Early in the novel, Dracula's "wives" attempt to seduce Jonathan Harker, a visitor to Castle Dracula, in order to vampirize him. When they're on the verge of attacking Harker, the count unexpectedly returns. Flinging them off from Harker—"this man belongs to me!"—Dracula vampirizes him.

Dracula arrives in London and begins seducing two beautiful young English ladies who are both engaged to be married, Mina Murray and Lucy Westenra. Dracula has designs on Mina, Jonathan Harker's fiancée, after he views a photograph of her that Harker accidentally displays in Transylvania. Mina's love for Harker makes Dracula's plan more difficult, at the same time transforming the seduction into an act of violation. Dracula's seduction of Mina seems more poignant and unsettling than it would if she were sexually active.

On the other hand, Dracula's seduction of Mina's friend Lucy is less poignant because of Lucy's modernistic, hedonistic behavior. Unlike Mina, who professes eternal love for Jonathan, Lucy vacillates among three suitors, revealing a far more sensual nature. She asks Mina, "Why cannot a girl marry three men, or as many as want her, without all this trouble?" Mina, herself a "New Woman" by early Victorian standards, exemplifies a late-Victorian version of "True Woman," serving as monogamous wife and mother, while Lucy belongs to the "New Woman" movement in which women satisfy their appetites and express their views regardless of conventions. At one point Mina and Lucy consume copious amounts of food after a long walk, and Mina jokes to Lucy, "I believe we should have shocked the 'New Woman' with our appetites." Writer Katharina Mewald argues that Mina corresponds to "the ideal Victorian woman," whereas Lucy conforms to the "polygamous" New Women.[23]

In 1931 Universal Pictures released its classic version of *Dracula*, directed by Tod Browning, in which Bela Lugosi reprised his successful Broadway role as the aristocratic vampire. Edward Van Sloan played Professor Abraham Van Helsing, the most famous vampire hunter of all time. Recognizing the box-office potential of Stoker's novel, Universal production chief Carl Laemmle, Jr., envisioned horror star Lon Chaney as his vampire, but Chaney died suddenly before production commenced. Lugosi's success in the Broadway version helped him secure the role. In Browning's adaptation, Lugosi appears supremely Byronesque, complete with genteel manners, exotic accent, and aristocratic appearance. His attacks—mainly on women—function as seductions, but instead of romance, his penetrations symbolically amount to rape. He drinks his victims' blood while infecting them with the mythical disease of vampirism, symbolic of sexually transmitted diseases such as syphilis and gonorrhea. Beneath his aristocratic demeanor, Dracula poses a dire threat to Victorian sexual mores and a challenge to the social order.

When Dracula meets Dr. Seward (Herbert Bunston), Mina (Helen Chandler), Lucy (Francis Dade), and John Harker (David Manners), he makes quite an impression on the young ladies. Lucy seems to flirt with him as she recites an old poem about death. He responds, "To die, to be really dead, that must be glorious." Lucy exclaims, "Why, Count Dracula!" He replies that "there are far worse things waiting man than death." Then he stares intently at Lucy and begins hypnotizing her. When Mina makes fun of the count, Lucy says, "Laugh all you want, I think he's fascinating!" Later Dracula appears at her window in bat form, then reappears in her bedroom in human form. As he approaches her bed, his fingers extend like claws as he brings his mouth to her throat. This scene must have titillated audiences back in 1931, shortly before the film industry's restrictive Hays Code began to be enforced. After the code's enforcement in 1934, a film with the obvious sexual overtones and undertones of *Dracula* likely wouldn't have been allowed.[24]

Dracula attacks Lucy again outside Dr. Seward's house, causing her death. She soon returns as a vampire preying on young children. Mina describes an encounter: "The most horrible expression came over her face, she was like a hungry animal: a wolf. Then she turned and ran off into the dark." Mina also receives Dracula's advances and begins to transform into a vampire. However, as in Stoker's novel, Mina regrets no longer being a True Woman. She explains to her fiancé, "It's all over, John, our love, our life together." She tells him, "I love you, John, you," but she says, "It's a horror. He [Dracula] wills it." As in the novel, Nina survives (barely) Dracula's seductions, returning to fully human form after Professor Van Helsing drives a stake through Dracula's heart. Mina is saved because, as a True Woman, she deserves to survive—unlike her friend Lucy, the New Woman in this film.

When he attacks Van Helsing, Dracula becomes a fearful monster. But when he seduces Lucy and Mina, he is a Byronic rake vampire. Stoker combined these two metaphors in an unforgettable character. He invokes the threat of seduction posed by the rake/libertine and the threat of personal violence posed by recent immigrants. To Victorians, Count Dracula represented the destruction of the last remnants of puritanical morality. He literally feasts off whomever he desires.

Leslie Selander's film *The Vampire's Ghost* (1945) features a Byonic vampire character named Webb Fallon (John Abbott) who owns a nightclub in a mythical African village. Fallon is a "fallen angel," a vampire who has been walking the earth for 400 years under a curse he received after causing the breakup of two passionate lovers. This curse demands that he continue to break up young lovers for eternity. His friend Roy Hendrick (Charles Gordon), a local plantation owner, sees a native spear thrown directly at Fallon without killing him, though the weapon sinks deeply into his chest. Fallon hypnotizes Hendrick and commands him to forget the incident and not think of him as a vampire. Hendrick must instead concentrate on placing Fallon's body under the full moon with his head on a box of soil from his native country, to keep him from dying.

Under the spell of the curse, Fallon transforms into a seducer whenever he encounters young lovers and attractive females, including the beautiful Julie Vance (Peggy Stewart), Hendrick's fiancée. Weary and dispirited by having to obey the curse, Fallon seeks the peace of the grave. He becomes the classic Byronic vampire: seductive, brooding, and doomed to prey upon humans because of his past sins.

Erle C. Kenton's *House of Dracula* (1945) updated the seductive Byronic vampire metaphor with John Carradine as Count Dracula and Lon Chaney, Jr., as the Wolf Man. In this World War II-era sequel to *House of Frankenstein*, Dr. Franz Edelman (Onslow Stevens), who specializes in rare diseases, substitutes for Dr. Frankenstein—although Frankenstein's monster appears, played by Glenn Strange. Count Dracula asks Edelman to cure him of vampirism as a ruse to get closer to Edelman's beautiful nurse, Melissa Morelle (Martha O'Driscoll). Using his occult powers, Dracula nearly seduces Morelle, but Edelman saves her by exposing Dracula's coffin to sunlight and opening the lid, turning him to dust.

As in many pop culture vampire narratives, apparent death proves misleading and plots need not always be logical. It turns out that Dracula had received a transfusion of Dr. Edelman's blood, at which time Dracula reversed the blood flow and tainted Edelman's blood with some of his own. Edelman begins to transform into Dracula, and the seemingly dead Byronic vampire springs to life once again in the person of Edelman. Although he begins as a rake, he goes berserk and slaughters people, even reanimating the Frankenstein monster. At this point Dracula becomes a full-fledged villain. This metaphor warns of the inherent danger of deceitful licentiousness. When Dracula seduces women, his super-powerful hypnosis renders them helpless—effectively making them innocent victims and placing moral blame squarely on him.

In the late 1950s, the British company Hammer Film Productions—known for its horror films—decided to compete directly with Hollywood for audiences. In 1957 Hammer released *The Curse of Frankenstein*, featuring Peter Cushing as Dr. Frankenstein and Christopher Lee as the Frankenstein monster. The less-rigid British production code allowed Hammer to symbolize sexuality relatively blatantly, and the cinematic collaboration between Cushing, Lee, and director Terence Fisher proved especially effective. The film was extremely profitable at the box office, grossing $7,000,000 in the United States alone after a production budget of only £65,000 ($100,689 using today's values), thanks to a marketing agreement between Hammer and Warner Bros.[25]

After this success, Hammer decided to revive and reinvent the vampire genre in 1958 with *Horror of Dracula*. Christopher Lee starred as the count, while Peter Cushing received top billing for his depiction of Van Helsing. Lee depicts Count Dracula as a Byronic rake, while Stoker's Lucy Westenra transforms into Lucy Homewood (Carol Marsh), Jonathan Harker's fiancée. Seduced and vampirized by Count Dracula, Lucy begins preying on young girls. In the film, the Mina of Stoker's novel becomes Lord Homewood's wife Mina (Melissa Stribling). As in the novel, Mina opens her window and invites Dracula in to feed from her blood, thereby proving to be an easy conquest for Dracula. *The Horror of Dracula* established Hammer's brand of vampire films by featuring vampires that were simultaneously seductive and menacing. Lee's Dracula—the first vampire to grow canine fangs since the 1847 novel *Varney the Vampyre*—hypnotizes victims by staring directly into their eyes and assuming control of their minds.

Critics now consider the "Hammer Horror" films made in England from the mid–1950s through the 1970s to be artistic classics and feminist expressions. During this period Hammer relied on the relatively lax British censorship code to create popular films that included sex (often featuring shots of bare female breasts) and violence, complete with graphic gore. Hammer films proved popular in the U.S., and the British company co-produced horror films with several Hollywood production companies over the next two decades.

Hammer dominated the horror market for decades, producing sci-fi, werewolf, and other horror films as well as television shows. Producers aimed at a youthful, male British audience and ended up attracting viewers worldwide. Hammer films contained more sex and violence than Hollywood films until the late 1960s, when American films such as *Bonnie and Clyde* (1967), *The Wild Bunch* (1969), *Butch Cassidy and the Sundance Kid* (1969), and *Easy Rider* (1969) began attracting large audiences. Hollywood studios began producing films with sexy plots, graphic violence, and, increasingly, shots of bare female breasts.

Hammer's *Taste the Blood of Dracula* (1970), directed by Terence Fisher, tells the story of three elderly, upper-class British gentlemen—William Hargood (Geoffrey Keen), Sam Paxton (Peter Sallis), and Jonathan Secker (John Carson)—who slip off one night each week for debaucheries with prostitutes, while claiming to be engaged in charitable work. These men epitomize hypocritical bourgeois Victorian men consorting with prostitutes while pretending piety. One night a young English peer, Lord Courtley (Ralph Bates), flings open the door to the brothel parlor in which the three men are cavorting with scantily clad young prostitutes. The elegantly attired Courtley looks the women over and, with a snap of his fingers, beckons one of them. She abruptly quits Hargood and exits with Courtley. Outraged yet intrigued, Hargood later asks Courtley to dine with them. Sensing the men's moral depravity, Courtley invites them to sell their souls to Satan in exchange for eternal life. They readily agree after Courtley shows them relics of Count Dracula, including his cape and ring and his dried blood. He commands them to purchase these objects and to bring three crystal glasses to Dracula's abbey at midnight.

This scenario satirizes Victorian morality. The three gentlemen represent a retrograde paternalism that, even before the feminist vampires of the 1970s, seems shockingly corrupt. They meet Lord Courtley and begin participating in the ceremony but at the last minute refuse to drink Dracula's blood. Courtley drinks it instead, just as the three "gentlemen" turn on their mentor, kicking and beating him to death. As Courtley dies, he transforms into Dracula (Christopher Lee), who immediately plots vengeance and vows, "They have destroyed my servant, they will be destroyed." Dracula easily seduces Hargood's daughter Alice (Cinda Hayden), who slays her father on his command. Next Dracula seduces and vampirizes Lucy Paxton (Isla Blair) and persuades her to kill her father. Finally Lucy visits Jeremy Secker (Martin Jarvis), the third gentleman's son, and persuades him to kill his father. Thus Dracula enacts final judgment against three badly flawed humans, exacting a terrible penalty for their attempt to murder him.

The libidinous Courtley/Dracula of the film evokes the figure of Lord Ruthven and, ultimately, Byron himself. Like Byron, Courtley/Dracula comes from the highest social ranks and behaves licentiously, rejecting Victorian morality. He enters the room let by the "gentlemen" and imperiously summons one of the prostitutes, and she follows him with alacrity. He becomes the ultimate sexual predator, against whom females stand little chance. As such, he conforms perfectly to the Byronic rake model.

After prematurely abandoning hopes of starring Christopher Lee as Dracula, Hammer had decided to cast Ralph Bates in the lead role. But when Lee changed his mind, the studio incorporated the role of Courtley with that of Dracula.[26] Courtley/Dracula continues the association of vampirism with upper-class greed and arrogance. For Hammer fans, the tall, athletic, and handsome Lee embodied the image of the Byronic hero. Although Lee portrayed fierce and dangerous vampires, his contagious smile and commanding presence helped make him an ideal rake vampire. As J. Gordon Melton observes, "Lacking any clear direction from the production staff, Lee developed Dracula as a complex human who had great positive qualities—leadership, charm, intelligence, and sensuality—coupled with a savage and ferocious streak that would lead to his eventual downfall." In addition, in Lee's depictions "Dracula also had a tragic quality, his undead immortality."[27]

During this same period, other filmmakers also created vampire films featuring rakes. One of these was *Count Yorga, Vampire* (1970), a low-budget horror film originally conceived as a soft porn movie titled *The Loves of Count Yorga, Vampire!* Fear of an unfavorable rating from the Motion Picture Association of America led the filmmakers to reframe their movie as a more serious melodrama and give it a new title. Still, the film retained much of the sexuality of the original. In the film, Romanian Count Yorga (Robert Quarry) seduces Donna (Donna Anders) and Erica (Judy Lang) at a local séance through hypnosis—one of the Byronic vampires' most useful powers. He orders them through thought projection to come to him, then begins sensuously kissing and caressing them before biting them and sucking their blood.

The sexual nature of the original concept continues in this "serious" movie, as audiences behold a lengthy scene in which Erica and her boyfriend Paul (Michael Murphy) make love in the back of a minibus. Count Yorba lusts after every attractive female, including Donna's mother, played by porn star Marsha Jordan. One after another, all the principal females are seduced and devoured by Yorba. His rapacity far outstrips that of Lord Ruthven, reflecting 1970s sexual liberation. The movie became a surprise box-office hit, spawning a sequel called *The Return of Count Yorga* (1971). It also helped prepare the way for *Blacula* (1972) and its sequel, *Scream, Blacula, Scream* (1973), starring William Marshall, as well as a number of more sexually explicit vampire thrillers.

Anne Rice's Vampire Chronicles novel series arrived in 1976 with *Interview with the Vampire,* followed by *The Vampire Lestat* (1985) and *The Queen of the Damned* (1988). The books became bestsellers and instant classics. In 1994 Hollywood released the film version of *Interview with the Vampire*, directed by Neil Jordan. A well-respected cinematic rendering of Rice's story, Jordan's film—like the novel—is considered classic by critics. It relies on the Byronic vampire's seductive powers in the person of Lestat de Lioncourt (Tom Cruise), who entices Louis de Pointe du Lac (Brad Pitt) to transform into a vampire. True to Byronic form, the two men have breeding, wealth, and aristocratic backgrounds. In the Romantic tradition, they form a partnership that contains strong subliminal elements of homoeroticism in their exchange of blood, friendship, and cooperation.

After being bitten by Lestat, Louis fights his own vampirism and refuses to drink human blood or take human life, preferring to dine on the blood of rats he finds in the sewers. He soon tires of rat blood, however, and begins to partake of human blood for survival. Lestat, on the other hand, openly preys on humans and demonstrates a prodigious appetite for their blood. As Louis relates, "Lestat killed two, sometimes three a night. A fresh young girl,

Queen Akasha (Aaliyah) awakes from centuries of hibernation when she hears the music of the Vampire Lestat, who recently awoke from a two hundred year sleep and became an openly vampire rock star. Akasha kills her husband by drinking his blood dry, then seduces Lestat to be her new king in *Queen of the Damned* (2002) (Kobal Collection at Art Resource, New York).

that was his favorite for the first of the evening. For seconds, he preferred a gilded beautiful youth. But the snob in him loved to hunt in society, and the blood of the aristocrat thrilled him best of all." Lestat has eclectic tastes, preferring women but preying at times upon men and even children, while Louis favors women. The two form a friendship that finally fractures under the weight of gender and sexuality. Their open bisexuality paved the way for modern bisexual male vampires.

In 2002 Michael Rymer released *Queen of the Damned*, based on Rice's third Vampire Chronicles novel. Like *Interview with the Vampire*, Rymer's film features Lestat (Stuart Townsend). Audiences first meet Lestat as he slowly awakens in his coffin, where he has lain for centuries until the rhythmic beat of a local rock and roll band awakens him. Once awake, Lestat quickly assumes a rock star persona, transforming the garage band that woke him into a vampire band. At this point Lestat comes out in the open about his vampirism and calls on other vampires to follow his example, daring them to "come out, come out, wherever you are!" This enrages vampires who prefer to continue preying on humans covertly, and they vow to kill Lestat at a Burning Man–type rock concert.

Lestat's seductive powers ramp up after his music awakens Akasha (Aaliyah), the original vampire queen in ancient Egypt from whom all vampires originated. Akasha seduces Lestat, who in turn sucks blood from her arm in order to assimilate her power. He then joins the Order of Ancient Vampires to destroy her and end her threat to humanity. In director Rymer's hands, Aaliya's performance—especially her seductive dance movements—highlights female sexuality, while Townsend as Lestat pleased both fans and critics.

Lestat develops a relationship with Jesse Reeves (Marguerite Moreau), a paranormal researcher who finds him irresistible. In the final scene Lestat transforms Reeves into a vampire, saving her life and creating a mate for himself. The two slowly walk away together. As in Polidori's "The Vampyre," Lestat survives and attains freedom from domination by other vampires, including the seductive Akasha. In the process he frees himself from enslavement to his own outsized rock-star personality.

In 1991 author L. J. Smith published *The Vampire Diaries*, a trilogy of novels aimed at young adults; a fourth novel was added to the series the following year. The series features dramatic events in the life of Elena Gilbert, a seventeen-year-old high school student from Fells Church, Virginia—a town situated at a major junction or "nexus" of invisible power structures, including ley lines connecting ancient historic sites. Gilbert drops her long-time boyfriend in favor of two youthful-appearing but very old vampire brothers, Stefan and Damon Salvatore. She bonds with both of them, Stefan because he plays the "good boy" role by being "nice" and "decent," and Damon because he acts as a Byronic rake and is "exciting," "aggressive," and "playful." By a strange coincidence, back in Renaissance Italy both brothers had fallen in love with and competed for the affections of Katherine—who looked identical to Elana. Katherine had turned the youths into immortal vampires before they murdered each other in a sword fight, and she committed suicide when it appeared she couldn't have them both.

In the present, the brothers compete fiercely for Elena's love, but she adamantly opposes dropping one in favor of the other and decides to keep both as lovers. She dies and becomes a vampire herself, then later is cured of vampirism and returns as a human. Damon also dies and returns as a human, then is transformed once more into a vampire. Characters in the novels often transform into vampires, witches, or demons and then change back into humans. In fact, many paranormal characters slip back and forth between the supernatural realm and the human domain, creating a mysterious, surreal atmosphere.

The novels fueled the popular *Vampire Diaries* television series (2009–present). Series developers Kevin Williamson and Julie Plec changed the setting from Fells Church to Mystic Falls, Virginia. Nina Dobrev plays Elena, Paul Wesley plays Stefan, and Ian Somerhalder plays Damon. In the television series, a sexier version of Elena named Faith joins the cast and functions as a seductive vamp. The shows showcase both Byronic rake vampires (Damon and Stephan) and vamps (Elena and Faith).

J.S. Cardone's film *The Forsaken* (2001) stars Kerr Smith as Sean, a young man who accepts a job driving a vintage Mercedes sports car to Florida. Despite the fact that he's been forbidden to pick up hitchhikers or damage the car in any way, and in spite of his initial reluctance, he stops for Nick (Brandon Fehr)—seemingly a drifter—to help pay for gas. The two form a Byronic friendship similar to the Romantic-era male bonding between Lord Byron and John Polidori. They are quickly overtaken by a carload of vampires, including Kit, played by Jonathan Schaech, and Pen, played by Simon Rex, both of whom are male models referred to as "eye candy." Reviewer Dennis Hensley observes that while Kit "isn't gay, he does enjoy sucking on a few good men."[28] Nick turns out to be a vampire hunter searching for the vampire that had bitten him a year earlier, landing him in a hospital. One of the hospital employees had recognized vampire marks on Nick and helped him survive with special medication. The capsules contain a formula of amino acids, antigens, and proteins developed to slow HIV. They offer Nick a respite, but ultimately he must kill the vampire that infected him.

One night outside a restaurant somewhere in the Southwest, Nick encounters a sick young woman named Megan (Izabella Miko). He befriends her and takes her to the Palm Inn Motel. Realizing that Megan is suffering from the early stages of vampirism, Nick shocks her by throwing her into an icy bath. While Nick holds her down, Sean administers a shot of morphine, but in the confusion Megan bites Sean and infects him with vampirism. From that point they must seek out and destroy the head vampire, a member of the original "Forsaken" group of vampires, or they will surely transform into vampires themselves. Their mission cements the bonds of friendship.

In 2008 the seductive Byronic vampire Edward Cullen (Robert Pattinson) thrilled millions of young women worldwide upon the release of *Twilight*, the first movie in a series based on novels by Stephenie Meyer. In the series, Cullen falls in love with human/vampire hybrid Bella Swan (Kristen Stewart), a fellow high school student in Forks, Washington. Cullen refrains from seducing the young woman he finds so attractive and, in so doing, breaks vampire conventions. He requires no sleep and therefore needs no coffin. He endures daylight, unlike Count Dracula, but avoids bright sunlight, which makes his skin sparkle like diamonds. Furthermore, he avoids sexual intimacy with Bella, delaying their physical gratification—like a neo–Victorian—until after they marry. He and the rest of the Cullen vampire clan avoid drinking human blood, preferring to live off the blood of wild animals they hunt in the woods. The Cullens think of themselves as "vegetarians" for their refusal to feed on humans.

Edward Cullen appeals strongly to female audiences. Being a vampire makes him dangerous. "I'm the world's best predator, aren't I?" he

Vampire Edward Cullen (Robert Pattinson) protects human hybrid Bella Swan (Kristen Stewart) from predatory vampires in *Twilight: Breaking Dawn Part 1* (2011). Cullen, part of a new breed of vampires, walks freely in daylight, shuns drinking human blood, and loves and protects Bella (Kobal Collection at Art Resource, New York).

asks Bella. "Everything about me invites you in—my voice, my face, even my *smell.*" His seductiveness reminds us of typical Byronic vampires, except that his sexual restraint actually enhances his romantic appeal. He falls in love with Bella's scent and struggles against two drives: to have sex with her and to drink her blood. Novelist Meyer describes Cullen as physically attractive, even godlike: "He lay perfectly still in the grass, his shirt open over his sculpted, incandescent chest, his scintillating arms bare. His glistening, pale lavender lids were shut, though of course he didn't sleep. A perfect statue, carved in some unknown stone, smooth like marble, glittering like crystal." Cullen's mental abilities match his physical attributes, and in the novels he garners undergraduate and graduate degrees by studying at night (he doesn't need to sleep). His tenure at Forks High School challenges his tolerance, since his knowledge exceeds the curriculum.

Cullen departs from the seductive womanizer model and instead embodies the tortured, conflicted Romantic hero of the nineteenth century. As one critic observed, "He isn't just the bad boy, he's the bad boy who can be saved *if only the good girl loves and trusts him enough.* He really is a romance addict, dangerously seductive, proudly resentful, drawing Bella in with those most irresistible words: *Stay away from me for your own good.*"[29] Audiences didn't stay away, and *Twilight: New Moon* garnered $141 million during its opening week, the third-highest opening in movie history. Surprisingly, many in the audiences—eighty percent of whom were females—weren't teenagers but forty-something women remembering their own early romances.[30]

Bella's attraction for Edward alters the traditional vampire metaphor. In past cycles, love between vampire and human ends tragically after the vampire attacks its love interest. In the *Twilight* cycle, however, Cullen and his family fight their vampire nature and protect Bella rather than consume her. This allows her to join their family, shielding her from rogue vampires. The union between Edward and Bella in effect joins the vampire and human races and promises a bright future for both. The relationship symbolizes diversity, reflecting increasing acceptance of ethnic, racial, and gender differences. CNN reports that interracial marriage in the United States reached an all-time high in 2010.[31] The fact that Edward and Bella both appear to be Caucasian renders their "interracial" marriage symbolic, conveyed through vampirism.

HBO's hit television series *True Blood* (2008–2012) features seductive vampires of the Byronic aristocratic mold. Civil War veteran Bill Compton (Stephen Moyer) and Viking Eric Northman (Alexander Skarsgård) provide sex appeal for fans worldwide. Filmmaker Alan Ball chose Bon Temps, Louisiana, as his fictional setting in a state where vampires "come out of the casket" and mix freely with humans. Both men compete for the affections of

Sookie Stackhouse (Anna Paquin), a sexy young human hybrid who's a waitress at a local diner. Compton becomes a spokesperson for local vampires in their struggle against evangelical Christians waging a bitter religious war against them, while Northman serves as "sheriff" of the local vampire community.

True Blood employs both carnal metaphors and direct depictions. "The image of the sexy vampire is everywhere," observes the *Huffington Post's* Emma Gray. "They're alluring, irresistible, almost inhumanly beautiful and virtually always sexual in nature."

"Overwhelmingly (though obviously not exclusively), the fan bases of these television shows, movies and novels are women," says Gray. "Where *Twilight* idealizes repression, *True Blood* embraces play." Taken together, the two series illustrate the conflict between Victorian attitudes and today's secular sexual diversity. Gray concludes, "Most TV shows and movies don't come close to representing the complexity of real sexual interactions, but Edward, Bella, Bill and Sookie might be helping us get a step closer."[32]

True Blood's Bill Compton and *Twilight's* Edward Cullen conform to the Romantic image of brooding, flawed heroes. As typical Byronic heroes, they have a "desperate need of rehabilitation," says a Fox News "sexpert." As a result of both their flaws and their overwhelming gifts, "Women can't help but be drawn to these mesmerizing, misunderstood, moody bad boys."[33] These potentially savage carnivores, as Lady Caroline Lamb once said of Lord Byron himself, appear "mad, bad, and dangerous to know" (see Chapter One).

Dark Shadows (2012), Tim Burton's cinematic homage to the 1970s television series of the same name, stars Johnny Depp as Barnabas Collins, a seductive 200-year-old vampire who escapes captivity in a coffin. In 1776 Collins' pretty maid Angelique Bouchard (Eva Green) had fallen in love with her employer and attempted to seduce him, but when Collins scorned her she revealed her identity as a powerful witch and imprisoned him in the coffin. When workers accidentally free him in 1972, Collins heads for Collinwood, his ancestral manor house near the American seaside town of Collinsport. Announcing that he is an English cousin come to pay a visit, he quickly ingratiates himself with the entire household. He earns the admiration of all, including Victoria Winters (Bella Heathcote). The two share an intimate kiss that's seen by his former captor, Angelique Bouchard, who competes with Collins' fishing business. Using her seductive and magical powers, she persuades local fishermen to abandon their contracts with Collins and sell to her instead. To quench her jealousy, she intends to enrich herself at the expense of the Collins family. But Barnabas turns the tables by using his own hypnotic powers, forcing a confrontation with Bouchard. She decides to make him an offer he can't refuse:

Bouchard: I'm going to make an offer to you, Barnabas. My last. You can join me by my side and we can run Collinsport together as partners, and lovers … or I'll put you back in the box.

Collins: I have already prepared my counter-proposal. It reads thusly: You may strategically place your wonderful lips upon my posterior and kiss it repeatedly!

As they test each other's powers, Bouchard exclaims, "I worshipped you!" Collins replies, "You plagued me!" She replies, "I adore you!" He retorts, "I despise you!" Eventually Collins proves the stronger, and Bouchard tears out her heart and offers it to him, exclaiming, "I really did love you!" Collins, in a modern rendition of the Byronic vampire, proves more powerful than the Carmilla-inspired Bouchard.

During the U.S. presidential election campaign of 2012, a low-budget vampire farce titled Trapped by the Mormons *received media attention by attracting thousands of online viewers. A politically motivated website included links to the election campaigns of both Barack Obama and Mitt Romney, with the following warning: "MITT ROMNEY IS … A MORMON!!! … AND MORMONS ARE … EVIL!!!!!!"*

Available for free viewing long after the election, the film included the vampire-as-sexual-seducer metaphor as well as the savage monster metaphor. Shot in black and white, and silent except for 1920s organ music, *Trapped by the Mormons* was a 2005 remake of a 1922 British movie that had the same name and a similar plot, minus vampires.

The 2005 version stars Johnny Kat as Isolde Keane, a nineteenth-century Mormon recruiter on a mission to seduce and kidnap young London women and bring them to Utah to enhance his growing harem of wives. He falls for Nora Prescott (Emily Riehl-Bedford), a young shopgirl he meets on the London streets. Keane immediately succeeds in mesmerizing her and placing her under his control. He commands her to break off her upcoming engagement to a young army officer and to introduce him to her girlfriends. At a park, Prescott and her friends witness an obviously staged event in which Keane seemingly restores a dead man to life. (The "dead man" is his accomplice and fellow Mormon.) Convinced by this demonstration of Keane's healing powers, Prescott agrees to slip out of her home and marry him. But after joining Keane in his church, Prescott has second thoughts about the marriage, scheduled for the following morning. One of Keane's other wives confirms her suspicions, but Keane and his henchmen tie up the wife and attempt to drug Prescott. She escapes before the police raid the house, where they discover Keane's many wives—who have become ravenous, zombie-like vampires whom they must kill.

The negative characterizations in *Trapped by the Mormons* reveal much about the diversity of the Byronic rake vampire metaphor. In *Trapped by the Mormons*, the vampires force polygamy on unwilling victims. In the hands of *True Blood* creator Alan Ball, on the other hand, attractive vampires seduce willing humans. In today's atmosphere of greater tolerance for GLTB identities, handsome male vampires may symbolize sexual predation, homosexuality, and bisexuality. Diverse interpretations of the original Byronic model show the continuing appeal of powerful, seductive male vampires and female vamps.

Vamps

Female rakes exploded in popularity during the Romantic era. Eighteenth-century poet Alexander Pope gave voice to their presence when he observed:

> Men, some to Business, some to pleasure take;
> But ev'ry Woman is at heart a Rake.[34]

Referred to as "vamps," female rakes appear youthful and often dazzlingly beautiful. Such women have populated stories for thousands of years. Lilith,a female demon from Jewish mythology, supposedly was married to Adam but left because she refused to be subservient to him. She reputedly captured and strangled children and seduced men, producing demon offspring.[35] Lamiai or Lamia, also female demons who sucked the blood of children, assumed the vampire role in ancient Greek mythology. In *The Life of Apollonius*, the Greek writer Philostratus (c. 170 to 247 AD) relates that Apollonius's student Menippus planned to marry a wealthy young woman. However, Apollonius perceived that the lady, though beautiful, possessed vampire qualities and threatened to drain Menippus of life. He warned Menippus in time to prevent disaster.[36] Other mythical vampires include female Caribbean and South American entities called loogaroos, soukouyant, and asemas that attack their victims at night. She allegedly divided her time between seducing men (succubus) and stealing and then devouring children.[37] This theme—of females secretly preying on others—speaks to male insecurities regarding adultery and female promiscuity.

Unlike male vampire seducers depicted in films and literature as charming, irresistible, brooding, and mysterious, pop culture's female seductresses often receive negative treatment as immoral, dangerous, monstrous, and evil, like the Sirens and Medusa in Greek mythology.[38] These gender disparities continue in contemporary popular culture, where seductresses often fare poorly while seducers assume hero status. Nineteenth-century vampire literature, however, presents some notable exceptions. By creating potent female characters who functioned independently of males, Romantic-era writers inaugurated powerful, seductive roles that, though mainly negative, reflected the era's proto-feminist politics.

The real life of infamous Transylvanian (Hungarian) Countess Elizabeth Bathory (1560–1614) presents pop culture with one of history's most powerful female characters. Bathory sprang from one of Hungary's oldest aristocratic families. Her ancestor Stephen Bathory had fought alongside Vlad III Dracul (aka The Impaler) against the Ottoman Turks a century earlier, and another relative had ascended to the Polish throne. She was not only noble by birth but also possessed great beauty, acute intelligence, and a mastery of four languages. Unfortunately, early in life she showed antisocial, sadistic, and psychotic tendencies. By age four she is said to have suffered from epileptic seizures, and as she grew older she began to exhibit violent, uncontrollable rages. Like many aristocrats of the era, she appeared to be suffering from genetic disorders resulting from inbreeding.[39]

Bathory also exhibited precocious sexuality, reputedly being impregnated by a local commoner while barely in her teens. Her family sequestered her in a remote area until the baby was born, then married her off to warrior count Ferenc Nadasdy. He adopted his wife's family name of Bathory, a nobler name than his. Only fourteen at her wedding, Bathory had already experienced sex and childbirth, and she had a penchant for violence.

She assumed command of the count's castle and lands while he was away fighting Ottoman armies. During his absences she eventually kidnapped, imprisoned, tortured, and murdered hundreds of young girls and women over a twenty-year period. Initially she ordered servants to kidnap peasant girls, but she eventually turned to the young daughters of the area's lesser gentry. While they were chained to cells in the castle basement, Bathory supposedly drained their blood to use for her bath, believing that virgin blood would keep her face and body from aging.

Bathory allegedly tortured and sexually abused her captives until they finally died. Rumors about her activities grew insistent, and in 1611, despite her formidable lineage and royal connections, the king of Hungary reluctantly ordered her brought to trial for murder. Evidence against her included a list in her handwriting of more than 650 young women, many of whom had mysteriously disappeared over the years. She was convicted of multiple counts of murder and mayhem.[40] Bathory's rank served her well: the court sentenced her not to death or prison but to be walled inside her rooms, fed through a small opening, and never allowed to go outside or speak to anyone. She died in 1614 at age 54 after two years of imprisonment. The association with blood, and accusations that she ate human flesh and tortured and sexually abused her victims, made the connection with vampires inevitable. Today popular culture knows her as the "Blood Countess" and "Countess Dracula."[41]

Inspired by the story of Elizabeth Bathory, or by ancient mythology or nineteenth-century news reports, Romantic writers such as John Keats and Samuel Taylor Coleridge created the first female vampire characters in English literature. Coleridge's lengthy poem *Christabel* (published in 1816) relates the meeting of a beautiful young virgin named Christabel ("beautiful Christian"), daughter of wealthy baron Sir Leoline, with the richly clad and mysterious Geraldine. They first meet in the forest beside a huge oak tree as Christabel prays for her absent lover. Geraldine narrates a fantastic tale in which five mysterious warriors riding white steeds had abducted her, then left her beside the tree but threaten to return at any moment. Christabel invites Geraldine to her home, where she collapses and Cristabel carries her over the threshold. In Christabel's room, Geraldine begs her to lie down on the bed while Geraldine prays. Then Geraldine partially disrobes in front of Christabel:

> The cincture from beneath her breast:
> Her silken robe, and inner vest,
> Dropped to her feet, and full in view
> Behold! Her bosom and half her side-
> A sight to dream of, not to tell!

Geraldine lies beside Christabel and begins sensually and tenderly caressing her. When they awaken in the morning, Geraldine appears refreshed and radiant—implying vampirism, a lesbian relationship, or both.

Bracy, a poet friend of Sir Leoline, dreams of a huge green snake devouring a helpless dove that resembles Christabel. Geraldine as a snake evokes Lamia, a mythological half-woman, half-snake vampire who seduces young women and drinks their blood. Christabel catches a glimpse of Geraldine's eyes transforming into those of a snake, and she begs her father to expel Geraldine from the house. But the aged Sir Leoline falls under Geraldine's spell and refuses Christabel's urgent pleas, instead walking off hand in hand with the vampire. His decision seals both his and his daughter's doom.

Christabel allegedly inspired novelist Joseph Sheridan Le Fanu to write a novel that developed the characters of Christabel and Geraldine more fully. Le Fanu's *Carmilla* appeared in 1872, featuring a female vampire that seems to be a combination of Countess Bathory and Coleridge's Geraldine. Le Fanu's story takes place in Styrgia, a mountainous region in Austria where a young girl named Laura dreams that a beautiful woman visits her bedroom and bites her on the chest. A few years later, a more mature Laura receives an unexpected visit from Carmilla, the beautiful woman of her dream. Carmilla and her mother emerge from an opulent carriage that has just been in an accident, and the mother asks Laura's father to allow Carmilla to stay with them while she attends to urgent business elsewhere. The father agrees, and the two young ladies seem to enjoy each other's company.

However, Laura has disturbing dreams of being visited in her bed by a supernatural cat and eventually by Carmilla herself, who seduces her sexually. Laura later recalls that Carmilla "used to place her pretty arms about my neck, draw me to her, and laying her cheek to mine, murmur with her lips near my ear, 'Dearest, your little heart is wounded; think me not cruel because I obey the irresistible law of my strength and weakness; if your dear heart is wounded, my wild heart bleeds with yours.'" After another nocturnal encounter with Laura, Carmilla says, "Now I live through your warmth and life, but you will die—how sweet to die for me and because of me. I can do nothing to change it. Even as I feed on you, so will you feed on others and come to know the ecstasy of the cruelty that is love. I live in you and you must die for me. I love you, terribly and eternally." She prophesies that "as I draw near to you, you, in your turn, will draw near to others, and learn the rapture of that cruelty, which yet is love; so, for a while, seek to know no more of me and mine, but trust me with all your loving spirit."

Gradually Laura's health fades, and her father decides to visit the village of Karnstein where Carmilla originated. He meets General Spielsdorf, who had lost his niece to a beautiful visitor—in this case named Millarca (an anagram of Carmilla). The two men realize that Carmilla and Millarca are the same person, anagrams of Countess Mircalla Karnstein, supposedly killed years earlier by a local hero who was the region's first vampire hunter. His descendent, Barren Vordenburg, meets Laura's father and General Spielsdorf and offers his assistance. They locate Countess Karnstein's tomb and uncover her body, which shows no signs of decay despite 150 years of interment. They drive a stake through her heart, decapitate her, and then burn her body, thereby releasing Laura from her vampire spell.

Le Fanu barely conceals Carmilla's (and Laura's) lesbian tendencies, at one point describing Carmilla as longing to caress a female victim's breast. At another point Laura becomes sexually aroused by Carmilla's scent. Female characters in this novella exhibit both strength and sexuality. Laura's father remains ineffective throughout the encounters between his daughter and Carmilla. Despite the mortal threat Carmilla poses, Laura falls in love with her as an escape from her life within a paternalistic society. Although Carmilla dies at the hands of Baron Vordenburg, Le Fanu implies that Laura, too, will transform into a vampire, renewing the cycle. Female vampirism, like female liberation, proves impossible to suppress for any length of time. Le Fanu implies that the lesbian vampire cycle—metaphorically related to Victorian feminism—cannot be suppressed but will continue forever.

Carmilla and her successors reflect tensions about the Victorian cult of domesticity that decreed all women should aspire to piety, purity, submissiveness, and domesticity.[42] Carmilla fails to conform to those ideals. Instead, she more closely resembles the Victorian "New Woman." Scholar and critic Trudi Van Dyke suggests that killing off Carmilla and other "New Woman" vampires "could be interpreted as a culturally acceptable way to metaphorically control the New Woman, thereby keeping the existing patriarchal domination unblemished and intact."[43]

Carmilla was an important source for Bram Stoker's *Dracula*, and Le Fanu's influence in Stoker's novel seems unmistakable, from staking vampires through the heart to Stoker's Lucy Westenra character.[44] Lucy, Count Dracula's initial conquest in London, conforms to the New Woman stereotype. Like Dracula's other "brides," he turns seductive after her transformation into a vampire. As Lucy's living soul expires, she "opened her eyes, which were now dull and hard at once, and said in a soft, voluptuous voice, such as I had never heard from her lips, 'Arthur! Oh, my love, I am so glad you have come! Kiss me!'"

Lucy proves to be an avid vampire, aggressively preying on neighborhood children. Newspapers dub her the "Kensington Horror," the "Stabbing Woman," and the "Woman in Black." The local children label her the "bloofer lady" who lures children away by offering to walk with them. Van Helsing traps her vampire body in its coffin by sealing the tomb with blessed Communion wafers. He lifts the lid to reveal a new Lucy—"a nightmare of Lucy as she lay there, the pointed teeth, the blood stained, voluptuous mouth, which made one shudder to see, the whole carnal and unspirited appearance, seeming like a devilish mockery of Lucy's sweet purity."

Lucy's persona evoked Victorian fears about women becoming predacious. According to the mores of the late nineteenth century, nice women didn't exhibit sexual feelings. If women became noticeably sexually aroused, they weren't considered proper ladies. Women's revolt, resulting in the "New Women" of the age, is prophesied by Bram Stoker in *Dracula*. In the novel, Count Dracula—the one responsible for creating New Women vampires like Lucy—warns, "My revenge is just begun! I spread it over centuries, and time is on my side." Trudi Van Dyke observes, "Indeed, Dracula's promised threat comes true. The New Woman does resurface [in the twentieth century], biting back in a revamped, contemporary, and above all culturally acceptable form."[45]

By contrast, Stoker includes the female character of Mina initially as a "True Woman," Harker's fiancé and later his wife, who acted with piety, purity, submissiveness, and domesticity. Described throughout as pretty, Mina earns the esteem of all the other characters. Dr. Seward implies that she has a mysterious destiny to help rid the world of evil. "Ah, that wonderful Madam Mina! She has man's brain, a brain that a man should have were he much gifted, and a woman's heart. The good God fashioned her for a purpose, believe me, when He made that so good combination." He calls her "one of God's women, fashioned by His own hand to show us men and other women that there is a heaven where we can enter, and that its light can be here on earth." Mina epitomizes the ideal True Woman, "so sweet, so noble, so little an egoist, and that, let me tell you, is much in this age, skeptical and selfish."

Infatuated with Mina, Dracula performs the "ceremony of blood" by drinking her blood and forcing her to drink his. His appetite for the chaste girl seems more of a violation than does his preying on Lucy, who by her seemingly promiscuous relationships with many suitors almost invites his seduction. Once vampirized, Mina reluctantly assumes the role of "New Woman." The two English women symbolize different ideas about Victorian women. In the era's cult of domesticity, society expected women to adhere to certain standards of behavior, including piety, purity, submissiveness, and domesticity. "True Women" were expected to remain chaste and exhibit feminine delicacy and reticence.[46] Dracula's power over the pure Mina seems to demonstrate the threats to British womanhood. As Mina begins transforming into a vampire she begs her friends, "You must promise me, one and all, even you, my beloved husband, that should the time come, you will kill me." Mina prefers death to life as a "New Woman" like Lucy.

Stoker's novel became the most important source for subsequent vampire characters, but Rudyard Kipling's poem "The Vampire," also published in 1897, inaugurated a new cycle of predatory female vampire characters. At the time, Kipling belonged to a Freemason lodge that embraced many aspects of the occult, and he corresponded with members of the Golden Dawn Society, a popular esoteric cult of the era.[47] His immersion into mysticism helped inspire one of the most influential seductive female vampires.

The Vampire
by Rudyard Kipling
The verses—as suggested by the painting
"The Vampire" by Philip Burne Jones (1897)

A fool there was and he made his prayer
(Even as you and I!)
To a rag and a bone and a hank of hair

(We called her the woman who did not care),
But the fool he called her his lady fair
(Even as you and I!)

Oh the years we waste and the tears we waste
And the work of our head and hand,
Belong to the woman who did not know
(And now we know that she never could know)
And did not understand.

A fool there was and his goods he spent
(Even as you and I!)
Honor and faith and a sure intent
But a fool must follow his natural bent
(And it wasn't the least what the lady meant),
(Even as you and I!)

Oh the toil we lost and the spoil we lost
And the excellent things we planned,
Belong to the woman who didn't know why
(And now we know she never knew why)
And did not understand.

The fool we stripped to his foolish hide
(Even as you and I!)
Which she might have seen when she threw him aside—
(But it isn't on record the lady tried)
So some of him lived but the most of him died—
(Even as you and I!)

And it isn't the shame and it isn't the blame
That stings like a white hot brand.

It's coming to know that she never knew why
(Seeing at last she could never know why)
And never could understand.

The two characters in Kipling's poem, the male fool and the female "vampire," were ensnared in a dangerous and disastrous relationship. Although the vampire takes everything from the fool, from his goods to his toil, stripping him to his "foolish hide," he insists on calling her his "lady fair." Finally, "the most of him died" indirectly by her hand.

Although no blood is shed or consumed in his poem, Kipling titled it "The Vampire," and it provided a model for future writers and filmmakers. The first film inspired by the poem, now lost, also bore the title *The Vampire*. Produced in the United States by William Nicholas Selig in 1910, it depicted a seductive female psychic vampire who preyed on unsuspecting men. Robert Vignola's classic 1913 *The Vampire* depicts Sybil (Alice Hollister), a psychic vampire who pursues young Harold Brentwell (Harry Millarde). He moves to a temptation-ridden city to take a new job, but Sybil distracts and seduces him. She abandons him after he becomes an alcoholic and is addicted to her charms.

In 1915 Frank Powell directed an influential film called *A Fool There Was*, starring Theda Bara in her screen debut. Powell's movie directly parallels Kipling's poem by introducing a "fool" character named John Schuyler (Edward Jose), a wealthy statesman with a wife and daughter. Schuyler falls helplessly in love with Bara, billed only as "the vampire." She seduces and abandons wealthy men, who end up dead by suicide or stress-induced heart failure. At one point aboard an ocean liner, Bara famously commands a desperate former lover to "Kiss me, my fool" as he raises a pistol to his head and commits suicide. A steward later tells an officer, "Only a boy he was, sir, and she was standing there laughing like the Devil."

Bara's performance as *The Vampire* cemented her reputation as a screen star and launched the "vamp" style that was popular for over a decade. The actress famously remarked, "The reason good women like me and flock to my pictures is that there is a little bit of vampire instinct in every woman."[48] During the 1920s, vamp characters also became known as "gold diggers." Vampire-like characters played by Clara Bow, Jean Harlow, Mae West, and Barbara Stanwyck achieved wide popularity over the next two decades.

Although the 1920s and early 1930s abound in vamp seductresses, Jack Conroy's *Red-Headed Woman* (1932) glorifies the character like few others. In Conroy's film, Lil (Jean Harlow) seduces her happily married boss, Bill Legendre, Jr. (Chester Morris), resulting in his wife's divorcing him. After Lil marries Legendre she immediately begins an affair with a wealthy older man. In an epilogue we see her riding in a limousine with an even wealthier older Frenchman while exchanging glances with her chauffeur Albert (Charles Boyer), with whom she has been conducting a secret affair. Audience sympathies lie with Lil, not with the boring and easily seduced businessmen, and in the end she's truly happy and seemingly on top of the world. This is the diametrical opposite of Kipling's villainous and uncaring woman in *The Vampire*, in effect glorifying a predatory female who epitomizes the seductive, gold-digging vamp character.

In 1932 Danish director Carl Dreyer released *Vampyr*, loosely based on *Carmilla* without the novel's references to lesbianism. The central character in Dreyer's film, Allan Gray (Julian West), appears derived from Le Fanu's Dr. Hesselius, the occult doctor who serves as Le Fanu's narrator. Dreyer made his Carmilla an elderly noblewoman, Marquarite Chopin (Henriette Gerard). She preys on beautiful young women for their blood—thus extending the vampire-as-lesbian metaphor to include older women. The village doctor (Jan Hieronimoko), a pawn of Chopin, meets his death trapped inside a flour mill that gradually fills with flour, slowly suffocating him. As this happens, Chopin's face dominates the screen. Alain Silver and James Ursini observe that Dreyer's film transforms Le Fanu's beautiful and apparently youthful Carmilla into an elderly crone-like woman who feeds upon youth and epitomizes evil.[49]

John Cromwell's 1934 American film *Of Human Bondage*, based on the 1915 Somerset Maugham novel, depicts a vamp in the character of cockney waitress Mildred Rogers (Bette Davis). She seduces a club-footed, love-struck medical student, Philip Carey (Leslie Howard), who serves as the victim. Like the couple in Kipling's "The Vampire," Rogers and Carey seem mismatched and dysfunctional. After Carey meets Rogers in a London café he tells her, "I've been looking for you all my life." Rogers displays indifference or outright rejection, never expressing pleasure at seeing Carey and accepting the dates he offers with an offhand "I don't mind." A friend of Carey's finds her "ill-tempered and contemptible." Rogers makes life unbearable for him, but when

Lil (Nan Gray, left) is interviewed by Countess Marya Zeleska (Gloria Holden) for a modeling position while being seduced by the countess. Later that night Lil is found in a "post hypnotic trance" with telltale red marks on her neck in *Dracula's Daughter* (1936) (Kobal Collection at Art Resource, New York).

he threatens to leave after she starts seeing another man, she disdainfully says, "Good riddance to bad rubbish!" Finally the indifferent and scornful Rogers quits Carey and takes up with another medical student, but she returns when she becomes pregnant and her new relationship fails.

In the meantime, Carey finds himself enjoying a new relationship with Nora (Kay Johnson), who loves him selflessly. However, he sets Rogers up in an apartment and pays her bills, eventually breaking up with Nora. Angered, Nora exclaims, "It's always the same. If you want a man to be nice to you, you have to be rotten to him." Carey comes to his senses in the final scenes and proposes marriage to a new love, Sally Athelny (Sandra Dee), a beautiful young upper-class woman who loves him deeply. Unlike Kipling's fool, Carey overcomes his vamp.

During the 1930s, Hollywood ushered in lesbian vampire characters. Universal produced a sequel to its successful *Dracula* film in 1936: *Dracula's Daughter*, homage to Le Fanu's *Carmilla*. Lambert Hillyer directed the film, which begins with Count Dracula dying at the hand of Van Helsing (Edward Sloan). Hillyer's film features Countess Marya Zaleska (Gloria Holden), a vampire who dreams of transforming into a human. While she loathes her vampire desires, she finds herself unable to resist her instincts. Countess Zaleska preys on beautiful young females and enlists the help of renowned psychoanalyst Dr. Jeffery Garth (Otto Kruger) to overcome this addiction.

Zaleska, through her assertiveness and explorations of the dark side, represents the New Woman. A second New Woman in this film is Janet Blake (Marguerite Churchill), a baron's daughter who serves as Dr. Garth's assistant (and probable girlfriend). She and Garth play at lovers' quarrels after Countess Zaleska enlists Dr. Garth's aid. Blake appears remarkably modern in her outlook, being jealous of Countess Zaleska and possessive of Garth, then tormenting him with telephone calls intended to interrupt his visits with the countess.

Countess Zaleska seduces young women by luring them to her house as artists' models, then hypnotizing them (using a ring with a magic gemstone) before drinking their blood. The countess, typical of the Carmilla model, prefers the blood of beautiful young women. In one scene pulsating with sexual energy as well as horror, a young model named Lili (Nan Grey) senses that something's amiss after the countess stares at her hungrily.

Lili: Why are you looking at me that way? Will I do?
Countess Marya Zaleska: Yes, you'll do very well indeed. Do you like jewels, Lili? It's very old and very beautiful, I'll show it to you.
Lili: I think I'll pass tonight. I think I'll go if you don't mind. Please don't come any closer.

At this time lesbianism topped the list of taboo movie subjects in U.S films, policed by the Motion Picture Producers and Distributors of America under what's known as the Hays Production Code. Named after Will Hays, the powerful MPPDA president, the code began being enforced in 1934. Although the Hays censors allowed the film in its present form, it generated controversy—chiefly in the form of a protest essay written by Dr. Theodore Malkin in which he charged that lesbians seduce and prey upon youth. Universal Studio executives actually hoped that protests like Malkin's might generate audience interest and increase the box-office receipts. Although there's no evidence that this happened, *Dracula's Daughter* remains a favorite among vampire film fans.[50]

The Hays Production Code officially banished lesbians, gold diggers, vamps, and psychic vamp characters from Hollywood. Instead, Hollywood quickly became enamored of screwball comedies—featuring oddballs instead of gold diggers—such as *It Happened One Night* (1934), *Bringing Up Baby* (1938), and *His Girl Friday* (1940). Predatory females remained banned from cinema until World War II distracted the Motion Picture Producers and Distributors of America and the Hays Office allowed psychic vampire types in the gritty new genre called *film noir*. The females in these movies, dubbed "femme noir," share many characteristics with earlier vamp characters, including greed, selfishness, and heartlessness. The movie posters often featured sexy artwork of the leading ladies in seductive poses.[51] The films themselves feature "bad girls" manipulating and often murdering males. "Bad girl" classics include Ida Lupino in *They Drive by Night* (1940); Mary Astor in *The Maltese Falcon* (1941); Barbara Stanwyck in *Double Indemnity* (1944); Ann Blyth in *Mildred Pierce* (1945); Ann Savage in *Detour* (1945); Lana Turner in *The Postman Always Rings Twice* (1946); Martha Vickers in *The Big Sleep* (1946); Jane Greer in *Out of the Past* (1947); Joan Bennett in *Scarlet Street* (1948); Rita Hayworth in *Gilda*; and Peggy Cummins in *Gun Crazy* (1950). These femme fatales seduce men and often manipulate them into committing murder and robbery. They most often fall into villain or antihero roles. Femme noir characters share many similarities with earlier females as vamps.

In Billy Wilder's film noir classic *Double Indemnity* (1944), actress Barbara Stanwyck—star of pre-code "gold digger" films such as *Baby Face* (1933)—plays the seductive Phyllis Dietrichson, who convinces insurance agent Walter Neff (Fred MacMurray) to murder her husband so they can collect his life insurance. Neff reminds her of the "double indemnity" clause that pays double in the event of an accidental death, so they make it look as if the husband had fallen off a speeding train. In an example of the sexually charged dialogue, this exchange occurs between the two:

Phyllis Dietrichson: There's a speed limit in this state, Mr. Neff. Forty-five miles an hour.

Walter Neff: How fast was I going, officer?

Phyllis: I'd say around ninety.

Walter: Suppose you get down off your motorcycle and give me a ticket.

Phyllis: Suppose I let you off with a warning this time.

Walter: Suppose it doesn't take.

Phyllis: Suppose I have to whack you over the knuckles.

Walter: Suppose I bust out crying and put my head on your shoulder.

Phyllis: Suppose you try putting it on my husband's shoulder.

Although Dietrichson rebuffs Neff's advances, her banter convinces him that she's available, and he begins to fantasize about her. Ultimately Neff is seduced into an adulterous relationship with her. A bullet wound from Dietrichson's pistol eventually kills him, proving her to be "the woman who doesn't care" of the vamp metaphor.

Femme noir characters like Phyllis Dietrichson match the profile of the Kipling seductress—cold, uncaring, and self-centered. They are copies of Kipling's and Theda Bara's "vampires" calmly tearing the petals from flowers. The frequent use of voice-over flashback narratives sends the leading men into the past, and they quickly become "a fool there was." While some noir male leads survive at film's end, most of them, like Walter Neff, succumb to the seductive powers of their female counterparts and end up dead. Violent images of dying men with uncaring women seem to highlight powerful tensions between genders. As psychologist Scott Snyder observes, "the femme noir femme fatale" became for Hollywood "a composite of power, lust, and greed."[52] These duplicitous, narcissistic, and deadly females maneuver males into committing murder, robbery, and fraud. On one level they represent male fears of rising female economic and political power during World War II.

Sexy female vampires returned with a vengeance to pop culture during the 1970s, an era of rising feminism. In 1970 Hammer Film Productions released *The Vampire Lovers*, the first of three Hammer films based on *Carmilla* and known collectively as the Karnstein Trilogy. The tag line promised viewers they could "Taste the deadly passion of the blood-nymphs." The film stars Peter Cushing as General Spielsdorf, who throws a party for his niece Laura (Pippa Steele) and invites a local countess (Dawn Adams) to attend. As in Le Fanu's novel, the countess is called away on the sudden death of a close friend but leaves her daughter Mircalla (Ingrid Pitt) to stay with the Spielsdorf family. Mircalla and Laura become such good friends that Laura refuses to see her other friends, even her boyfriend.

Laura grows weaker daily and dreams repeatedly that a huge cat is suffocating her. Mircalla comforts her and then disappears after Laura dies.

Only on her deathbed do others notice the faint pinpricks on Laura's throat. Later Mircalla resurfaces as Carmilla, also played by Pitt. She befriends Emma Morton (Madeline Smith), becomes her invited guest, and—as in Laura's case—begins seducing and draining Emma. Emma's father Roger Morton (George Cole), away in Vienna, receives an urgent summons to return home. On the way he meets General Spielsdorf and Baron von Hartog (Douglas Wilmer). The baron is descended from a man who had responded to a plague of vampires by staking them—all except for Mircalla. Hartog, Spielsdorf, Roger Morton, and Laura's ex-boyfriend Carl Ebhardt (Jon Finch) visit Karnstein Castle and discover a painting of the former Countess Mircalla, who looks exactly like Carmilla. Finding her in her casket, they stake and behead her.

The 1971 Hammer film *Lust for a Vampire* (1971), starring Yutte Stensgaard, bears the tag line "A Vampire's lust knows no bounds." Count and Countess Karnstein (Mike Raven and Barbara Jefford) conduct a satanic ceremony to resurrect the body of their daughter Mircalla. After being revived as an apparent teenager, she is enrolled in a fashionable local finishing school and immediately meets Richard LeStrange (Michael Johnson), a writer of occult books. He falls in love with Mircalla and arranges to teach at her school in order to be close to her. The two form an intimate bond, but she doesn't vampirize him. Later Mircalla's roommate Susan (Pippa Steele) turns up dead, with two tiny pinpricks in her neck. Eventually the villagers storm Karnstein Castle and set it afire. LeStrange rushes in to save his vampire lover, but a burning beam pierces Mircalla's heart, ending her life.

Twins of Evil (1971), the third film in the Karnstein Trilogy, stars sexy identical twins Mary and Madeline Collinson (also featured in *Playboy*). They play Maria and Frieda Gelhorn, sisters who go to live with their Uncle Gustav (Peter Cushing) and Aunt Cathy (Kathleen Byron) at Karnstein after the death of their parents. Uncle Gustav leads the Brotherhood, a group of sanctimonious, psychopathic vigilantes obsessed with burning suspected fornicators, adulators, witches, and vampires. Count Karnstein (Damien Thomas), who aspires to be a vampire, is unaffected by the Brotherhood because of his ties to the Emperor. The count reanimates Countess Mircalla (Katya Wyeth), who immediately grants his wish by vampirizing him. Frieda is drawn irresistibly to Karnstein Castle, and once the vampire count sees the beautiful young blonde he attacks and vampirizes her.

Hammer's sexy features capitalized on the growing power of feminism and a rising counterculture movement that rejected neo-Victorian morality. Hammer vampire films of the 1960s abundant gore and more sex than American censors permitted. By the 1970s, however, says film critic Tom Fallows, "subtext could go to hell and beauties (often ex-models or Playboy bunnies) and bare breast became the order of the day. *The Vampire Lovers* (1970) sees the curvaceous Ingrid Pitt as a vampire seducing and feeding upon a number of buxom young women. This vamp preferred biting breasts to necks, and the gratuitous lesbianism shocked many. Producer Anthony Hinds referred to these new films as, 'soft porn shows,' and retired shortly after."[53]

Hammer's *Countess Dracula* (1971) reintroduces the Countess Elizabeth Bathory character, here called Countess Elizabeth Dodosheen (Ingrid Pitt). In this film, a sexy female seducer of both men and women abducts, imprisons, tortures, bleeds, and murders young females—even children—to satisfy her fixation on bathing in a virgin's blood. Like the real Countess Bathory, Countess Dodosheen tortures and murders her victims, seducing and betraying men as well as women—although the real Bathory reputedly seduced many more young men and women than this film depicts. The Hammer vampire films caught a prevailing mood of emerging sexual freedom and rising feminism. According to the American Movie Classics website, "These films took advantage of the new morality, and were characterized by deeply saturated color, bright-red blood, gothic horror, suggestive soft-core sex and graphic nudity, vampire brides, lesbian overtones, plunging necklines, and a bevy of 'Scream Queen' stars such as Ingrid Pitt."[54]

Tony Scott's 1983 film *The Hunger* stars Catherine Denueve as centuries-old Egyptian vampire Miriam Blaylock and Susan Sarandon as Dr. Sara Roberts, a scientist who is seduced by Blaylock and eventually seduces victims of both sexes to satisfy her own sexual and blood needs. In 1984 a satirical comedy called *Vampire Lesbians of Sodom*, written by Charles Busch about two competing vampires, premiered off-Broadway. The Succubus, also known as La Condessa or Magda Legerdemaine, clashes with a virgin-turned-vampire known as both Madelaine Astarte and Madelaine Andrews. The two survive the downfall of the mythical Biblical city of Sodom and immediately struggle for dominance. Eventually they arrive in 1920s/1930s Broadway and Hollywood and pass themselves off as silent film stars. In the last scene, set in Las Vegas in the 1980s, they finally reach a truce. A *New York Times* critic described "costumes flashier than pinball machines, outrageous lines, awful puns, sinister innocence, harmless depravity—it's all here."[55]

The film *Tales From the Crypt: Bordello of Blood* (1996) updates the sexy vampire killer metaphor through a combination of feeble humor and sleazy scenes of sexy, partially nude female thralls in a whorehouse run by vampires. The heroes, two adolescent boys, learn the hard way that seemingly free sex isn't always what it appears. Ironically, the lesson learned comes in the form of soft pornography designed to titillate teenage audiences. Also presenting the vampire-as-prostitute theme is Robert Rodriguez's *From Dusk Till Dawn* (1996), which depicts the vampire as an exotic dancer and prostitute. Quentin Tarantino co-wrote the script. The action takes place in the Mexican desert at a bar called the Titty Twister, where Satanico Pandemonium (Salma Hayek) performs a sexy barroom dance complete with boa constrictor, capturing the admiration of the male patrons—until the sight of blood transforms her into a hideous monster. It turns out that the bar is a coven of vampires. Heyek's performance endeared her to fans, but it owes much to Cecilia Pezet's depiction of a prostitute/vampire in Gilberto Martinez Solares's Mexican cult film *Satanico Pandemonium* (1975). That film chronicles a Catholic nun who is seduced by Satan and attempts to corrupt all the nuns in her convent. *Lesbian Vampire Killers* (2009) continues the pattern of "innocent" human boys confronted by sexy but deadly female vampires. This film resembles the real-life case of Tracey Wigginton, who murdered a man in 1989 and drank his blood. The press labeled her "the lesbian vampire killer."[56] In the film, two young men, Jimmy (Matthew Horne) and Fletch (James Cordon), encounter Carmilla (Sylvia Colloca) and her lesbian vampire thralls in a remote English mountain village. After their first encounter Fletch exclaims, "Yep, lesbian vampires. Just another one of God's cruel tricks to get on my tits. Even dead women'd sooner sleep with each other than get with me it would appear. But eatin' me alive, oh no, that's fine." The film's comedic tone undercuts its abundant antifeminist sentiments. It serves up a combination horror/sex vampire narrative in which the metaphor of vampirism substitutes for lesbian sexuality.

Neil Jordon's *Byzantium* (2012) further updates the Carmilla-type lesbian vampire trope. Jordon's earlier *Interview with the Vampire* introduced Anne Rice's complex male vampires, and this more recent film introduces sensitive lesbian vampires. Gemma Arterton plays Clara/Carmilla, a 200-year-old vampire who lives with her daughter Eleanor (Saoirse Ronan), who is also 200 years old but appears to be sixteen. Clara pretends to be Eleanor's older sister and legal guardian. Clara supports them through prostitution, occasionally feeding on clients. Both women are unabashed feminist advocates. Clara declares her intention "to punish those that prey on the weak—to curb the power of men." Arterton asserts that *Byzantium* succeeds as "a girl power movie without it being about 'girl power.'"[57]

Lesbian vampires, in vogue since the Romantic era, currently are experiencing mixed popularity, receiving vilification in some pop culture depictions and near deification in others. Perhaps this ambivalence occurs because strong elements of Puritanism and neo-Victorianism remain entrenched in American society, enjoying a virtual renaissance during the last decade. It also recalls pop culture's perennial conflict between sexy, promiscuous characters and restrained, chaste examples, representing a diversity of lifestyles.

Necrophilia and Bestiality

Necrophilia—a sexual attraction to dead bodies—forms a powerful subtext in vampire lore. The medical meaning of the term, also called *necromania*, includes "an abnormal fondness for being in the presence of dead bodies" and "sexual contact with or erotic desire for dead bodies."[58] Ever since the publication of *Dracula,* vampires have been associated with necrophilia, drawing power and pleasure from fornicating with dead bodies.[59] Part of the sexual appeal of vampires stems from their status as dead, or rather undead. Taking this into consideration, sex between Bella Swan and Edward Cullen in the *Twilight* series constitutes necrophilia, due to Cullen's undead status.

The idea of sex with a dead person—even one who acts alive, like a vampire—immediately conjures up taboos. So, too, does the notion—however contemplative—of sex with an animal, including a werewolf. These taboos add to the forbidden pleasures associated with vampires and werewolves. Most vampires manifest little or no body temperature, feeling cold to the touch, like a dead human body. But sex with Count Dracula or any other vampire constitutes a reversal of the standard necrophilia encounter. In these cases vampires often initiate the sex, or bloodletting, not the humans. Humans tend to become inert at the first contact with a vampire and often act as willing, unresisting victims under the vampire's powerful hypnosis, causing a necrophilia role reversal.

Sexy Vampires

Sexy vampires of every sexual orientation may more accurately reflect actual human sexuality than is generally acknowledged. Dan Bergner, author of *What Do Women Want? Adventures in the Science of Female Desire,* observes that neither females nor males appear especially programmed for monogamy. In fact, when women and men feel safe to freely discuss sex, both genders experience sex with multiple partners over their lifetimes. Bergner argues that because of their ability to experience multiple organs, females might be anatomically adapted to experience sex with multiple partners, placing them on a par with males regarding sexual promiscuity.[60] *New York Times* writer Elaine Blair notes, "For some reason—maybe for many reasons—the story of the libidinous male and sexually indifferent female doesn't make sense to us anymore."[61] When we understand promiscuity as closer to a social norm instead of sinful aberration, the enduring popularity of sexy vampire "rakes" becomes readily understandable.

The popularity of sexual vampires continues unabated, and the most recent twists include the embracing of neo-Victorian sex standards. The *Twilight* series, for instance, emphasizes Edward Cullen's surprising prudery when he forces his girlfriend, Bella, to wait until they marry before they can make love. As one film critic recently opined, "You name it, the vampire can symbolize it: religion, capitalist exploitation, death and decay, addictions and sexuality or indeed *Twilight*-style abstinence."[62] *Twilight*-style abstinence seems to apply only to the characters, not necessarily to the actors portraying them. In 2012 the tabloids and online sources erupted with the news that Kristen Stewart, who plays *Twilight's* Bella Swan, had split with costar and longtime boyfriend Robert Pattinson after word of her secret affair with director Rupert Sanders was leaked to the press. The costars eventually reconciled and appeared inseparable—but Stewart's admission of the affair resulted in her being labeled with the epithet "trampire."[63]

Realistic depictions of seduction energize and empower pop culture's vampire narratives, attracting film audiences, readers, and gamers of all ages. An analysis of sexuality through metaphor in vampire culture reveals changing societal dynamics and evolving issues. The increasing acceptance of sexuality as a normal part of human relationships will continue to inspire realistic sexual narratives. Social scientists may profitably analyze pop culture's depictions of vampires for evidence of nascent attitudes and beliefs about sexuality.

THREE

Genders

Gender roles date back at least to the first book of the Bible. In Genesis, after God creates Adam and then forms Eve from one of Adam's ribs, Adam gazes upon Eve and says, "This is now bone of my bones and flesh of my flesh; she shall be called Woman, for she was taken out of Man."[1] The idea of woman being "taken out of man" appears to assign females to a subordinate position, as wives. Christians may argue that the role of wife and husband corresponds to that of the church to Christ. Wives, as well as the church, were intended to play subordinate roles to husbands and Christ. On the other hand, vampire metaphors, instead of enshrining traditional gender roles, depict a variety of "gender schema"—including heterosexual, gay, lesbian, bisexual, and transgender orientations.

Sociologists define gender schema as deeply embedded cognitive frameworks that define gender roles, as inculcated by socializing agents such as parents, teachers, peers, pop culture, the Internet, and religion.[2] Of these, pop culture may offer a wide range of gender models. Clinical social worker Caitlin Ryan notes that young people increasingly define themselves in terms of nontraditional gender classifications: "Gender has become part of the defining way that youth organize themselves and rebel against adults." She says that young people often experience a "fluidity of gender" as part of their personality development."[3]

Vampire lore exists within a general climate of heterosexism, and vampires as metaphors challenge traditional patriarchal roles. Researcher Shannon Winnubst observes that writers and filmmakers "use the trope of the vampire to unravel how whiteness, maleness, and heterosexuality feed on the same set of disavowals—of the body, of the Other, of fluidity, of dependency itself."[4] When Count Dracula (or one of his many successors) pierces a male victim with his teeth and drinks his blood, thereby exchanging bodily fluids, the scene subliminally evokes homosexuality, as it does when Dracula orders his "wives" not to touch Jonathan Harker. "How dare you touch him, any of you?" he jealously warns them. "How dare you cast eyes on him? This man belongs to me!"[5] On the other hand, when vampires nurse their brood of thralls by allowing them to drink from their bodies, a maternal image arises, as when Dracula cuts his chest and forces Mina Harker to drink from the wound. Critics note that this scene "presents a perverse mockery of the nursing mother: rather than giving life by offering milk, the count tries to ensure Mina's death by feeding her his blood."[6]

The seeming contradictions of conventional gender roles disappear if we regard vampirism as a "pangendered construct in which traditional male and female genders are combined to form a whole."[7] Pangender refers to "having mixed gender identity, not identifying as one static gender."[8] In fact, when we regard vampirism as a series of gender metaphors, we must conclude that most vampires qualify as pangendered. It may be premature to pronounce gender roles obsolete, but judging by pop culture's vampires, heterosexism increasingly appears weakened.

Victorian vampires arose in a patriarchal, heterosexual society, and writers who wanted to depict gender diversity relied increasingly on vampires as gender metaphors. As Victorianism ended at the turn of the twentieth century and was replaced by more egalitarian social structures, the dominance of patriarchy weakened. In part this resulted from Eastern and Western European immigration to England and the U.S., challenging traditional social structures and creating anxiety as a result.

Continental Europe experienced changes in gender relations as feminism and female emancipation became celebrated causes. Women's voting rights were codified in Weimar, Germany in 1919. F.W. Murnau's classic German Expressionist film *Nosferatu* (1922) provides a striking example of gender role changes. Murnau's vampire, Count Orlok (Max Schreck), inhabits a paternalistic, heterosexual world in which females serve as prizes and prey. Accordingly, Orlok falls in love with Ellen (Greta Schroeder), a newlywed bride, and attacks both her and her husband, Hutter (Gustav von Wangenheim). Realizing her sexual power over Orlok, Ellen turns the tables on the vampire and seduces him into spending the night with her. When dawn breaks, Orlok is incinerated by the sunrise—thereby releasing Ellen from her growing dependence on him. The fact that a female, not a male, outwits and destroys this monstrous vampire serves as a poignant metaphor for the era's feminism.

By the 1940s, heterosexism as a value had continued to weaken, as evidenced by pop culture's vampires. Lew Landers' film *The Return of the Vampire* (1944) continued along the trajectory of ever-weakening patriarchy/heterosexism. The plot begins in 1918, when vampire Armand Tesla (Bela Lugosi) preys on a female child named Nicki (Sherlee Collier), the granddaughter of Oxford professor Walter Saunders (Gilbert Emery). Saunders saves Nicki through a blood transfusion, and then he and Lady Jane Ainsley (Frieda Inescort) pursue Tesla and drive a stake through his heart. Flash forward to 1941, when cemetery workers inadvertently release Tesla, who then finds the grown-up Nicki (Nina Foch) and feeds from her once more. Lady Ainsley and her associate Andreas (the Wolfman, played by Matt Willis) track down Tesla once again, and during the confusion of a German air raid, Andreas drags the vampire into the sunlight, where he perishes. Preying on a young girl renders Tesla a pedophilic heterosexist, and Tesla's characterization foreshadows the eventual upending of male heterosexual vampires into more complex, gender-nuanced characters.

While early vampire characters bent traditional gender roles and undermined patriarchy and heterosexism, the transformation of vampires into gay, lesbian, bisexual, and transgender characters (GLBT) really exploded during the 1960s and 1970s. Homoerotic vampire literature and films that achieved great popularity included Anne Rice's Vampire Chronicles series (1976–2003), featuring sexually complex vampires with homosexual or bisexual tendencies. Male vampires began biting the necks of male humans in literature and film. Professor George E. Haggerty remarks that Rice's vampires are filled with "homoerotic desire."[9]

Crypt of the Vampire (1964) exemplifies the "feminist" vampires of the 1960s. The film stars Christopher Lee as Count Ludwig Karnstein and Audrey Amber (Adriana Ambesi) as Laura Karnstein, the count's ailing daughter. Count Ludwig believes that his ancestor Scirra Karnstein, a witch, wants to inhabit Laura's body in order to return to the realm of the living, so he hires a doctor to save his daughter from her. Lyuba (Ursula Davis) enters the story when a carriage accident strands her at Castle Karnstein. Lyuba begins an intimate friendship with Laura, whose health apparently improves. Gradually Lyuba becomes the most powerful figure in Laura's life, supplanting her father. In the final scene at the ruins of the old Karnstein Castle, Count Ludwig and others open the witch Scirra's tomb to discover Lyuba lying in it. They destroy her, and Laura's health improves. The implied sexual relationship between Lyuba and Laura identifies this film with 1970s feminism and lesbianism. Lyuba serves as a modern update of the Victorian New Woman, becoming a seductress with power to disrupt the entire countryside by her actions. Her final death inside her coffin may symbolize at some level a weakening of feminism.

The "Turbulent Seventies"—or the "Feminist Seventies," as many characterize this period—witnessed a more militant form of feminism, prospering through the 1980s and known as "Second Wave Feminism." Feminists such as Gloria Steinem, Angela Davis, and Jane Fonda were outspoken in their support of woman's rights. In 1978 the National Woman's Liberation Conference in Britain presented Seven Demands for gender equality:

1. Equal pay for equal work
2. Equal education and job opportunities
3. Free contraception
4. Free 24-hour community-controlled childcare
5. Legal and financial independence for women
6. An end to discrimination against lesbians
7. Freedom for all women from intimidation by the threat or use of male violence

In summary, the conference called for an end to the laws, assumptions and institutions which perpetuate male dominance and men's aggression towards women.[10]

Some during this period compared feminists and vampires, because both seemed "selfish, too interested in sex, and non-nurturing." In the words of one observer: "The female vampire, like the witch, is suspect because she acts outside the accepted norms for women in our society. She is self-contained, she doesn't rely on men, she goes out and gets what she wants no matter the consequences, she 'forces' people to do things that are against their nature, and she is certainly not nurturing!"[11] Female vampires—armed with superpowers, immortality, and eternal youth—comprise potent feminist metaphors. One interpretation sees Stoker's *Dracula* as a story of feminine liberation and empowerment: Lucy's encounter with Count Dracula transforms her from a silly, giggly girl to a powerfully erotic woman. This emphasizes Lucy's encounter with her own sexuality, something Victorian culture labeled as deviant and forbidden. Lucy's symbolic embrace of sexuality defied Victorian traditions.[12]

The 1970s also witnessed "blaxploitation," the depiction of African Americans using positive stereotypes[13] In the 1972 blaxploitation film *Blacula,* directed by William Crain, Count Dracula (Charles Macauley) bites the African prince Manuwalde (William Marshall), cursing him with the name Blacula—"like myself, a living fiend ... never to know that sweet blood which shall be your only desire." The "sweet blood" may symbolize physical blood or a sweet, satisfying relationship with another being. Blacula's love interest is his wife, Luva (Vonetta McGee). Later, after being released from Dracula's sealed casket, he falls in love with Tina (Vonetta McGee), Luva's reincarnation, whom he turns into a vampire. Eventually Manuwalde succumbs to modernity; unable to stand being undead after Tina is staked, he walks into the sunlight and expires.

In 1973 Bob Kelljan released *Scream, Blacula, Scream*. William Marshall again plays Blacula (Prince Mumuwalde), and this time he's paired with legendary Pam Grier as Lisa Fortner, Blacula's star-crossed lover. Lisa is elected to succeed a popular voodoo leader who has recently died, but a jealous cult member exhumes Mumuwalde's body and resurrects the undead vampire. Lisa agrees to help Mumuwalde break an ancient curse against him, but she retracts her allegiance after he goes on a rampage and tries to kill her and a small army of law enforcement officers sent to apprehend him. Proving himself a metaphorical bisexual in the film, Blacula bites anyone and everyone, regardless of gender. William Marshall—who stood 6 feet 5 inches tall—had a commanding presence that resonated with contemporary black power movement. Pam Grier epitomized the era's Afro-feminist, providing a counterpoint to Marshall's bombastically macho performance.[14] The two actors evoke both 1970s Black Power and Second Wave Feminism.

As discussed in Chapter Two, growing public acceptance of bisexuality and lesbianism led to a trilogy of lesbian vampire films by Hammer Film

Vampires Lestat de Lioncourt (Tom Cruise) and Louis de Ponte du lac (Brad Pitt) attack a tavern girl (Melissa George) in *Interview with the Vampire: The Vampire Chronicles* (1994), based on Anne Rice's 1976 book (Kobal Collection at Art Resource, New York).

Productions modeled on *Carmilla,* now labeled the Karnstein Trilogy. Although previous Hammer vampire films had raised the bar on female nudity and sexuality, *The Vampire Lovers* (1970), directed by Roy Ward Baker, openly depicted vampire lesbianism for the first time. Baker's film features Ingrid Pitt as Marcilla/Carmilla/Mircalla Karnstein, a beautiful young Austrian noblewoman who goes by various anagram aliases while seducing young women—and occasionally men—for their blood. The sexy horror film relies on female nudity and saucy dialogue. First the vampire invites Gretchen (Janet Key), the local forester's young daughter, into her bedroom as she is bathing. She convinces Gretchen to disrobe in order to try on a beautiful dress Carmilla is offering. As the two semi-nude young women playfully chase each other around the bedroom, audiences behold full nude shots from behind, along with numerous shots of bare breasts. The two wind up on top of the bed, and as the camera fades Gretchen emits a piercing scream of pleasure.

In her various aliases, Carmilla seduces other young women through suggestive repartee and sensual caresses. When beautiful Laura (Pippa Steel) grows anemic from having her blood sucked, Marcilla—a temporary resident of Laura's family castle—visits to offer comfort. As the vampire embraces her victim, Laura exclaims, "Ah, Marcilla, you're so kind to me. I swear I shall die when you leave." At this point Marcilla coos reassuringly and menacingly in a memorable line initially penned by Le Fanu, "I will never leave you, my dearest Laura," as she begins caressing and kissing Laura's breast. Scenes such as this assured the financial success of *The Vampire Lovers* and emboldened studio executives into commissioning sequels.

As the second installment of their Karnstein Trilogy, Hammer Film Productions released *Lust for a Vampire* (1971), directed by Jimmy Sangster. In the first scene, a beautiful Austrian maiden strolls along a forest path and encounters a grand coach drawn by magnificent black horses. A hooded figure invites her in, but once she's inside she utters a piercing scream—at which point the driver lashes the horses into a gallop. In the next scene the same girl lies unconscious and bound in a cathedral where a black-robed priest intones a Satanic mass. A beautiful woman wielding a huge curved knife slits the girl's throat, and her blood drains into a golden chalice. The dark-robed man pours the blood into a coffin containing an ancient, shriveled cadaver. Slowly a reddish light begins to grow and pulsate, and blonde Mircalla/Carmella Karnstein (Yutte Stensgaard) emerges from the coffin, looking gorgeous in a skimpy costume dripping with the blood of her sacrificial victim. Reborn after centuries, she enrolls in an exclusive finishing school connected with the Countess Hermptzen (Barbara Jefford). There she seduces

Susan Kelly (Pippa Steel), then attacks her during an unauthorized moonlight skinny-dip in a local lake.

In this film Mircalla also targets men, including Richard Lestrange (Michael Johnson), a handsome young author who falls deeply in love with her and even arranges to become a teacher in her school. Lestrange's impetuousness and genteel breeding owe much to the legend of Lord Byron, the model for the earliest seductive vampires. But unlike Byron, Lestrange never transforms into a vampire himself. Mircalla, though smitten at first by this handsome man, ultimately attacks him and intends to drain his blood and kill him, but villagers rescue him from the wreckage of the burning Karnstein Castle just in time. Though his infatuation with Mircalla nearly cost him his life, Lestrange never grew bored with the bisexual vampire.

John Hough released *Twins of Evil* in 1971, completing the Karnstein Trilogy. Hough's film features beautiful Viennese twins Maria (Mary Collinson) and Frieda (Madelaine Collinson), orphans who go live with their uncle Gustaf Weil (Peter Cushing) and Aunt Cathy (Kathleen Byron). Uncle Gustaf heads a local vigilante gang called the Brotherhood, whose hooded members capture, torture, and burn at the stake those suspected of being vampires and witches—and also local maidens they find in acts of copulation with local men. This calls to mind the actions outlined in the *Malleus Maleficarum*, or "Hammer of Witches," a fifteenth-century treatise on witches written in Germany—a "Bible" for witch-burning and other tortures for those accused of vampirism or witchcraft.[15]

Weil and the Brotherhood attempt to arrest a young woman in her woodland cottage, but there they discover her lover, Count Karnstein (Damien Thomas). The count is well connected with the emperor, and he threatens that he will use his influence against them if they arrest her. Karnstein dabbles in the black arts by conducting Satanic masses in which his servants sacrifice virgins at his command. Later he sacrifices a virgin and spills her blood into an ancient casket containing the remains of Countess Marcilla Karnstein (Katya Wyeth), in order to resurrect her. Resurrected as a vampire, she immediately attacks and vampirizes Count Karnstein.

Meanwhile, Aunt Cathy enrolls Frieda and Maria in school, where choirmaster Anton Hogger (David Warbeck) falls in love with Frieda. However, Frieda has different ideas. After hearing about Count Karnstein's scandalous parties, one night she escapes from her bedroom and begs a ride in Karnstein's carriage to the castle. Once there she soon encounters the count, and he immediately vampirizes her. Later her Uncle Weil comes upon Frieda attacking a man and drinking his blood. He exclaims, "The Devil has sent me twins of evil!" He orders Frieda imprisoned and returns home to seize Maria, but

Aunt Cathy prevents it. At this point Count Karnstein abducts Maria as a hostage and a substitute for Frieda.

Choirmaster Hogger, upset at losing Frieda to the count, complains to the church elders that the Brotherhood's practice of burning their victims fails to destroy vampires. "By burning," complains Hogger, "you char the body. The soul will only re-create itself in another body and continue with its carnage. Only a stake through the heart or decapitation will end their tormented evil." Inflamed by this speech, the villagers form a mob and lay siege to Karnstein Castle, setting it ablaze. The count and his female thralls perish in the fire, impaled by burning beams. In the end, good triumphs over evil as the Satanic vampires receive lasting death from the villagers.

The Karnstein Trilogy encompassed many social issues of the period, including the rise of feminism, lesbianism, and permissive sexual mores. Film buffs consider these films classics. Their success attests to the lasting impact of Sheridan Le Fanu's novel *Carmilla*, which has inspired more than a dozen vampire films featuring deadly, seductive females, as well as novels, comics, graphic novels, anime, and video games.

In 1971 Hammer Productions released a movie about fifteenth century Hungarian countess Elizabeth Bathory, who allegedly murdered hundreds of young women to drain their blood, that bore the provocative title *Countess Dracula*, directed by Peter Sasdy. Polish beauty Ingrid Pitt stars as Countess Elizabeth Nordosheen, a stand-in for Elizabeth Bathory. Countess Elizabeth rules her domain with an iron fist, aided by Captain Dobi (Nigel Green), her castle steward. Sasdy takes many liberties with the Bathory story, toning down her 650 murders to just a few. Although the film depicts Countess Elizabeth bathing in blood, a voice-over intones "the more she drinks, the prettier she gets," strongly implying a vampire nature—hence the title *Countess Dracula*. While some films depict Bathory as a deranged psychopath, this movie perpetuates the myth of vampirism.

The year 1971 also witnessed another classic horror film—*Let's Scare Jessica to Death.* John D. Hancock directed and co-scripted this loose adaptation of Le Fanu's predatory female vampire. Emily (Mariclare Costello) is a young woman who squats in an unoccupied farmhouse until the new owners, Jessica (Zohra Lambert) and her husband Duncan (Garton Heyman), move in. Emily bonds well with the couple and their friend Woody (Kevin O'Conner), who are New York counterculture enthusiasts planning to farm apples. Emily turns out to be Abigail Bishop, a twenty-year-old woman who had disappeared in 1880 and still haunts the area as a vampire.

Emily begins seducing Jessica with the intention of vampirizing her, but Jessica proves resistant—despite Emily's telepathic messages beckoning her to follow wherever she leads. Finally, Emily warns: "I'm still here.... I won't go away.... You can't get rid of me.... I'm in your blood.... You want to die." Everywhere Jessica turns, she encounters hostile, mysteriously bandaged locals with incriminating throat wounds. She leaps into a rowboat after an infected ferryboat man tells her that "the ferry isn't running for you," but a threatening hand arises from the lake and grabs hold of the boat. Jessica seizes a pickaxe and repeatedly stabs the person—who unfortunately turns out to be her husband.

Jessica looks toward the shore to find Emily and the locals staring at her with hostility. Sometime later she remarks, "I sit here, and I can't believe that it happened!" She gazes into the distance and says, "And yet I have to believe it. Nightmares or dreams? Madness or sanity? I don't know which is which!"

In the end, director Hancock leaves viewers with some discomforting thoughts. Although Jessica seemingly eludes death at the hands of Emily and the locals, she inadvertently kills her husband in the process. And who can tell when it will end? Will Emily leave her alone now, after having "selected" her to become one of her thralls? The answer seems uncertain at best. Emily now inhabits Jessica's body. Metaphorically, vampire lesbianism seems like something inherited, within one's DNA, and immutable.

Let's Scare Jessica to Death holds a favored position in the canon of feminist films because of Emily's potency as well as her menace. Like Carmilla, she enters and commandeers victims while consuming their life's blood. The vampirism that she transmits seems somewhat like a sexually transmitted disease, since she first seduces through smiles, sweet words, kisses, and caresses before moving on to bites. She relies on relentlessness as well as seduction to slake her desires. While this behavior renders Emily less than attractive, she has a strong appeal by portraying unconscious, taboo sexual desires. Like Carmilla, Emily seduces by blending into the family and then undermining it. This film arrived at a time of traumatic national events—such as the National Guard shootings at Kent State University in 1970 and continuing protests against President Richard Nixon's handling of the Vietnam War—and the characters' counterculture behavior seems a reaction to these dramatic events.

Spanish director Vicente Aranda's *La Novia Ensengrentada* (1972) appeared in the U.S. as *The Blood Spattered Bride* in 1975. In Aranda's rendering of *Carmilla*, Mircalla Karnstein (Alexandra Bastedo) returns from the grave to re-enact the ancient murder of her husband (Simon Andreu) on their wedding night. Modern bride Susan (Maribel Martin) feels sexually repulsed by her husband on their wedding night after dreaming that he rips off her wedding dress and rapes her—a dream later actualized, as he does just that. She finds his sexual aggression (including forcing her to perform fellatio) increasingly repugnant, setting the stage for her upcoming revolution. She complains about the "realization of my violated virgin's shuddering sense of horror." Sexual abuse sets the stage for the couple's estrangement and her future attachment to Mircalla.

Susan first encounters Mircalla seated in a car at the resort hotel where she and her husband expect a brief honeymoon. Then she catches visions of a beautiful blonde woman in a purple wedding dress. Her husband tells her of one of his ancestors marrying Mircalla, who was enraged by his sexual demands and stabbed him to death on their wedding night. The next day they discover Mircalla lying next to his dead body, seemingly alive yet fallen into a tenacious trance. After failing to revive her despite prolonged efforts, the family eventually has her pronounced dead and buried.

Next, the newly married Susan goes to live with her husband in a large castle and begins seeing visions of the mysterious blonde woman in the purple wedding gown. These visions increase and intensify, and the blonde woman as ghostly apparition visits Susan in her bedroom, where she dreams of murdering her husband sleeping beside her by plunging a large dagger repeatedly into his chest. After a real dagger appears in her bed, her husband buries it deep in the woods. However, it keeps turning up, and Susan continues experiencing visions of a mysterious woman and a dagger.

Eventually the husband discovers Mircalla alive and buried in beach sand. He carries her nearly nude body to the castle, where she bonds instantly with Susan. Mircalla turns out to be the mysterious woman of Susan's nightmares, and she attempts to brainwash Susan into stabbing her husband—the reincarnated groom murdered decades earlier. Now Mircalla wants to finish the job and recruit a new vampire to take her place. But she fails to kill her reincarnated husband, and he tracks her to her crypt and shoots her and Susan numerous times with a high-powered rifle as they lay nude in a coffin. "They'll be back. They cannot die," warns Carol (Maria Rosa Rodriguez), a young staff member also transformed into a vampire. He shoots her, too, and carves the hearts out of all three women. The final screen shot is of a newspaper headline: "Man cuts out the hearts of three women." The husband survives vampire attacks but will likely be executed for killing his vampire attackers.

Despite the film's brutality against women, it sends a strong message about female power. This, coupled with strong performances by the cast, explains the continued popularity of *The Blood Spattered Bride*. Feminists appreciate the anti-male, pro-female overtones, and men like the dramatic action and the husband's strong final act of disposing of three female vampires. However, his success is illusory, as the newspaper headline foreshadows his upcoming trial, probable conviction, imprisonment, and possible execution—while the female vampires will never die. Men may seek vengeance, but women prevail in the long run, possessing a kind of immortality. During this era, one group of feminists known as "lesbian separatists" declared their intent to dispense with heterosexuality entirely, because men were paternalistic, disagreeable, and ultimately dispensable![16]

The Spanish film *Hannah: Queen of the Vampires* (1973) continues the Carmilla story, with some new twists. Ray Danton directed the American version, and Lou Shaw wrote the screenplay. The film depicts the accidental resurrection of a vampire queen (Teresa Gimpera) entombed on a remote Mediterranean island. The story begins as Professor Bolton (Mariano Garcia), an archaeologist, happens upon an ancient underground tomb containing an elaborately carved marble casket. As he gazes at it, a wild man (Ihsan Genik) and his accomplice attack and kill him. He falls beneath the marble tomb, which rests on four pillars. The attackers use sledgehammers to break the pillars, and the heavy casket falls on top of Professor Bolton. Bolton's son Chris (Andrew Prine) journeys to the island to bury his father, but first he must remove the heavy casket. But locals believe the casket contains the remains of a vampire queen that will unleash an attack on the island's inhabitants, and they are reluctant to help.

Chris refuses to listen to vampire stories, and he undertakes the removal of the casket. He personally breaks the casket's seal in order to remove it in pieces, lid first. Once the casket is unsealed, the remarkably preserved and lovely body of Hannah (Teresa Gimpera) begins to awaken. At first Hannah leaves her tomb by shapeshifting into a wolf that roams the countryside each night searching for animals to kill for their blood. Flushed with the blood of the wolf's victims, Queen Hannah rises and flies away in search of fresh human blood. She drinks Peter's (Mark Damon) blood, transforming him into a vampire. Armed with crosses and stakes, Chris leads the villagers on a vampire hunt. He eventually finds Hannah and Peter and stakes stakes, seemingly freeing the islanders from the island's vampire curse.

The film's epilogue shows a very young female vampire attacking a young boy. Hannah, it appears, remains at large in the guise of this child and will continue the vampire cycle, presumably forever. Hannah's story carries a feminist message that despite whatever defense men launch, she will triumph and continue as an immortal. Nothing can restore patriarchy, the film implies, because youth no longer embrace it.

In the 1974 film *Vampyres*, female vampires Fran (Marianne Morris) and Miriam (Anulka) inhabit a seemingly deserted English castle. One evening a vacationing couple, John (Brian Deacon) and Harriett (Ally Faulkner), search nearby for a parking space for their camper before night falls. They encounter Fran and Mariam and decide to camp in a scenic location beside the castle, where they remain for a few days—unaware that Fran and Ally prowl the night seeking men to seduce and murder. They weaken them with wine, make passionate love with them, and end the evening by drinking their blood. A victim named Ted (Murray Brown) manages to survive for three nights. On the third night he escapes and seeks help from John and Harriett. But Fran and Miriam easily dispatch John and then turn to Harriett, whom they devour with almost sexual relish. Ted apparently escapes. These two vampires clearly symbolize bisexual women possessed of robust, animalistic sexuality. This theme gains in popularity over time.

Tony Scott's haunting *The Hunger* (1983) dissects the bisexual vampire trope on several levels. Head vampire Miriam (Catherine Deneuve) and her husband John Blalock (David Bowie) prey on young partygoers, seducing and then stabbing them with ancient Egyptian pendants in the shape of ankhs—ironically, a symbol of eternal life that they both wear. After piercing the bodies, they consume the blood of their victims, who rapidly age but remain alive in coffins hidden in the couple's attic. One day John experiences difficulty sleeping and begins aging rapidly, adding decades every few hours. In desperation he visits Dr. Sarah Roberts (Susan Sarandon), an eminent researcher of the aging process. Believing John to be crazy, Roberts tricks him into waiting for two hours in her patients' lounge, during which time he transforms from a man in his 30s to someone who's apparently in his 80s. He confronts Roberts, who now realizes he was telling the truth, and he rushes out of the clinic and tries to revive himself with the blood of a teenage music student. That fails to reverse his symptoms.

Roberts attempts to visit John but instead meets Miriam, who seduces her and drinks her blood, transforming her into a vampire with a raging blood thirst. Roberts and her colleagues at the clinic use all their medical acumen to seek a cure for the disease that racks her body, without success. Roberts returns to Miriam's mansion to confront the vampire, who assures her that she will never age as long as Roberts is her vampire lover. Roberts struggles against the transformation taking place within her body, and she ends up stabbing and killing her own human lover, Dr. Tom Haver (Cliff de Young). Miriam decides to drain Roberts' blood once again and attempts to place her in an attic coffin—but her previous victims have risen from their coffins and now attack her en masse. In the next scene we find the Blaylock mansion for sale and both the Blaylocks deceased. In the postscript, a brief scene shows a now-vibrant Roberts surrounded by her own lovers/thralls.

Miriam Blaylock symbolizes bisexual females seducing and feeding off both females and males. John Blaylock prefers feeding from adult women, but his bloodlust drives him to vampirize a young girl. The metaphor of vampires as amoral bisexuals and pedophiles equates vampirism with pangenderism, and the resulting portrait appears to be a cautionary tale against sexual promiscuity. Scott's movie has become a cult classic, partly because of its primordial, insistent sexuality. Bowie and Deneuve deliver memorable performances as sexual predators, and Susan Sarandon also deserves commendation for her depiction of Dr. Sara Roberts descending into vampirism and eventually mastering Miriam Blaylock. The movie resonates with sexually driven hunger, serving as a metaphor for sexual addiction.

Joel Schumacher's *The Lost Boys* (1987), yet another cult classic, includes a subtext in which the protagonists—brothers Sam (Corey Haim) and Michael (Jason Patric)—encounter a vampire biker gang led by David (Kiefer Sutherland). The brothers end up deeply entwined in a seemingly homoerotic youth gang culture led by David, who tells Michael, "Sleep all day. Party all night. Never grow old. Never die. It's fun to be a vampire." He summarizes, "Now you know what we are, now you know what you are. You'll never grow old, Michael, and you'll never die. But you must feed!"

Sam characterizes gayness, with posters of actor Rob Lowe on his closet doors and with his enjoyment of bubble baths. Older brother Michael drinks seductively from David's cup, which contains his vampire blood. Gradually Michael undergoes vampirization and gains the superpowers necessary to defeat the local vampire clan. The gang's eventual defeat ends their existences of riotous outlawry and narcissistic hedonism.

Interview with the Vampire (1994), Neil Jordon's adaptation of the Anne Rice novel, strongly hints at a bisexual relationship between Louis de Pointe du Lac (Brad Pitt) and Lestat de Lioncourt (Tom Cruise) after Lestat bites Louis and transforms him into a vampire. Louis attempts to resist Lestat's vampirism, but he ultimately fails and comes under Lestat's sway. "No one could resist me, not even you, Louis," boasts Lestat. "I tried," Louis replies. Smiling, Lestat says, "And the more you tried, the more I wanted you." The obvious erotic subtext in this exchange symbolizes the characters' bisexuality. Through the course of the novel and film the two handsome vampire males create a child vampire, Claudia. The resulting nontraditional family mocks the one-man and one-woman heterosexual family model.

The Vampire Armand (1998), Anne Rice's sixth Vampire Chronicles novel, features Armand, another bisexual vampire. When Armand comes "of age"—about fifteen or sixteen years old—his mentor, Marius de Romanus, sends him to a Venetian brothel to learn about heterosexuality, then to a male

African Prince Mamuwalde (William Marshall) transforms into a powerful vampire after being bitten by Count Dracula, who dubs him "Blacula" in *Scream, Blacula, Scream* (1973). The film immediately provoked controversy among those who perceived it as "Blaxploitation" versus a manifestation of the era's "Black Power Movement" (Kobal Collection at Art Resource, New York).

brothel to round out his bisexuality. However, Armand passionately remembers Marius's embrace:

> Once I lay half asleep. The air was rosy and golden. The place was warm. I felt his lips on mine, and his cold tongue move serpent like into my mouth. A liquid filled my mouth, a rich and burning nectar, a potion so exquisite that I felt it roll through my body to the very tips of my outstretched fingers. I felt it descend through my torso and into the most private part of me. I burned. I burned.

In 2002 Michael Rymer directed *Queen of the Damned*, based on Anne Rice's third Vampire Chronicles novel, *The Queen of the Damned* (1988). In the film version Lestat (Stuart Townsend) awakens after a couple centuries of sleep into a world of rock bands and mass media. He quickly vampirizes a rock group living in his old house and inaugurates a new group, "The Vampire Louis Lestat." He writes vampire music and vampirizes several humans, in the process jumping on and killing two young groupie girls. His music eventually awakens Akasha (Aaliyah), queen of all vampires, who decides to make him her new king and rule over all humans until they are dead or vampires. When Louis challenges all vampires through a television journalist, "Come out, come out, wherever you are," Rice and Rymer evoke the metaphor of vampires as homosexuals. The idea of "coming out" connects Lestat with gays coming out of the closet. At one crucial juncture, Louis says to the Lestat, "I love you because you are so perfectly what is wrong with all things male. Aggressive, full of hate and recklessness, and endlessly eloquent excuses for violence—you are the essence of masculinity."[17] *Queen of the Damned*, like *Interview with the Vampire*, challenges older vampire lore and introduces complex, rounded characters that symbolize more realistic gender roles than pop culture previously offered.

Uwe Boll's *BloodRayne* (2005) features Rayne (Kristanna Loken), a half-human/half-vampire hybrid, or "dhampir," who wars against her father Kagan (Ben Kinsley), a master vampire who raped and killed her mother and now plans to rule the world as a vampire king. To accomplish his plan, he needs three magic talismans: a heart, a rib, and an eye. Only Rayne and a confederation of vampire slayers named Brimstone stand in his way. Rayne uses her vampire powers as well as her martial training to obtain the eye and the heart. She desires them only to gain access to Kagan, then kill him. Possessed of the ability to seduce both men and women, she makes love only once in the film, with one of the (male) slayers. She functions as a sexually potent "bad girl" who lives up to the film's tagline: "She's one hell of a heroine ... literally!"

By the late 1980s, feminism had reinvented itself as "Third Wave Feminism." In their book *Manifesta: Young Women, Feminism and the Future*, Jennifer Baumgardner and Amy Richards discuss the transformation:

> Consciousness among women is what caused this [change], and consciousness, one's ability to open their mind to the fact that male domination does affect the women of our generation, is what we need…. The presence of feminism in our lives is taken for granted. For our generation, feminism is like fluoride. We scarcely notice we have it—it's simply in the water.[18]

The same year as the *Manifesta* appeared, Gabrielle Beaumont directed a remarkable television adaptation of *Carmilla*, set in a Southern plantation on the eve of the Civil War. Beaumont's film begins with a violent carriage accident, after which Carmilla (Meg Tilly), too injured to travel, begs the owner of a nearby antebellum plantation to be allowed to stay there to rest and recuperate. He agrees, and Carmilla befriends Marie (Ione Skye), the beautiful but lonely young daughter of the plantation owner. The two become bosom companions, sharing long walks through the woods on the plantation grounds. Soon they begin to behave like lovers, and Carmilla begins feeding on Marie's blood. After her maid dies mysteriously, Marie herself becomes progressively weaker. Inspector Amos (Roddy McDowell) launches an investigation. He suspects Carmilla, but soon Amos also dies mysteriously. Emboldened by desperation, Marie's father Leo (Roy Dotrice) follows Marie and Carmilla to a crypt. Leo eventually persuades Marie to come outside, and his assistants stake Carmilla and two other female vampires they also discover—including Marie's mother.

Marie's will to resist Carmilla's deadly seduction slowly grows stronger, and her father renders assistance by staking Carmilla's relatives in their crypt. Carmilla, however, escapes and continues to pursue Marie by shapeshifting into a white rat that leaps onto Marie's bed, but Marie shrieks and jumps off the bed. Carmilla assumes her human form and throws Marie onto the bed to feed from her one final time. But Marie acquires super strength from her growing vampirism and throws Carmilla onto a pointed finial, staking her through the heart. Leo opens the curtains and allows sunlight in to complete the execution.

Author/professor Nina Auerbach observes that this film denigrates males "by caricaturing all the men so no one can take them seriously." She describes Marie's father as "a neurotic tyrant" and Roddy McDowell's character "over-played" as a "boorish vampire killer." Against these weak males, this film portrays vampirism as "women's friendship as a rebellion against parental control."[19] And the film retains a hint that Marie might retain essential elements of Carmilla's personality in her own psyche and that through her, Carmilla might yet escape death.

In 1992 Fran Rubel Kuzui directed *Buffy the Vampire Slayer*, about a heterosexual high school vampire killer. The film became an instant hit, grossing well over $16 million and spawning a popular television series (1997–2002).[20] Kuzui's film, scripted by Joss Whedon, stars Kristy Swanson as Buffy and Donald Sutherland as Merrick. Buffy was descended from a long line of vampire slayers—always young women—while Merrick had been reincarnated many times as a trainer of vampire slayers. Rutger Hauer plays Lothos, the original vampire, who despite appearing to be middle-aged intends to marry the teenage Buffy. He offers her the gift of eternal life if she'll acquiesce. But she prefers the role of a high school cheerleader who then goes to college and gets married. Lothos forces her to choose between becoming a vampire slayer—like her ancestors—or his vampire bride.

At first Buffy is a reluctant hero, refusing Merrick's invitation to accompany him to a graveyard at night. However, he finally persuades her. At the cemetery, they encounter two vampires freshly raised from their graves. Instinctively, Buffy drives stakes through their hearts. Merrick continually challenges her, at one point throwing a knife directly at her head. She deftly catches it. "Only the chosen one could have caught it!" he exclaims. He continues to sharpen her skills, first allowing only one vampire and later more than one to attack Buffy. Each time she manages to kill them, using her continually improving skills together with her vampire-killing heritage.

Buffy's confidence improves along with her skills as she learns to cope with an ever-increasing number of new vampires infected by Lothos. He conforms to the Byronic vampire model, dressing in stylized black and red formal attire, playing a violin or stroking a cat, and comporting himself like an aristocrat. He epitomizes Lord Ruthven/Lord Byron. But seductive rakes pose no threat to Buffy, and in the end she defeats Lothos with gymnastics as well as speed, agility, and advanced martial arts skills. She relies on training as well as instinct, but she possesses no superpowers beyond her status as the "chosen one." Instead of serving as the victim of a seductive male vampire, this young, beautiful human teenager slays one.

Buffy conforms to the Victorian social phenomenon known as the "New Woman" in which women exercised shocking (for the times) individuality. As Ilona Gaul observes, Carmilla both symbolized and challenged Victorian gender roles.[21] In addition, female vampires were stand-ins for the New Women of the era, noted for their independence and sexual liberation.[22] Essayist Trudi Van Dyke argues that in recent times the human vampire killer Buffy exemplifies the Victorian New Woman, assuming that status as a contemporary feminist.[23]

Buffy's ascension from victim to victor illustrates the rise of feminism during the past decades. Buffy joins ranks with other powerful female action heroes such as Zena the Warrior Princess—the popular 1990s television action hero who defeats arrogant males—she exemplifies a complex feminist perspective. As feminist blogger Megan Karius writes, "Buffy inhabits multiple spaces simultaneously, thereby refusing easy categorization, and in this way, she exemplifies many ideals of third-wave feminism."[24]

David DeCoteau's television series *The Brotherhood* (2001–2008) exploits a strongly homoerotic subtext involving "eye-candy" young males and sadomasochistic fraternity rituals, including drinking one another's blood. DeCoteau's film stars Sam Page as Chris Chandler, an attractive, athletic, but naive freshman at Drake College. On his first day at college, Chandler runs afoul of the legendary Doma Tau Omega fraternity, an elitist organization of immortals headed by Devin Eisley (Bradley Stryker). They select, seduce, and sacrifice handsome young men to Satan, tricking their victims into drinking each other's blood before being sacrificed. Vampires make excellent metaphors for a variety of social outsiders, including LGBT.[25]

Post 9/11

The terrorist attacks of September 11, 2001, dramatically affected pop culture in nearly every respect, and they profoundly impacted feminism and the role of women. In his book *Post-9/11 Horror in American Cinema*, Kevin Wetmore observes that 9/11 altered feminism in two important ways. On one hand, the terrorist attacks and the wars that followed commanded central attention and immediately rendered feminism and other pre–9/11 issues irrelevant. Concern for race, gender, and class were forgotten as public attention turned to defense against future attacks and reprisal against the perpetrators and their allies. In the paranoia and rage that followed, gender issues no longer seemed relevant. "A collapsing building or crashing plane does not care about one's gender, orientation with one's father," notes Wetmore. "Random and anonymous death is not concerned with oppression or gendered identity."[26] On the other hand, journalist Susan Faludi argues that although the terrorist attacks and subsequent events didn't display gender bias or rely on gender identity per se, gender issues infused the manner in which the events were presented in the media. A feminist author, Faludi was besieged by reporters in the aftermath of 9/11 wondering if feminism suddenly had become irrelevant and might even constitute an invitation to terrorism by "feminizing" the American male. Instead of liberated women, some Americans called for a return of manly men who could protect America from terrorists. She observed, "Of all the peculiar responses our culture manifested to 9/11, perhaps none was more incongruous than the desire to rein in a liberated female population. In some murky fashion, women's independence had become implicated in our nation's failure to protect itself." Furthermore, Faludi noted that critics of feminism believed the movement might bear indirect responsibility for failures in U.S. foreign policy leading up to the attacks.[27]

Despite the immediate relegation of feminism to the past, by 2008 the issue began manifesting itself once more in pop culture. In 2008, *Buffy the Vampire Slayer* comics depicted the teenage Buffy sleeping with another female vampire slayer, a beautiful Asian woman named Satsu. Co-creator Joss Whedon reassured readers, "We're not going to make her gay, nor are we going to take the next 50 issues explaining that she's not. She's young and experimenting, and did I mention open-minded?"[28] The television series had often focused on Buffy Summers' romantic relationship with Spike (James Marsters). By making her bisexual, Whedon appears to be broadening his audience. Recent studies indicate that sixty-nine percent of adolescents self-identifying as bisexual have experienced sexual intercourse, a higher percentage than either gay or heterosexual adolescents.[29] In addition, a variety of studies indicate that perhaps as many as ten percent of the adult population have had sexual intercourse at least once with a member of their same gender.[30]

Sleepwalkers (1992), directed by Mark Garris and based on a novel by Stephen King, features psychic vampires Mary Brady (Alice Krige) and

Charles (Brian Krause), a mother and her son. A definition of the film title explains the characters' origins:

> Sleepwalker (n). Nomadic shapeshifting creatures with human and feline origins. Vulnerable to the deadly scratch of the cat, the sleepwalker feeds upon the lifeforce of virginal human females. Probable source of the vampire legend.[31]

Mary Brady and her son must feed upon young virgin females, and Charles zeroes in on Tanya (Madchen Amick), who is teased by her high school girlfriends for her virginity and lack of experiences with boys. Her innocence and beauty make her a perfect victim for the two "sleepwalker" vampires. For some reason, cats become agitated and aggressive by the presence of Mary and Charles Brady. Cats hate them, and ordinary housecats become as aggressive as tigers in their presence. In a high school English paper, Charles explains how it feels to be a shapeshifter:

> They were sleepwalkers, hiding in human roles, feeding on virtue, loving to feed, eating to breed, so in the end they ran. In the end Robbie and his mother always had to run, for one night the men would come, in their old cars. Men

Psychic Vampire Charles Brady (Brian Krause) attempts to drain virginal Tanya Robertson's (Madchen Amick) life force, which he plans to share with his mother, another psychic vampire. The mother/son vampire couple celebrate their psychic meals by having incestuous sex in *Sleepwalkers* (1992), based on a Stephen King short story (Kobal Collection at Art Resource, New York).

with lights and guns, just a boy and his mother, their curses and the screams of rage always sounded the same. Like the laughter of cruel gods. Time passing, too brief to be anything but golden, had run out.

The mother and son enjoy sexual intimacy with each other. Kissing her son's lips seductively, Mary says, "I'm famished! I'm famished!" She hungers for Tanya's life force and expects to partake of it through Charles after he extracts it from Tanya. When Charles and Tanya spend an afternoon making gravestone rubbings at the local cemetery, Charles starts kissing her. As they become passionate he begins inhaling her life force, which takes the form of a greenish, glowing light (a depiction of psychic energy favored by filmmakers). At this point a cat jumps on Charles's back and starts biting and scratching him until he releases Tanya and drives home. The housecats then start gathering in the Brady yard, growling and acting increasingly menacing toward the shapeshifters.

Desperate to feed off Tanya, Mary Brady visits Tanya's home bearing a vase of roses. Tanya's father (Lyman Ward) attempts to stop her, and she smashes the vase, cutting his face. When Mrs. Robinson (Cindy Pickett) comes in to see what the commotion is, Mary throws her out the window. Events become increasingly chaotic as Mary kills two police officers and destroys their squad cars. Then she knocks Tanya out and brings her back to her house, where she forces the girl to dance with Charles. When Charles attempts to suck her life force once again, Tanya pokes his eyes out with her fingers. Mary screams, "You killed my only son!" at which point the police break into the house. Some of the assembled cats rush in and leap onto Mary, biting and scratching. This somehow causes Mary to burst into flames, but she pulls herself together one final time and leaps on the windshield of the patrol car in which Tanya has sought refuge. "You killed my son, my only son!" she shouts before expiring.

Albert Rolls, in *Stephen King: A Biography,* argues that director Garris failed to let the film make a statement condemning the horror genre as misogynistic.[32] However, Tanya's strength and her vampire-slaying abilities place her in close proximity to Buffy, essentially qualifying her as a feminist.

Buffy-type heroes defend society against an onslaught of deadly vampires. No longer content to serve as victims, these bisexual heroes defeat both males and females. Buffy and Tanya arrived amid a rash of other powerful female characters, including monster-slayer Ripley (Sigourney Weaver) in *Alien Resurrection* (1992) and murderous bisexual writer Catherine Tramell (Sharon Stone) in *Basic Instinct* (1992). The success of *Buffy* on the big screen and later on television and in comic books paved the way for other powerful female characters: vampire and werewolf slayer Selene (Kate Beckinsale) in the *Underworld* film series (2003–2012); Catwoman (Halle Berry) in *Catwoman* (2004); and vampire slayer Saya (Gianna Jun) in *Blood: The Last Vampire* (2009).

A remake of *Carmilla*, this time with a trendy zombie plot, appeared in 2004 in the form of Vince D'Amato's *Vampires vs. Zombies*. In the film, a man named Travis Fontaine (C.S. Munro) and his blonde teenage daughter Jenna (Bonny Giroux) seek a cure for a strange disease that transforms people into vampire/zombies. While driving through a thick forest, they encounter a woman standing beside a car in the middle of the road (Brinke Stevens). She introduces her daughter Carmilla (Maritama Carlson) and begs them to take Carmilla with them so she can rush her other daughter, infected with vampire/zombism, to the hospital. Travis agrees, despite stiff opposition from his daughter. At this point in the low-budget film, D'Amato inserts bizarre elements that include a curmudgeon-like vampire hunter named The General (Peter Ruginis) and a witch who makes a car disappear. Zombies and vampires threaten the protagonists at every turn.

True to form, Carmilla seduces Jenna, who comes under her influence as a thrall. D'Amato treats audiences to scenes of the two young women kissing, fondling, and stripping, fully exploiting the lesbian sexual element. He also includes gory scenes with zombies and vampires, adding offbeat humor in the process. Although critics generally panned this film for being confusing, amateurish, and poorly acted, a few ardent fans emerged. Online critic Scott Davis praised the film for "tons of originality." Says he, "We've all seen zombie movies, we've done the vampire thing, we've even seen *Carmilla* adapted for the big screen…. But we haven't seen all three brought together with such quirky tweaks and with some psychological spiraling that comes in later."[33] In the finale, female vampires defeat male and female zombies and destroy Fontaine and the General for good measure. However, Carmilla falls into the hands of zombies, and they devour her. Vampires die while zombies survive. If vampires represent feminists, this film appears to be post-feminist.

Stephenie Meyer's *Twilight* (2005) signaled a return to more heterosexist pop culture vampires. The novel features Bella Swan, a seventeen-year-old high school student in Forks, Washington, who falls in love with Edward Cullen, an apparently high-school-age vampire who's actually over a hundred years old. In her article "Vampire Love: The Second Sex Negotiates the Twenty First Century," feminist Bonnie Mann expresses her initial shock at reading *Twilight*, Meyer's first in a popular series of novels that then became films. "The female protagonist struck me as an idealized woman of my mother's generation, transposed into twenty-first century circumstances." Bella Swan assumes a subservient role, while Edward, the vampire, takes a dominant role. Mann concludes that "the infantilization of females as objects of male desire has intensified." However, she also points to a feminist subtext in the relationship between Edward and Bella, that "he, not she, puts the brakes on their erotic encounters." In addition, Edward's female vampire "sisters" Rosalie and Alice are strong, dominant personalities who refuse to take orders from Edward (although they follow the leadership of Carlyle Cullen, their adoptive father).[34]

HBO's popular vampire series *True Blood* (2008–2012) serves as an extended metaphor for gender diversity. Director Alan Ball set his series in a community in which vampires "came out of the closet" and live openly with humans. First aired just a couple of months before the passage of California's Proposition Eight denied gays the right to marry, the initial episode featured footage from the Civil Rights marches along with a road sign blaring "God Hates Fangs." Reviewers promptly labeled the series a "gay-rights analogy." In the series, a hate group calling itself "The Obamas" because of their trademark Barack Obama masks wages war against "the supes," supernatural minorities.[35]

LGBT characters in *True Blood* include lesbians and a gay couple, Russell Edgington (Denis O'Hare) and Talbot (Theo Alexander). Director Ball explains that creating attractive LGBT vampires was "not the main point of the show; that's just kind of some fun window dressing." Gay and lesbian allusions are "a symbol for the gay and lesbian community because that's what's going on right now," he explains. "I mean, fifty years ago it would have been African-Americans, 100 years ago it would have been women and their struggles for equality and the right to vote, that kind of thing."[36]

True Blood references and symbolizes potent lesbian relationships between characters. Pam de Braufort (Kristin Bauer van Straten) and Sophie-Anne Leclerq (Evan Rachel Wood), two vampires on the series, at one point drink blood from human women's inner thighs. This act, clearly symbolic of lesbianism, appears pleasurable for both humans and vampires. However, lesbian vampires in the series are dressed and groomed as traditional heterosexual women. Ball avoids "butch" stereotypes while depicting metaphorical lesbianism.

Ball makes clear his own support for gay marriage by including angry protests for equal marriage rights for vampires and humans in *True Blood*. Writer Eve Dufour also notes Ball's inclusion of powerful female vampire characters such as Sophie-Anne, Vampire Queen. Although vampires in the series depict powerful females and show great gender diversity, she points out that *True Blood* also reinforces traditional gender roles.[37]

The British film *Vampire Killers* (2009), directed by Phil Claydon and originally called *Lesbian Vampire Killers,* was renamed after producers opted for a less controversial and antifeminist title. An update of Le Fanu's *Carmilla,* the film features Sylvia Colloca as Carmilla, a vampire slain hundreds of years earlier by Baron Wolfgang MacLaren after he discovered her seducing his wife. Before she's killed by Baron MacLaren's magic sword, Carmilla curses all the village women to become vampires when they turn eighteen. Flash forward to the present as two young men from London, Jimmy (Matthew Horne) and Fletch (James Corden), try to change their lives by going camping in the Scottish mountain village of Cragwitch—a journey that's meant to help Jimmy forget being jilted by his girlfriend. In the village, a local vicar (Paul McGann) informs Jimmy that he is descended from the family of the Baron MacLaren who had slain Carmilla centuries earlier.

An innkeeper offers the boys free beer and lodging at nearby Mircalla Cottage, Carmilla's old haunt. Coincidentally, a busload of college girls also arrives at the cottage, and the youth take advantage of the free beer to engage in a round of partying. But as the party progresses, the young women gradually turn into vampires, and the young men (with the assistance of the local vicar) began fighting them. Jimmy's ex-girlfriend Judy (Lucy Gaskell) arrives to attempt a reconciliation, but she, too, turns out to be a vampire. After a long hiatus, this film suggests, audiences may once again enjoy strong female characters overpowering males—even if they end up being slain.

Vampire Killers appeals to a teenage audience with its heavy-handed comedy, bringing a light tone and slapstick and humor to the Carmilla narrative and demonstrating the continuing popularity of the Le Fanu's theme. Lesbians are the chief villains, while the two young males represent the heterosexual perspective. After Jimmy and his friends manage to destroy the lesbian vampires—including former girlfriend Judy—stability returns and lesbianism recedes. In this film, Lesbianism is weakened and ultimately destroyed. Carmilla and the other lesbian vampires appear evil, not admirable, while the two men form a Byronic male bond as they hone their vampire-slaying skills. This transforms the Carmilla metaphor, disempowering females while empowering males. Feminist reviewer Milly Shaw declared that the film is "not just a spoofy excuse to leer at faux-lesbians, it's a cold and deeply unfunny 86 minutes of hatred against women."[38]

By contrast, *Life Blood* (2009), directed by Ron Carlson, glorifies lesbian vampires Brooke Anchel (Sophie Monk) and Rhea Cohen (Anya Lahiri). On New Year's Eve of 1969, the two women are vampirized by God (Angela Lindvall), a female. She intended to vampirize only Rhea—the good member of the couple—but Rhea pleas for Brooke to be transformed as well. God explains Rhea's new role as an avenger: "You shall kill to survive, and the truly wicked are the ones you want to destroy." Back at the New Year's Eve party, Brooke had attacked and stabbed Warren James (Justin Stilton), a handsome actor she found raping a young fan (Taylor-Compton). James fits the category of the "truly wicked" mentioned by God, but Brooke lacks the wisdom to limit her killing to wicked people and begins attacking random victims.

Much of the action takes place at the Murder Gas Station, where Brooke and Rhea go after Brooke murders and vampirizes two men on the nearby highway. Reminiscent of the gas station scenes in *From Dusk Till Dawn* (1996), Brooke murders a husband and wife who stop to use the bathroom and purchase a soda. When two police officers try to arrest her, Brooke kills them and drives away in a stolen car. God enters the gas station and revives Rhea, who then frees a young girl named Lizzy (Electra Avellan) who's trapped in a car. She commandeers a police car to go in search of Brooke. When she meets her former lover, Rhea strikes her with one powerful blow that sends Brooke flying through the air. She lands on a sign that sends a stake through her heart, and Rhea departs with Lizzy, now an apprentice vampire. At a diner, as God waits nearby in the guise of a waitress, Rhea explains to Lizzy:

> Honey, we're all God's creatures. You see, there came a time when the world became so evil that God made it rain for forty days and forty nights, killing all those who were corrupt. And so it came to be that only two of each creature were left. She started over. And to keep control of the evil that exists here on Earth, she created angels in her image to do her work. We serve the highest purpose. It is up to us to rid the world of these people.

This speech characterizes lesbian vampires as angels, not demons. Rhea focuses on eradicating the earth of evil, identified in this film with paternalism.

Life Blood serves as a strong metaphor about female power. More directly than most other films, this film depicts men as weak, impotent, irrelevant, sexist, egotistical, and clueless, while depicting women as strong, assertive, and aggressive. They challenge male authority, which has no power over them. Women seek and find solace and strength from other women, valorizing female friendship and empowerment. God—female—selects Rhea and Lizzy to rely only on each other, representing a more feminist metaphor than Buffy—who required a male trainer.

Recent vampire narratives such as *Twilight, True Blood,* and *Vampire Diaries* showcase a new breed of vampires—like *Twilight's* Edward Cullen—that possesses a sense of morality and self-control unknown in earlier pop culture vampires. In addition, they increasingly function as female protectors. After Edward Cullen (Robert Pattinson) saves Bella Swan (Kristen Stewart), he asks, "Did you follow me?" "I ... I feel very protective of you." Vampires in *The Breed* (2001), *Daybreakers* (2009), *Life Blood* (2009), and *Abraham Lincoln: Vampire Hunter* (2012) protect humans against other, more savage vampires.

Recent Carmilla–type films fall into two distinct categories. On the one hand, *Lesbian Vampire Killers* (2009), with its vicious, ball-busting vampires, conforms on the surface to a paternalistic, macho ethos in which men emerge triumphant. Male heroes rise to the occasion, bond like Romantics, and kill every lesbian vampire they encounter (before being killed *by* them). The resulting metaphor respects the power of lesbianism and feminism by dooming the powerful antagonists to death at the hands of two young men. On the other hand, *Life Blood's* vampires dispatch macho males unmercifully, with Rhea becoming more powerful than Brooke due to her morality. All males in this film seem destined to die, and only lesbian females survive—including the female God. Lesbians symbolize social justice, while heterosexuals are misogynistic morons, and paternalism appears to be doomed. But female vampires like those in *Lesbian Vampire Killers* and *True Blood* reinforce patriarchy through reliance on heterosexual (therefore paternalistic) female norms of grooming and dress, and they assume subordinate roles to male vampires and humans. Yet even when males attempt to dominate or slay them, female vampires still symbolize female strength and potency, thereby reinforcing LGBT gender roles.

Powerful female characters increasingly appear in pop culture, suggesting an underlying feminism. But when feminist journalist Helen Lewis asked readers what they considered the single biggest issue for modern-day feminists, this was one of the most thought-provoking responses: "[the] single biggest issue should be to work out why [the] vast majority of women don't think feminism represents them." Asks Lewis, "Is it because the big battles have been won? That must be something to do with it. Is it because first-world feminists don't talk enough about the struggles of women elsewhere?" Finally, she asks, "Is it because feminism doesn't seem very fun?"[39] This ambivalence about feminism's fate reminds us of the ambivalence in recent depictions of female vampires. At times they are vilified (as in *Lesbian Vampire Hunters*), at other glorified (as in *Life Blood*). In the 1970s, when pop culture featured many powerful Carmilla-type vampires, no such division appeared between pro- and anti-feminist sentiments. Only recently do we witness it—perhaps signaling a change in attitudes toward gender.

Today's LGBT vampires reflect rising acceptance of gender diversity. *Esquire* critic Stephen Marche believes that LGBT vampires symbolize "a quiet but profound sexual revolution and a new acceptance of freakiness in mainstream American life." Notes Marche, "Vampire fiction for young women is the equivalent of lesbian porn for men: Both create an atmosphere of sexual abandon that is nonthreatening." He thinks people want sex that's "risky but comfortable, gooey and violent but also traditional and loving. In the bedroom, we want to have one foot in the twenty-first century and another in the nineteenth."[40]

Vampire narratives serve as dynamic, socially acceptable ways of representing gender roles. During the Victorian era, vampires safely evoked feminism (as the New Woman), bisexuality, and homosexuality. By the 1920s, pop-culture creators were experimenting with more powerful female roles. In recent times, vampires display more human sensitivity than in the past, and female vampires have become ever more powerful in response to developments in feminism and the family. Pangender vampires continue to symbolize society's diverse gender roles and may signal increased acceptance of the LGBT population.

• Four •

Monsters

Vampire metaphors often reference human aggression, savagery, and violence—behavior that dates back to humanity's origins. Since early Christian times, wrath has been designated as one of the "seven deadly sins," transgressions so serious that they threaten life itself. Psychologists believe that the roots of human aggression lie intertwined in sexuality. Like the sex drive, violence springs from deep within the brain's hippo-campus region.[1] Both drive behavior powerfully. Sigmund Freud linked the two: Eros (procreation, survival) and Thanatos (aggression, death). In *Beyond the Pleasure Principle* (1922), he observed that as a result of human aggress-ion, "their neighbor is for them not only a potential helper or sexual object, but also someone who tempts them to satisfy their aggressiveness on him, to exploit his capacity for work without compensation, to use him sexually without his consent, to seize his possessions, to humiliate him, to cause him pain, to torture and to kill him. *Homo homini lupus*. (Man is a wolf to man.)"[2]

Every life, according to Freud, revolves around the conflict between these two powerful forces. He believed that each person has a "will to die," a subconscious drive that deeply affects the decision-making process.[3] Mon-strous vampires express this death wish by threatening murder and mayhem, and by their nature as "undead" creatures bereft of life as we understand it. They represent the tremendous power of the subconscious, even in an age of science and technology.

Freud labeled threatening fictional characters like vampires "monsters from the id" and identified them as "debased dreams of hellish delight."[4] Nov-elist Anne Rice, creator of *The Vampire Chronicles* novels, observed that "the mind of each man is a Savage Garden ... in which all manner of creatures rise and fall."[5] Monstrous vampires derive from the wellspring of human imagination, deep within the psyche, born of fears of vulnerability. Bestial vampires serve as cautionary metaphors, instructing us to beware the full moon, ancient or dark and isolated settings, and unexpected individuals who appear in these places. Vampire pop culture favors such settings because they stimulate fear and titillation.

Essayist Amanda Podonsky observes that sexuality forms a powerful subtext in Bram Stoker's *Dracula*, joining with issues of sexual identity to create villains who are both socially and sexually deviant. In the Victorian Age, sex and *homosexuality* were controversial topics. Caution and awareness were constantly emphasized in regard to sexual matters, and an overall chaste and modest lifestyle was encouraged.[6]

Humanity's aggression/death instinct fuels perennial fascination with violence and aggression. Consumers *demand* violence and aggression. In popular culture, monstrous vampire characters represent humanity's dark side, from Count Orlok in F.W. Murnau's 1922 film *Nosteratu* to the rogue vampires that threaten the Cullen family in today's *Twilight*: savage, aggressive, murderous, monstrous, and deadly. Critics often label such threatening vampires as Nosteratu, a tribute to Murnau's pioneering film. The term has come to serve as a synonym for "monster."

Vampires symbolize—and therefore lessen—real life-threatening dangers that might prove uncomfortable to audiences if depicted directly. *Dungeons and Dragons*, a popular fantasy role-playing game, relies on vampires to express brutal and dangerous human characteristics. The vampire character in the game assumes the role of "a chaotic evil, night-prowling creature whose powerful negative force drains life energy from victims."[7] *Dungeons and Dragons* vampires can represent all sorts of existential fears—about crime, lawlessness, dismemberment, wild animals, aliens, war, and terrorism may symbolize nativism, racism, and homophobia. *Dungeons and Dragons* vampires often become ravenous monsters desperate to obtain blood. While these differ from the seductive vampires discussed in Chapter Three, some transform easily from seducers to monsters when it suits them. Many appear handsome or beautiful at first in order to lure their victims, after which they shed their benign disguises and assume more monstrous appearances.

A demon might be defined as anything that has evil characteristics. According to myth, vampires are "evil."[8] However, the definition of "evil" varies between groups or individuals. As an example, to property developers the excavation of land inaugurates a creative process of community building, while to politicians it represents jobs and tax revenue. But to many Native Americans, excavating land for commercial use is a heinous activity carried out by monstrous spirits against Mother Earth. Just as some Native Americans might attribute such activity to storm deities and death lords, pop culture relies on vampires to symbolize death. Like ancient death lords, vampires celebrate the vital role played by the spirits in the life-death cycle.

Vampires once symbolized anti–Semitic prejudices and fears, as Jewish immigrants flooded Europe and the U.S. fleeing pogrom and seeking jobs. Parallels between Bram Stoker's Count Dracula and popular stereotypes of Jews are striking. Dracula, like most Jewish immigrants of the period, originated in Eastern Europe and emigrated to Europe, but his evil intentions included preying on humans everywhere. The parallels between Stoker's characterization of Dracula and nineteenth-century stereotypes of Jews begin with Dracula's dark features and pale-skinned "hook nose." Stoker's appropriation of negative Semitic stereotypes includes Dracula's depiction as selfish, materialistic, and evil, possessing a "child's brain."[9]

Murnau's *Nosteratu* survives today because of illegal copies kept after Florence Stoker, Bram Stoker's widow, successfully sued the producers, charging that the film was an unacknowledged and illegal appropriation of Stoker's novel. The film's Count Orlok, a thinly disguised Count Dracula, is a stereotypical Eastern European Jew. Close-ups of actor Max Schreck's long, pointed nose and the use of shadows to theatrically darken his bushy eyebrows against a large, pale forehead conform to widely held images of Jews at that time, as do costumes accentuating Orlok's lack of masculine physique.[10] When Orlok encounters Thomas Hutter (Gustav von Wangenheim), a local real estate agent, he observes a photograph of Hutter's young bride, Ellen (Greta Schroder). He immediately falls in love with her image, lecherously asking, "Is this your wife? What a lovely throat!" After purchasing a house next door to the Hutters, Orlok stares out his window at Ellen. She reads a book about vampires titled *Nosteratu* and then opens the window, seemingly to let Orlok inside. He enters and falls onto her in bed to feed from her blood. By her sacrificial act of keeping Orlok away from his casket until the sun rises, she saves humanity from the deadly monster. In Murnau's hands, vampirism emerges as a powerful metaphor for unwanted groups.

In 2000, E. Elias Merhige released *Shadow of the Vampire*, a movie about the filming of *Nosteratu*. John Malkovich plays original director F. W. Murnau, while Willem Dafoe is Max Schreck, who played Count Orlok in the original film. Merhige relies on images of "a desolate castle, a rat-infested ghost ship and above all the hollow visage of Max Schreck in the title role." Merhige's scriptwriter Stephen Katz claims that Murnau's choice to play the vampire count could not have been more appropriate because, in fact, Schreck was actually a real vampire, making *Nosteratu* "the most realistic vampire film ever made."[11] In Merhige's homage to *Nosteratu,* the great German director Murnau emerges as a monster himself, willing to sacrifice cast and crew to feed Schreck's vampirism, allowing him to make one of the greatest examples of German Expressionism in existence.

Like *Nosteratu,* Tod Browning's 1931 film version of *Dracula* earned critical praise and today ranks among the most memorable of the classic vampire movies. Browning chose Hungarian actor Bela Lugosi to play Count Dracula. Lugosi's Hungarian could be mistaken for a Hebrew accent, and in the film he wore an eight-pointed star pendant, reminiscent of a Star of David. In fact, the emblem probably relates to Dracula's ancestor Vlad II Dracul, who belonged to the Order of the Dragon.

Count Dracula functions as a full-fledged monster with superpowers: shapeshifting at will into menacing beasts, hypnotizing his victims, and demonstrating super strength. When Renfield (Dwight Frye), a London reality agent sent to call on Dracula, asks the local innkeeper (Michael Visaroff) about the location of Castle Dracula, the innkeeper direly warns, "No. You mustn't go there! We people of the mountains believe in the castle there are vampires. Dracula and his wives—they take the form of wolves and bats. They leave their coffins at night and they feed on the blood of the living!" Later, after a semi-vampirized Renfield attempts to save Mina from Dracula's bite, the Count silently confronts him. Renfield pleads, "I'm loyal to you, Master, I am your slave. I didn't betray you! Oh, no, don't! Don't kill me! Let me live, please! Punish me, torture me, but let me live! I can't die with all those lives on my conscience! All that blood on my hands!" But Dracula easily lifts Renfield's body with his bony hands, instantly killing him. He murders without remorse, a true Nosteratu vampire.

Christian European aristocrats also found themselves labeled as vampires. In *The Vampire Bat* (1933), directed by Frank R. Strayer, the villain turns out to be a close substitute for a vampire, a German aristocrat who embodies wealth and privilege. Strayer drew on the mythologies of not only vampires but also the "evil scientist" motif that dates back to Goethe's seventeenth-century Dr. Faustus, who trades his soul to Satan in exchange for power and knowledge. Mary Shelley's original Dr. Frankenstein continued the tradition of a mad scientist trading immortality for worldly gain. In Strayer's film, Dr. Otto von Niemann (Lionel Atwil) trades his soul not for knowledge but for the lives of innocent victims sacrificed in order for him to obtain eternal life. Like Dr. Frankenstein, Dr. von Niemann abandons the orthodox world in which only God creates life.

Vampires evoke the Christian worldview that pits Jesus and his angels against Satan and his minions, which include vampires. However, this Manichean "black or white" perspective may cloud nuances and variations on the perennial battle between good and evil despite vampires' evil reputation—or perhaps because of it—millions remain fascinated with these creatures in fiction and film.

According to novelist Danny Phillips, savage vampires "kill their victims and drink their blood to survive. They rest in coffins because they are the 'living dead' who are only able to come out at night. They have no reflection in a mirror, and most times they can turn into something like a bat and fly away." Bad vampires "always sink their teeth into their victims and suck the blood from their bodies, leaving them dead. They are indeed creatures to be feared by normal humans."[12]

But vampires—like Satan in Milton's *Paradise Lost*—often seem dynamic and appealing even as they prey on humans. Vampires such as Count Dracula and all his personifications can appear more attractive than their hunters, who may come across as staid in comparison. Bella Lugosi's rendition of Count Dracula in *Dracula* transformed the Nosteratu monster into a suave, handsome, aristocratic seducer. Vampires' nocturnal habits resonate with youthful audiences, and their clothing influences today's Goth movement. Writer and religious scholar J. Gordon Meldon credits vampires as being the single most important element in Goth culture, in which adherents wear vampire-inspired black, formal clothing and attempt to replicate some of vampires' romantic attributes.[13]

At the same time, savage vampires are an ever-popular archetype that reveals much about what constitutes "evil" and "the other." They form in response to rising fears about immigration, drug addiction, criminal gangs, terrorists, or rapists; and as issues that sparked controversy and debate in earlier decades become less vexing, new fears arise.

The spectacle of monstrous vampires attacking peaceful civilians never fails to excite audiences. In Matt Reeves' *Let Me In* (2010), the vampire Abby (Chloe Grace Moretz), who appears to be a twelve-year-old, survives over the centuries by killing people and drinking their blood. She forces an older human known as her "father" to provide her with human blood, which he obtains by stalking and draining victims. When he fails to supply her with blood, Abbey kills him. She replaces him with a twelve-year-old neighbor boy named Owen (Kodi Smit-McPhee) after saving him from psychotic bullies intent on drowning him in a swimming pool. While underwater, Owen sees a severed head and other body parts that Abby has torn from his attackers. She is just one among the savage Nosteratu vampires inhabiting pop culture in recent times.

Nearly eight decades earlier, in 1932, Danish filmmaker Carl Dreyer's *Vampyr* featured a young man named Alan Gray (Julian West) who travels through Europe studying Satanism. His interest in the occult affects his judgment, leading him to aimlessly wander the countryside collecting biology specimens in a butterfly net until he comes to a village cursed by a vampire.

There he discovers a young woman who bleeds from tiny neck wounds and a sinister doctor who appears to be controlled by someone else. Eventually Gray learns about the vampire's curse and helps a servant drive a metal stake through the heart of an elderly woman named Marguerite Chopin (Henriette Gérard), who's inhabiting a tomb. Some of her victims recover, including a young woman named Gisele (Rena Mandel) but she reappears before the village doctor as a giant, terrifying him and sending him running into a flour mill. A servant traps him in a steel cage, and he suffocates under tons of flour. The curse finally lifts, and Gray and Gisele appear together in a final scene. In lieu of the typical monstrous male, Dreyer chooses to use an elderly female as his monster—reminiscent of Hungarian Countess Elizabeth Bathory (see Chapter Two).

Cold War

The bombing of Hiroshima and Nagasaki by the United States in the last days of World War II introduced new fears. Anxiety about voracious aliens gave way to fear of nuclear attacks by the USSR and other Cold War adversaries. By the late 1950s, vampires were attracting movie audiences in both England and the United States. England's Hammer Film Productions released a series of highly successful films starring tall, charismatic Christopher Lee as Dracula, pitted against Peter Cushing as Abraham Van Helsing. With generous infusions of nudity, sexuality, and graphic horror, these films captivated a generation of movie fans.

In Hammer's *Dracula* (1958), released in the U.S. as *Horror of Dracula*, Jonathan Harker (John Van Eyssen) encounters Count Dracula (Christopher Lee) and writes in his diary, "It only remains for me now to await the daylight hours where I will with God's help forever end this man's reign of terror." But Harker immediately comes under attack by one of Dracula's vampire wives, who bites his neck and would have sucked his blood dry had not Count Dracula violently intervened. When he discovers Dracula and his wife sleeping in their caskets he attempts to kill them both. He manages to drive a wooden stake through the heart of Dracula's wife. He attempts to do the same to the Count, but Dracula gains the upper hand and transforms Harker into an undead thrall by drinking his blood. Dracula next turns to Harker's fiancée, Lucy Holmwood (Carol Marsh), to avenge the killing of his wife. While only Dr. Van Helsing (Peter Cushing) appears able to save Lucy, her brother Arthur (Michael Gough), in denying the existence of vampires, obstructs Van Helsing's efforts. Finally he realizes the truth and lends his assistance. Arthur symbolizes human disbelief in the supernatural. In vampire literature and films, supernatural elements must be confronted and defeated, leaving no room for philosophical skepticism.

The *Dracula* vampire targets the young, beautiful, and chaste. He threatens to destroy British society by enslaving young and beautiful women like Lucy, who will then seduce and enslave men until everyone has been infected with vampirism. In the film's final scene, the Count confronts Van Helsing. A struggle ensues, and Dracula easily fends off Van Helsing—but even his super strength fails when Van Helsing thrusts a cross in his face and tears down the window curtains to allow in a flood of sunlight, killing him. Here Van Helsing represents scientific reasoning and technology, which ultimately prevails against the "monsters from the id." Yet science's victory over vampires often proves illusory, and vampires repeatedly rise again to threaten humanity. Sunlight in this case symbolizes openness and truth, two qualities to which Cold War vampires find themselves allergic. Science and technology, represented by Van Helsing, along with Christianity and the cleansing properties of sunlight, combine to defeat the foreign threat embodied by Dracula. During the Cold War era, vampires evoke Soviet and Chinese leaders who threaten humanity with nuclear annihilation.

Plague

Humans who've been bitten or "infected" by vampires become carriers of the vampire-transforming agent, similar to blood-borne diseases. In the film *Nosteratu,* the vampire's casket aboard a ship is infested with rats, an ancient symbol of pestilence. Rats also follow Count Dracula in Tod Browning's film *Dracula*. Dracula and many other pop culture vampires prefer ruined dank, drafty castles and abbeys frequented by rats, bats, and spiders—all of which symbolize disease and death, evoking the supernatural. Such Gothic elements only increase the romantic allure of vampires.

Perhaps Bram Stoker's association of vampirism with disease represents a true scientific insight. Biochemist David H. Dolphin of the University of British Columbia proposed thirty years ago that what observers and writers refer to as "vampirism" might in fact be porphyria, a rare disease that causes the body to waste away. Dolphin argued that "the effects of the porphyria diseases, which involve a malfunctioning in the body's manufacture of crucial chemicals, could have left victims grotesquely disfigured, turned them into creatures of the night and caused them to suck the blood of their brothers and sisters." Sunlight is toxic to those suffering from porphyria, causing most to adopt a nocturnal lifestyle.[14]

Also striking is the location of porphyria outbreaks. The disease appears most frequently in remote villages in the Carpathian Mountains in Romania, the region known as Transylvania. Sufferers of the disease report severely sensitive, itchy skin. Their bodies lose the ability to extract porphyrins, chemicals used in the production of hemoglobin. Side effects include insomnia, restlessness, abdominal and muscle pain, seizures, confusion, hallucinations, disorientation, paranoia, and red-colored urine. Interestingly, garlic appears to make the symptoms more severe.[15]

Perhaps Bram Stoker's accounts of vampirism sprang in part from reported outbreaks of vampirism/porphyria during the nineteenth century. Possibly Stoker was inspired by this unusual disease, and his vampire characters have led to hundreds of imitators over the years.

The disease metaphor continues to strike a familiar note in contemporary pop culture. During the 1950s and 1960s polio was a widespread public health threat. In the United States the epidemic peaked in 1952, with more than 58,000 cases of paralytic polio reported. After the introduction of the polio vaccine and widespread public inoculation in 1955, outbreaks declined to 2,500 in 1960 and fewer than a hundred by the mid-1960s.[16] Cancer, too extracted a heavy toll during this era. Among its victims were the celebrated actor Humphrey Bogart, who died in 1957 at age 57, and atomic physicist and Nobel laureate Enrico Fermi, who died in 1954 at age 53.

The Last Man on Earth (1964), based on a 1959 novel by Robert Matheson, presents a post-apocalyptic scenario in which all the people on earth seem doomed to become vampires as the result of a plague. These zombie-like vampires come out at night to feed on living humans until they've exhausted the local supply. After all the scientists at the Mercer Laboratory succumb to the infection except for research biologist Dr. Robert Morgan (Vincent Price) and Dr. Mercer (Umberto Raho), Morgan asks, "What's going to happen, Dr. Mercer? Is everybody in the world going to die before someone finds the answer?" Mercer replies, "No, I don't think so. I don't deny there's some strange evolutionary process going on, but mankind won't be destroyed. The fact that you and I are working here today is evidence of that." But Mercer perishes, leaving Morgan as the only uninfected human.

Morgan spends his days systematically searching for and destroying zombies/vampires, and the vampires spend their nights trying to break into his fortified house to get his blood. They appear disorganized and disheveled, and they move sluggishly. Morgan explains that "individually they're weak, mentally unconnected, like animals after a long famine." However, when they gather together they become an increasingly formidable force that poses a nightly threat to Morgan's life. These creatures do manage to kill him—but not before he cures one vampire with his own blood, providing a potent serum that allows a tiny human community to survive.

The Last Man on Earth references not only the fear of life-threatening epidemics and pandemics but also the era's paranoia of a Communist takeover. Matheson's army of zombie-like vampires mindlessly and savagely consuming and destroying every human evokes Cold War fears of "fifth columnists" and other traitors undermining American society so that Communism—an "alien" ideology—can conquer and dominate society.

Dracula: The Satanic Rites, directed by Alan Gibson, appeared in 1973, marking the final installment of the Hammer Films vampire series that began in 1958 with *The Horror of Dracula*. Here Professor Lorrimor Van Helsing (Peter Cushing) proclaims that vampirism "is like a plague." A radioactive, virulent version of bubonic plague renders its victims completely helpless and threatens to annihilate humanity. Professor Julian Keeley (Julian Jones), Nobel Prize–winner-turned-Satan-worshiper, plots to unleash this radioactive plague. Dracula, disguised as D.D. Denham (Christopher Lee), plots to destroy civilization so he can control earth. Van Helsing learns of his scheme and attacks Denham, armed with a silver bullet fashioned from a Catholic cross. But Denham escapes, captures Van Helsing, and warns him, "You are an interfering man, Professor. Do not meddle, or you will have to deal with me!" He taunts Van Helsing that "in the days to come you will pray for death." However, Van Helsing escapes and manages to entangle Denham in a Hawthorne tree, deadly to vampires. A fire engulfs the Denham building, destroying the plague virus and thus releasing Dracula/Denham's thralls.

Pulsating with deadly radioactivity, the plague virus symbolizes active antiwar and antiestablishment movements around the world. The nuclear-tainted virus substitutes for politicized concerns in the Vietnam War era, including fears about the dangers of nuclear medicine and nuclear power. The contagion threatened by Dracula/Denham may symbolize widespread fears of Communism and Communist sympathizers, radioactive fallout, and nuclear Armageddon.

Addiction

Literature professor Susan Zieger sees vampires' relationship to addiction as an accumulation of earlier fears about alcohol, opium-eating, and other compulsions.[17] Others describe vampirism as a powerful and effective metaphor for addiction During the nineteenth century, vampires symbolized many kinds of addictions, including alcohol, sex, and drugs. In the twentieth century, the vampire as a metaphor for drug addiction became increasingly common as drug use increased. In 1986 President Ronald Reagan signed the Anti-Drug Abuse Act, inaugurating the "War on Drugs." Federal funding to combat drugs reached $17.1 billion in the 1990s, when over a third of Americans admitted to having tried marijuana.[18]

Abel Ferrara's 1995 film *The Addiction* depicts a New York University doctoral student named Kathy Conklin (Lili Taylor) who's bitten by a female vampire. She begins a painful process of transformation into a vampire, driven by a growing hunger for blood. As an academic she has a wide knowledge of history and philosophy, which she attempts to apply to end her blood addiction. She tells another vampire, "Our addiction is evil. The propensity for this evil lies in our weakness before it." In another speech she likens blood addiction to alcoholism: "We drink to escape the fact we're alcoholics. Existence is the search for relief from our habit, and our habit is the only relief we can find."

Christopher Walken plays Peina, a 400-year-old vampire who attempts to break his own addiction through total abstinence. He says to Conklin, "You know how long I've been fasting? Forty years!" He employs drug terminology for his blood addiction, saying "the last time I shot up" to mean the last time he drank blood. He describes his last blood orgy: "I had a dozen and a half in one night. They fall like flies before the hunger, don't they? You can never get enough, can you? But you learn to control it. You learn, like the Tibetans, to survive on a little."

This plot relies on human willpower to control addiction. If Conklin had possessed the will to demand that the vampire leave her in peace, she would never have been bitten. Eventually she achieves the necessary willpower and seemingly triumphs over death after she's reborn as a human. In the film's finale, she places a flower on her own grave. Ferrara belabors his vampire-as-drug-addict metaphor a bit, but the trick works. *The Addiction* still enjoys a following as one of the notable vampire films.

The Thirst (2009), directed by Jeremy Kasten, stars Matt Keesler and Claire Kramer as Maxx and Lisa, recovering drug addicts who are transformed into blood-addicted vampires. While hospitalized with a rare blood disease, Lisa is vampirized by the "Night Nurse," actually a vampire controlled by Darius (Jeremy Sisto). Darius orders Lisa abducted so she can serve as a stripper in his Hell Club. Maxx discovers Lisa in the club, but a club bouncer gets in his way. Desperate to reconnect with her, Maxx hires himself to a sadist and enters the club wearing a collar and pulled on a leash. His visit to the club resembles a real descent into hell, and Maxx finds himself within a sex-crazed vampire clan. He lets Lisa vampirize him so he can be with her.

In the ensuing chaos, Maxx learns how to vampirize humans but also discovers human blood's addictive powers. Their previous drug addictions make Maxx and Lisa realize that blood addiction represents the same personal and spiritual degradation. Says Lisa, "Yes, I'm hungry, but I can't do what they do. I can't do that to someone else no matter how hungry I am." But as blood becomes ever harder to resist, Maxx kills his friend Macey (Charlotte Ayanna). Afterward he experiences a complete mental breakdown and a full-fledged identity crisis. Lisa assures him, "We're gonna get out of this!" The two vow to team together to defeat Darius and the "family." By combining their strengths and willpowers and going "cold turkey," they succeed in freeing themselves of blood obsession.

In 2009 Christopher Hutson released *Bled*, another entry in the vampire-as-drug-addict genre, with a tagline that reads, "Every addiction has its price." Renfield (Jonathan Oldham), a suave and mysterious European, gradually seduces Sai (Sarah Farooqui), a gifted but lost painter living in a New York City loft, into smoking a highly addictive, vampiric drug. It sends her into a vivid dream world in which a hideous vampire attacks her and drinks her blood. Sai grows increasingly addicted to the drug, gradually allowing Renfield—a monstrous vampire from another dimension—to materialize in this world. The movie trailer proclaims, "A beast walks in the skin of man. Waits to cross over to give us new life again." The beast, like substance addiction, imprisons Sai's will and ultimately devours her.

Crime

Public fear of criminal gangs expanded in the 1980s and 1990s during a period of rapid spikes in gang-related crime. In 1997 President Bill Clinton announced a "War on Gangs." Criminologists Jodi Lane and James W. Meeker observe, "The public's fear of crime and gangs became one of the strongest motivating forces behind legislators' calls for harsher policies toward criminals during the 1990s."[19] This era inspired films in which vampires symbolize gang members. Frances Ford Coppola's *Bram Stoker's Dracula* (1992) depicts the vampire Prince Vlad/Dracula (Gary Oldman) as a viscious monster who preys on Londoners in 1897. He begins his reign of terror by vampirizing Lucy Westenra (Julie Frost), but Mina Murray (Winona Ryder) serves as his primary attraction. She shares the spirit of Dracula's ancient bride, who flung herself into a river upon hearing the false report of Prince Vlad's death in battle. Dracula begins to seduce Mina, who finds him impossible to resist. She falls in love with "my Prince," but Professor Abraham Van Helsing

(Anthony Hopkins) challenges Dracula. Boasts Dracula, "I, who served the Cross? I, who commanded nations, hundreds of years before you were born?" Van Helsing replies, "Your armies were defeated. You tortured and impaled thousands of people." Responds Dracula, "I was betrayed. Look what your God has done to me!"

Under Coppola's direction, the actors deliver excellent performances. Dracula revels in torture and massive incarcerations. As the film progresses, Coppola makes Dracula increasingly loathsome and hideous. Yet Oldman depicts the villain with a romantic side, and this softer Dracula begs Mina to give him peace. She obliges by shoving a dagger deep into his chest until it emerges from his back. In this film Count Dracula the infamous monster emerges as a monster with a sad, former-human heart. Despite an overabundance of gore—or perhaps in part because of it—fans often rank Coppola's film among the top vampire movies.

John Carpenter's *Vampires* (1998) often appears on blogger lists of "Best Vampire Movies." Carpenter cast James Woods as Jack Crow, a vampire hunter who works clandestinely with the Vatican to find and destroy vampires. In the first scene, Crow and a team of vampire hunters destroy a cell of nine gruesome vampires in an abandoned New Mexico house but fail to destroy their master, who rises from his grave as the slayers depart. Crow and his team rent the pagan-sounding Sun God Motel, stock it with liquor, hire prostitutes, and throw a wild victory party. But Jan Valek (Thomas Ian Griffith), the oversized master vampire, enters the motel unnoticed. He rapes and bites Katrina (Sheryl Lee), one of the prostitutes. Then Valek brutally slays the other prostitutes and all the slayers except for Crow and his partner Montoya (Daniel Baldwin), who barely escape the bloody rampage.

Valek represents the Nosteratu type of vampire—violent, deadly, and unattractive. Crow explains:

> Well first of all, they're not romantic. It's not like they're a bunch of fuckin' fags hoppin' around in rented formal wear and seducing everybody in sight with cheesy Euro-trash accents, all right? Forget whatever you've seen in the movies: they don't turn into bats, crosses don't work. Garlic? You wanna try garlic?

Crow and Montoya emerge as macho action heroes who execute vampires with crossbows, spears, and firearms. Crow wears a black leather jacket and dark glasses, and he smokes cigarettes. Valek, a giant alongside the other characters, appears Gothic in a black leather jacket and long black hair. This film channels 1990s fears of violent criminal gangs.

Youthful biker gangs long ago established themselves in popular culture with films like *The Wild One* (1953), the Laslo Benedek cult classic starring Marlon Brando as the leader of an outlaw motorcycle gang that invades a small California town. Thirty-four years later, Joel Schumacher's *The Lost Boys* (1987) borrows the youth gang motif and applies it to vampires. Schumacher's film takes place in Santa Carla, California, a picturesque seaside community that also qualifies as the "murder capital of the world." The problems begin with vampire gang leader David (Kiefer Sutherland). Upon moving to Santa Carla, Michael (Jason Patric) gets involved with David and his motorcycle gang and inadvertently drinks some of David's blood, partially transforming himself into a vampire.

Michael's recently divorced mother Lucy (Dianne Wiest) begins dating a video store owner named Max (Edward Herrmann), who turns out to be the powerful vampire lord who secretly controls David's gang. In the end, Michael and other allies defeat and kill David and Max, and the community returns to normal after the long ordeal of killer vampires in its midst. In the final scene, Michael's grandfather opens a beer and says, "There's one thing about living in Santa Carla.... I never could stomach—all the damn vampires."

The Lost Boys channeled rising fears about violent youth gangs. Although youth gangs had long existed in the United States, dating back to the eighteenth century, their proliferation after 1980 fueled public fears about violent youth gangs. The 1980s witnessed a rise in gang-related violence along with a crack cocaine epidemic.[20]

A few years after *The Lost Boys,* films featuring vampire characters in stereotypical Mafia roles began appearing. John Landis's *Innocent Blood* (1992) goes out of its way to identify with the Mafia. Landis set this comedy in the Bloomfield neighborhood around Liberty Avenue in Pittsburgh, Pennsylvania, a neighborhood known as "Little Italy." Actors *Tony Sirico* and *David Proval* play supporting gangster roles, performances that seem prescient in light of their later work in the television series *The Sopranos*. Other characters include Tony (Chazz Palminteri) and Sal "The Shark" Macelli (Robert Loggia), the film's chief villain. Vampir Marie (Anne Parillaud) feeds solely on violent Pittsburgh criminals whose deaths may actually be society's gain. After reading newspaper articles about local Mafia activities, she decides, "I was sad, I was starved. It was time to treat myself. Then I thought—what about ... Italian!"

However, it turns out that if Marie stops feeding on a victim too soon, that victim may survive as a new vampire—a development that occurs when she feeds on Sal. Transformed into a vampire, Sal vampirizes his mob henchmen, inducting them as "made men" into a criminal world in which vampires with superpowers threaten humanity. His mob includes Mafia attorney Emmanuel "Manny" Bergman (Don Rickles). Sal threatens his rival mobs, "I'm going to grind you down to blood and screams!"

Marie grows attracted to undercover officer Joey Genaro (Anthony LaPaglia), and the two survive attacks by Sal and Manny. Manny dies after exposure to sunlight, and later Joey lights a gasoline fire that ultimately engulfs and kills Sal. By asserting their freedom from domination by Sal and Manny, Joey and Marie demonstrate the potential strength of an alliance of opposites: vampire and human. Joey comes to accept Marie's occasional need to kill for human blood, and she refrains from killing him. This unlikely union of hunter and hunted symbolizes the covert assistance that gangs sometimes receive from corrupt law enforcement officers. The new vampire Mafia members have superpowers and an insatiable thirst for human blood. Public fears of organized crime translate into paranoia about a super-powerful, rapacious Mafia. By drinking the blood of their victims rather than using more traditional means of abuse, mobsters become even more horrifying. However, the horror comes with an element of satire: this is, after all, a comedy.

Because of the syndicated structure of many vampire clans, the violent nature of vampirism, and the role of authority figures in vampire narratives, vampires make apt stand-ins for organized crime. The metaphor's popularity increases exponentially in times when the fear of gangs and Mafia activities is especially strong. Pop culture offers relief from anxiety about criminals in the real world by defeating and killing "criminal" vampires.

In the *Blade* film series (1998–2004), vampires infiltrate human society to form a shadowy but powerful empire, much like organized gangs. The world of ordinary reality exists only as a delusion. The series channels pessimism, fear of powerlessness, and a sense that the world of appearances is a sham. Blade (Wesley Snipes) is a vampire/human hybrid who hates vampires and has the superpowers necessary to exterminate them. Like many superheroes, he works with an assistant, a man named Whistler (Kris Kristopherson). *Blade* designates subgroups within the vampire community, including "purebloods" like Dragonetti (Udo Kier) and "turned" vampires like Deacon Frost (Stephen Dorff). Pureblood vampires—elite "natural" vampires—desire coexistence with humans so they can remain in control of a vast network of businesses. "Turned" vampires were humans until they were bitten by a vampire.

At the vampire council, Frost and Dragonetti clash over Dragonetti's plans to forge a secret treaty with humans that would allow vampires to continue their clandestine existence. Frost objects. "We should be ruling the humans, not running around making back alley treaties with them," he says. "For fuck's sake, these people are our food, not our allies!" As Frost tells young doctor Karen Jensen (N'Bushe Wright), who becomes one of Blade's assistants, "The world you live in is just a sugar-coated topping. There is another world beneath it—the real world!"

Through Dragonetti and the council, vampires covertly control the world of humans. They function much like the conspiracy theories involving the Illuminati, the Knights Templar, Opus Dei, and Communists. But ultimately Frost gains ascendency over the other vampires by executing Dragonetti and the other purebloods on the vampire council. Using blood taken from Blade, he acquires their powers by resurrecting the "Blood God." Frost explains vampire powers to Dr. Jensen:

> I'll tell you what we are, sister! We're the top of the fucking food chain. The Blood God's coming and after tonight, you people are fucking history. He's a hurricane, an act of God. Anyone caught in his path will instantly be turned. Everyone you've ever known ... everyone you've ever fucking loved ... it won't matter who's pureblood and who's not.

By resurrecting a powerful, evil demon, Frost plans to gain ascendency over the council. He also reveals his rage at the treatment he has received from the council.

Blade depicts a life-and-death struggle between vampires and humans, a struggle that neither side wins decisively. As Whistler says, "There's a war going on out there. Blade, myself, a few others, we've tried to keep it from spilling over onto the streets." This conflict between supernatural vampires and their vampire/human progeny closely resembles humans facing zombie attacks in the zombie branch of horror. Although Blade finally manages to kill Deacon Frost, he continues to ferret out vampires in other lands—as in the film's epilogue, when he closes in on a suave Russian-speaking vampire about to bite a beautiful woman. Clearly Blade, the vampire/human hybrid, represents the solution to the "good vs. evil" struggles depicted in recent movies.

Michael Oblowitz's *The Breed* (2001) was one of the last pre–9/11 vampire films, appearing just two months before the terrorist attacks. Oblowitz sets his film in a future-retro world in which the protagonists drive vintage 1950s cars and the government appears socialistic despite the presence of many Nazi icons. Oblowitz chose actual Jewish ghettos in Eastern Europe to achieve a Warsaw Ghetto Uprising and Holocaust effect. His vampires fall into two groups: good and evil. The first vampire seen in the film turns out to be a rogue, since most in the vampire community have already come out in the open and cooperate peacefully with humans. Audiences witness this blond male rogue draining blood from the body of a female college student strung up from the ceiling of an abandoned warehouse.

The movie's good vampires include Aaron Gray (Adrian Paul), a Jewish Holocaust "survivor," and Lucy Westenra (Bai Ling), a Chinese American vampire. To defeat the rogue, Gray partners with Steve Grant (Bokeem Woodbine), an African American human. Both work for the Soviet/Nazi-like

National Security Administration. Westenra and Grant fall in love. Oblowitz's film associates vampires with ethnic diversity (Jews, African Americans, blond Europeans, Asians).

The Breed's underlying conflict consists of a racial war between humans and vampires. Each group attempts to exterminate the other, evoking thoughts of the Jewish Holocaust and genocidal wars against Native Americans. But elements of Nazism emanate from humans as well as vampires, and ultimately their identities merge into a single species divided racially and culturally. The good vampires in *The Breed* assist and serve their human counterparts. Westenra vows to stay with Grant throughout his life. Gray saves partner Grant's life more than once, proving his loyalty to humans, not vampires. The metaphoric message becomes one of diversity. Monstrous rogue vampires pose deadly threats to humans, but they exist alongside friendly, courageous vampires like Gray and Westenra. Cooperative vampires are associated with "good," uncooperative ones with "evil."

Terrorists

After the attacks of September 11, 2001, the terrorists who attacked the World Trade Building and the Pentagon instantly supplanted previous bogymen. Acts of terrorism quickly became symbolized as attacks by deadly Nosteratu-type vampires, and vampires became deadlier, more savage, and increasingly ruthless. American mythology refocused on satanic figures. Before 9/11, fewer than sixty percent of Americans said they believed in the existence of Satan. But after the attacks, more than seventy percent admitted believing in the devil, while sixty-nine percent said they believed in a literal hell.[21]

Savage Nosteratu vampire characters channel fears of terrorists, gangs, addictions, and diseases.[22] A 2005 survey discovered that only four percent of Americans believe in the existence of vampires, whereas ninety-one percent believe in God, eighty-seven percent believe in heaven, eighty-four percent believe in miracles, and seventy-nine percent believe in angels.[23] Since overwhelming numbers of Americans regard vampires as fictional rather than real, they make ideal metaphors. While people may dislike seeing their real fears expressed in films, or the deities they worship depicted, they appear to relish being frightened by imaginary creatures.

Following the path blazed by *Blade* and *The Breed*, in which vampires unite in warfare, Len Wiseman's 2003 film *Underworld* depicts a vampire organization battling lycans (werewolves), not humans. *Underworld* stars Kate Beckinsale as Selene, an iconic vampire who hunts down and kills werewolves one by one as part of a centuries-old war. One night Selene notices lycans trailing a human into a New York subway station. With assistance from other vampires, she enters the subway to save the human. After a lycan murders one of Selene's comrades, she tracks down the human they followed, Michael Corvin (Scott Speedman). It turns out that Corvin is the only person on earth who is immune to vampire bites, through a rare element in his blood. Lycans especially want this blood element so they can turn it into an anti-vampire serum.

Underworld's focus on blood pathogens speaks to public fears about HIV, hepatitis B, and hepatitis C, transformed cinematically into the fear of vampire and werewolf "viruses" transmitted through bites. As knowledge of the human genome expands, awareness of the role of microstructures in the human circulatory system increases, and science appears poised to eliminate some ancient maladies. This may provide inspiration for writers and film-makers in the future.

Fears about blood pathogens correspond with increasing concerns about food safety. Today many people forgo red meat and foods containing trans-fatty acids. Some forgo all food that comes from animals because of health or animal rights sentiments, though the percentage of vegetarians in the U.S., always minuscule, remained just slightly above three percent. Some recent vampires might be compared to vegetarians, in their distaste for human blood. In 2008 the film version of *Twilight* appeared, marking the first installment of the financially successful movie franchise based on the novels by Stephenie Meyer. Directed by Catherine Hardwicke, the film stars Robert Pattinson as Edward Cullen, a pallid high school senior/vampire who refrains from drinking human blood, assuaging his sanguinary needs by hunting game animals in a nearby forest.

The character of Cullen more accurately conforms to the Byronic vampires discussed in Chapter Two, but *Twilight* also references Nosteratu vampires. Three "rogue vampires"—Laurent (Edi Gathegi), Victoria (Rachelle Lefevre), and James (Cam Gigandet)—kill and feed off humans. James turns out to be the most violent character in the film. Unlike Cullen, who suppresses his powerful desire to drink the blood of Bella Swan (Kristen Stewart), James lets his lust for Swan's rare and apparently highly succulent hybrid blood overpower his reason and tempt him into attacking her—despite the fact that the powerful Cullen family supports her. *Twilight's* rogue vampires threaten not only humans but even the "vegetarian vampires" of the Cullen family. As in *Underworld, Blade,* and *The Breed,* undead characters battle each other, with rogue vampires pitted against good vampires. Humans, relatively powerless against characters with superpowers, cannot defeat the rogue vampires without the help of good vampires. Audiences seem to be attracted to films featuring comforting, helpful, and powerful characters to protect them against the ferocious rogue vampires waiting to feed from them.

HBO's popular *True Blood* also pits "good" against "evil" vampires. Good vampires choose to subsist on "True Blood," an artificial blood product that serves their nutritional needs without draining blood from humans. The series premiered in 2008, and by the 2009 season its audience had grown by double digits each month—with two-thirds of the viewers being female.[24] The series features vampires that have "come out of the casket" to live in rural Louisiana, the only state that allows vampires equal rights with humans. Adapted by HBO from Charlaine Harris' *Southern Vampire Mysteries* novels, the series chronicles the attempted coexistence of vampires and humans in the fictional small town of Bon Temps. The first season features Sookie Stackhouse (Anna Paquin) as a telepathic bar waitress who falls in love with vampire Bill Compton (Stephen Moyer). The series focuses on the interactions and sexual relationships between the vampires and humans.

True Blood features both Nosteratu and Byronic vampires. Rogue vampires visit the café where Sookie works and pay an unwanted social call on Compton, revealing something about the hierarchy and diversity of vampire characters in this series. That makes the vampires in this series appear more realistic than in many more formulaic vampire films. Certain audiences, however, react strongly against *True Blood*, including white supremacy advocates. Stormfront "white pride" website, for example, charges that *True Blood* is "100% anti-white propaganda. The entire show is an obvious giant metaphor for the racial and sexual situation."[25] In addition to diversity, according to a reviewer for the site, "the show is loaded with meaningless sex, racial mixing, and preaching of tolerance." This revie wer praised only one aspect of the film, "in the opening credits when they are going through photos and videos of various historical events. One photo is of a little white boy in a KKK outfit. The picture was a sweet reminder of what our nation once was."[26]

On the other hand, reviewer Alison Herman argues that ethnic and sexual diversity is part of the reason for the continued success of *True Blood*.[27] Both *True Blood* and the *Twilight* movies (2008–2010; 2008–2012) along with the independent film *The Breed* (2001), equate anti-vampire discrimination with other forms of discrimination. Negative reactions reveal enduring racial and ethnic tensions in the U.S.

Michael and Peter Spierig's *Daybreakers* (2009) continues the subgenre of savage vampires battling noble humans. In their film, set in 2019, vampires vastly outnumber humans, constituting eighty-five percent of the total population. They enjoy majority status and control society, from schools and governments to police, the military, and corporations. One company, the Bromley Marks Corporation, supplies blood to vampires by connecting humans to wicked-looking blood harvester machines and selling the collected blood to the ever-increasing vampire population. As the film begins, dwindling blood supplies force many "feral" vampires to feed on each other. Then they degenerate, transforming into vile, demonic, zombie-like vampires called "sub-siders." As their demonic nature overpowers their higher human qualities, they descend—or "subside"—into a hellish existence.

Ethan Hawke stars as Dr. Edward Dalton, a hematologist who works for the Bromley Marks Corporation, frantically seeking synthetic blood to substitute for the nearly extinguished human blood supply. Dalton's boss, Charles Bromley (Sam Neill), pressures him to invent a substitute; otherwise the company will fail and the world will continue its descent into chaos. Dalton, however, sees problems with the blood substitute quest. After being transformed into a human once more by sunlight, he invents a cure for the virus based on the blood of those who have turned from vampire back to human.

By juxtaposing vampire savagery with vampire protectors, *Daybreakers*—like *Twilight* (2008) and *Let Me In* (2010)—exemplifies the latest dichotomy of Nosteratu and protector vampires. The Spierig brothers pit the sub-siders against the Edward Dalton "helpful" vampires who strive to save lives instead of taking them. The two kinds of vampires symbolize strengths and weaknesses in the human psyche, and both types make up the imagined world of the near future. The sub-sider vampires, preying on each other as well as unsuspecting humans, represent social destabilization.

Daybreakers illustrates a common direction in pop culture vampires, in which an Armageddon-type conflict threatens the stability of the entire planet. Stakes have grown far higher in post–9/11 vampire films; wars break out between vampires and humans, and between vampires and werewolves. The mix of characters in these films—lycans, sub-siders, and hybrids as well as good-versus-evil vampires—provides a rich mythology that yields interesting insights into current social/political issues.

Craig Gillespie's *Fright Night* (2011), a remake of a popular 1985 film, features a Nosteratu-type monster. Jerry (Colin Ferrell), Gillespie's vampire, lives in Las Vegas, a perfect place for a vicious vampire to capture young victims and slowly drain their blood over a period of days. Charley Brewster (Anton Yelchin) learns from his friend "Evil Ed" Thompson that Jerry, their new neighbor, is a vampire. Disbelieving at first, Charley derisively says, "You read way too much *Twilight*." Evil Ed replies, "That's fiction, okay. This is real. He's a real monster, and he's not brooding, or lovesick, or noble. He's the fucking shark from *Jaws*. He kills, he feeds, and he doesn't stop until everybody around him is dead. And I seriously am so angry you think I read *Twilight*." Charley matches wits and courage with Jerry and other vampires that appear later in the film. Charley's girlfriend Amy (Imogen Poots) becomes Jerry's prisoner and most relished victim.

Jerry's greatest appetite comes from human fear, which excites and compels him. Typical of a predator, Jerry feeds on the fears and emotions of his victims and obtains energy from their blood. His powers evaporate with the sunrise but return at sunset. In the end, sunlight burns and kills him, just as the light of day dispels fears. Like the energy sought by psychic vampires, this Nosteratu vampire has the ability to inflict psychic as well as physical wounds. *Fright Night's* vampire successfully terrifies audiences because he represents the "boy next door," a friendly serial murderer who plans to slay as many neighborhood people as possible.

Vlad the Impaler

In 2003 Michael D. Sellers's *Vlad* became the first big-budget film to feature the legendary warrior Vlad Tepes (Vlad the Impaler) as a prince. Sellers's film jumps between Tepes' rule in fifteenth-century Wallachia to the present. Three American graduate students—Jeff Meyer (Paul Popowich), his sister Elexa (KamHeskin), and Lensey Constantin (Monica Davidescu)—begin work on writing projects about Tepes. At the invitation of a Romanian university, they visit Vlad's homeland in the Carpathian Mountains. There they learn the true purpose of the invitation: to lure Constantine, who possesses an allegedly powerful medallion once owned by Tepes, to the vicinity of Tepes' tomb. The medallion's close proximity to the tomb will cause Tepes (Dracula) to rise from his grave.

The medallion creates visions of ancient Wallachia. After one such vision, a young woman named Ilona (Iva Hasperger) appears in the present, greatly resembling Tepes' fifteenth-century wife. Soon thereafter Tepes reanimate and kidnaps Ilona from among the students, killing one of her defenders in the process. At this point, the students visit Ilie (Guy Singer), a venerable holy man from the mountains, who explains that Tepes initially used brutality for the good of his country but became addicted to inflicting pain, so God damned him to an eternal existence. Ilie says that Tepes appeared because he sensed that his medallion was near. If they bathe it in sacred water and place it in a cup, he says, Tepes will immediately return to his grave. Ilie functions as the vampire slayer in this offbeat vampire film. Although he never slays vampires, he wields sacred knowledge to use against them.

Gary Shore's 2014 film *Dracula Untold* stars Luke Evans as Vlad Tepes, a sixteenth-century Romanian prince who willingly becomes a vampire in order to protect his people from rapacious Turks intent on conquest. Shore's film became the first big-budget solo vampire movie since *Dracula 2000* in the year 2000. In the film, Vlad begs a mysterious master vampire (Charles Dance) for "the power to destroy my enemies and save my family." But the master vampire warns, "There is always a price for power." That price is losing the support of his people, who turn on him after they witness his magical powers, including commanding a huge flock of bats and powerful winds that tear the Turks to pieces. Armed with his newly acquired superpowers, Vlad defeats a massive Turkish army intent on invading Europe. He is presumed dead but survives into present times and encounters the reincarnation of his beloved wife Mirena (Sara Gaden). The master vampire, who also has not aged, utters the film's closing line: "Let the games begin." Who knows what games Vlad, armed with superpowers, might play in contemporary society? He certainly symbolizes powerful war-making technology.

Vlad-based vampires often become martial heroes, only to be undone by the excesses of their aggression. In Romania today, Vlad/Dracula remains a hero for his successes in combating the fifteenth-century Turkish invaders.[28] Although Vlad/Dracula emerges in popular culture as heroic and ruthless, this reputation gets softened in pop culture by his devotion to his wife. The courageous, romantic vampire must be added to our list of popular Nosteratu vampire metaphors. Although Vlad the Impaler qualifies as a monster, for many he redeems himself by his courage in battle.

Currently pop culture embraces the warrior vampire metaphor. Vampires as symbolic warriors date back to Slavic mythology, in which they represent cosmic battles between good and evil and between God and Satan. To pre-modern Slavs, vampires explained every catastrophe from infant death, disease, loss of crops and cattle, to any other kind of adversity.[29] Pop culture vampires wage war against rogue vampires (*Twilight* series), werewolves (*Underworld* and *Twilight* series), Time Lords (*Dr. Who* series), wizards (*Dresden Files* series), Ottoman Turks (*Dracula Untold*), and mutants (*X-Men* series). All of these wars revolve around metaphors of vampires as warriors.

The Monster Within

In 2010, David DiSalvo described a "popularity war" being waged in pop culture between vampires and zombies as to which most appropriately symbolized the economic effects of the era's Great Recession. DiSalvo noted that although zombies initially seemed to be favored by fans because of their wasted, emaciated appearance, vampires became the recession's "go to" characters because they offer escape and because "the vampire is the monster for all seasons. When we're hurting they offer a way out, and when we're feeling good they offer excitement. They're the ultimate manifestation of power and terror, a combination that's as enduring as emotion itself."[30]

At their most basic level, savage Nosferatu vampires symbolize violent, aggressive drives within the human psyche. They symbolize humanity's violent potential, and its ancient fascination with violent supernatural beings and catastrophic events. Nosferatu vampires ultimately call forth deeply rooted, subconscious fears and anxieties. These powerful emotions and beliefs foster a Romantic concept of the universe, one that values emotions over reason and spirituality over materialism.

Hollywood's monstrous vampires reveal more about contemporary fears and anxieties than about the supernatural world. Nosferatu-type vampires provide a convenient substitute for terrorists, criminal syndicates, drug addiction, HIV, immigration, and other sensitive subjects. They display voraciousness, fierceness, inflexibility, and savagery—qualities attributed to criminals. They also reference the fears that followed the attacks of 9/11. Nosferatu vampires showcase the dark side, humanity's alter ego and sinister id. Vampires also may exemplify warrior virtues—often displaying courage, a highly prized martial value—but for maximum effectiveness, Nosferatu vampires must resonate with audiences' real fears and anxieties in the postmodern world.[31]

The continued success of Nosferatu-type vampires, carefully crafted to frighten audiences "out of their seats," reflects threatening real-world events. Villains may come and go, but few match Nosferatu vampires for sheer violence and savagery, masquerade and deceit. Their superhuman powers include the ability to cling upside down to ceilings and to make giant leaps and even to fly. Monstrous Nosferatu vampires symbolize many hated elements of society at a given time, from Wall Street traders and bankers to illegal immigrants, restive minorities, racists, slave owners, and gays. The dark side often attracts humans—like Lucifer in John Milton's *Paradise Lost*—but these "monsters from the id" ultimately threaten humanity. Nosferatu vampires, like all id monsters, must be faced to be defeated. Only the truly brave and virtuous prove able to do so. Often the vampire hunters turn out to be young men (*Fright Night, Vampire Movie, Blade*) or young women (*Underworld, Ultraviolet*). Killing monstrous vampires equates to the mythological slaying of dragons and other demons. Only heroes pure in heart and courageous in battle can overcome these deadly and powerful predators.

Today society is besieged almost daily with reports of mass murderers, serial killers, and foreign and domestic terrorists. These villains represent real threats. Pop culture avoids these, opting instead for fictionalized villains to stand in for our actual enemies. Nosferatu vampires also represent primitive, animalistic, instinct-driven behavior. Pop culture demonizes overly aggressive and authoritarian behaviors and personalities. However, during times of crises—terrorist attacks, financial collapses, crime waves, and warfare—those same character defects transform into crucial survival adaptations. In the final analysis, the monsters we fear most turn out to be hidden, suppressed aspects of ourselves.

FIVE

Psychics

Psychic vampires are sometimes also known as energy, psychological, prana, tantric, or sexual vampires. Unlike their blood-drinking cousins, these characters drain humans of their energy, souls, sexuality, and life force. Instead of fangs, psychic vamps are said to use invisible "feeding tendrils" or other predatory equipment to draw off vital energy from people. Psi and psychic also serve as synonym for "parapsychology." Mario Varvogolis explains that "a large number of phenomena or experiences are considered psychic, or at least legitimate topics of parapsychological inquiry: these include telepathy, clairvoyance, psychokinesis (or mind-over-matter), psychic healing, out-of-body experiences, poltergeists and a number of others."[1] Any being or demon that derives sustenance from human essences other than blood qualifies as a "psychic vampire." Attacking their victims with negativity rather than fangs, these energy vampires drain their prey of energy, vitality, and good spirits. Joe H. Slate observed the following symptoms of psychic vampirism: A significant loss of energy; chronic fatigue; difficulty concentrating; sleep disturbances; irritability; lowered tolerance for frustration; depressed mood; excessive anxiety; sexual indifference; and impaired memory.[2]

Some "psi" or psychic vampires revert at times to being sanguinary or "sang" vampires, feeding once again on human blood; or often they live on energy from human auras. Psychic energy conjoins with elevated nervous system activity to produce even more psi energy. Although the precise method of energy extraction may remain mysterious, psychic vampirism inspires a surprising variety of interpretations. Most people probably know someone who qualifies as an energy drainer, whether or not they fall into the "vampire" category. Once pop culture defines them as "vampires," a number of interesting metaphors appear. Although psychic vampires arose in pop culture more than two hundred years ago, their periodic reappearance assures their survival. Psychic vampires currently enjoy a renewed popularity in comics and movies, and especially on the Internet.

The notion of sexual vampires originated in antiquity. Gypsies (and their southern neighbors, the Slavs) perceived vampires as sexual beings. Suspected vampires were periodically exhumed to look for any physical signs of vampirism. If a male corpse had an erection, it was immediately decapitated and dismembered. It was believed that male vampires have an intense sexual drive that can be powerful enough to bring them back from the grave. They might return for nightly sexual intercourse with their widows, who grow exhausted and emaciated, according to myth, and eventually die.[3]

The idea of predatory beings feeding off human energy gained widespread popularity in late nineteenth- and early twentieth-century England and the United States. The Theosophical Society, an organization that studied and revered occult sciences, theorized about "magnetic vampirism" in a pamphlet published in 1891. The society warned that "magnetic vampirism is practiced every day and hour in social, most especially in conjugal, intercourse." In this form of vampirism, "the weak absorb strength from the strong, the sickly from the robust, the aged from the young." As for the actual mechanisms by which psychics feed on humans, the society explained, "One vampirizes by hand-shaking, by sitting close together, by sleeping in the same bed." With this kind of vampirism, "the full brains of the clever became drained or 'sucked' by the spongy brains of the stupid."[4]

The Theosophical Society ultimately identified two distinct varieties of psychic vampires. "Astral vampires" possess the ability to separate astral bodies from human material bodies while leaving their graves nightly to hunt for human energy. The second type, "magnetic vampires," function as living "psychic sponges," absorbing the energy emitted by surrounding people.[5] Friends may say that they are draining to be around, that they seem to suck the life from a room, and that they have erratic mood swings.[6]

Psychic energy corresponds to what French philosopher Henri Bergson (1859–1941) labeled *élan vital*, or "life force." Bergson introduced the concept in his 1907 book *Creative Evolution*. However, the idea actually dates back to Aristotle's time and the philosophy of Vitalism, which was concerned with invisible, extremely potent biological energy. Vitalism contrasts with "reductionism," the theory that all life can be explained through examination and experimentation with its physical components. For reductionists, life becomes the sum of the parts of an animal or plant. Vitalism, by contrast, values the energy created by the libido and the imagination.[7]

Although ignored by traditional science, including biology and medicine, Vitalism provides the philosophical foundation for various forms of holistic medicine Chiropractic medicine, for example, aims through therapy to combat "vertebral subluxation complexes" blocking the flow of the body's vital energy, though these complexes remain unverified. Acupuncture, reiki, and other "energy therapies" all claim to affect the *qi*, or vital energy, that is an invisible force permeating all life.[8]

Reiki therapy derives from a Japanese technique for stress reduction, relaxation, and healing. Practitioners heal weak or sick individuals by "laying on hands," based on the idea that an unseen "life force energy" flows through us and makes us alive. If one experiences low life force energy, illness follows, whereas high energy indicates bodily health.[9] Some therapists claim that reiki therapy protects against psychic vampirism.[10] Author and "occult expert" Michelle Belanger notes that "the parallels between attuning an initiate to reiki and awakening a potential vampire to his true nature are striking." In both cases the process is personalized to the individual. Says Belanger, "The Greater Initiation Rite, which was circulated on the Internet in the late nineties ... described a ritual of vampiric awakening that shared distinct parallels with the act of opening someone up to reiki."[11]

The process of feeding occurs when psychic vampires, using their astral bodies, travel to another person and "suck" the energy out of that person. Some people with psychic abilities can see the energy being transferred. Some even see a "chain" or "cord" connecting the vampire to the victim. Other psi vamps can drain energy through touching, breathing a person's scent, and even from objects with which a person has been in contact. The cord may appear hose-like. Therapists cut the psychic attachments formed by psychic vampires to drain victims of psychic energy.[12]

A minor industry has developed around psi-vampire "experts" who counsel concerned individuals about strategies for defending against psi vampires. The first step in any defense involves accurate identification of one's antagonist. A manual on self-protection against psychic vampires advises these strategies: Take an inventory of people in your life who give energy; set clear boundaries; meditate; walk away; and build an energy shield around yourself.[13]

Psychology

To Sigmund Freud (1856–1939), mental forces account for the emotional power of dreams and the unconscious. He theorized that humans feel compelled to respond to potent "drives" linked to the libido. These drives transmit psychic energy.[14] In *The Ego and the Id* (1923), he postulated the existence of powerful sources of energy in the libido, the theoretical structure from which sexuality emanates. Because of the libido's addictive pleasures, Freud referred to the "narcissistic reservoir of libido" and further explained that it consists of "desexualized Eros."[15]

Austrian psychiatrist Wilhelm Reich (1897–1957), a student of Freud in the 1920s, also became fascinated with the libido. Reich suggested the existence of universal energy, or "orgone." He believed that orgone, like other universal forces, is a blend of both negative and positive energies. In the 1930s and 1940s, Reich claimed to have detected and measured the existence of "etheric energy" by using a modified Geiger counter. He thought that stacking alternating layers of fiberglass (an organic substance) with steel wool (an inorganic substance) attracted and collected orgone/etheric energy of both the life-beneficial positive form—"OR" or "POR"—and harmful negative etheric energy—"deadly orgone" or "DOR."[16] In 1940 Reich began construction of his "Orgone Accumulator." Patients sat inside the device to reap the benefits of orgone. Reich envisioned orgone as being a luminous blue—a favorite color, along with green, for depicting one's psychic aura. In pop culture, these hues frequently are used to signify psychic energy.[17]

Orgone therapy—sometimes called psychic energy therapy—is still popular with a small number of psychotherapists. *The Journal of Psychiatric Orgone Therapy* serves as a conduit of information. In October of 2013 at the International Conference on Orgonomy in Rome, speakers gave presentations on "What Is Orgonomy," "Moving Toward Life Energy, Changing Concept of Energy Since 1955," "Where Do We Go from Here: Discussion on Research Directions in Orgonomy," and "Recovering Natural Atmosphere Pulsation: From Reich to Present Days." Reichian therapy remains vibrant and active.

Sexuality

Reich's work on human sexuality generated intense controversy, thanks to his emphasis on orgasms. According to Reich, "Psychic health depends upon orgiastic potency, i.e., upon the degree to which one can surrender to and experience the climax of excitation in the natural sex act."[18] Such statements resulted in high media attention and popularity during the sexual revolution of the 1960s and 1970s and anticipated interest in psychic vampirism that arrived decades later.

"Sexual" or "tantric" vampires constitute a separate category of psychic vampirism. The human body is said to contain six main chakras, or energy points—at the base of the spine, near the navel, near the heart, near the throat, between the brows, and most importantly at the genitals. Each represents a potential gateway to higher energy. Tantric vampire rituals focus on the need to unlock these energy portals to harmonize the flow of energy through the body. These rituals help individuals achieve elevated states of sexual awareness, according to practitioners.[19] Catherene NightPoe explains on her "Vampiric Studies" website, "The Sexual Vampire feeds off of the sexual energy, the sexual need, the dependence of their victims once a secure relationship is established." These vampires select particularly susceptible individuals as their victims:

> They pick a person who is vulnerable. Someone who just came from an abusive relationship, someone who has been alone for a long time. Someone not described usually as beautiful or attractive, someone perhaps very over weight or who has no close ties. Very young or inexperienced people, etc. because these individuals are easier to conquer.[20]

Eventually sexual vampires, having drained their human partners of vital sexual energy, abandon them in order to locate and exploit new victims. In Hollywood, femme fatale characters have played the sexual vampire role in movies since the 1910s and as recently as the 1990s. Femme fatale movies include *A Fool There Was* (1915), *Red Headed Woman* (1932), *Double Indemnity* (1944), *The Postman Always Rings Twice* (1946), *Cleopatra* (1963), *Basic Instinct* (1992), and *The Last Seduction* (1994).

To some non-Reichian therapists, psychic vampirism explains various psychological, psychiatric, and even social maladies. Author and psychologist Joe H. Slate defines psychic vampirism as a multidimensional phenomenon with a wide range of psychological manifestations. Not only individuals but also corporations and institutions practice psychic vampirism, he says, and "global vampirism" as practiced by large corporations and institutions poses a dire threat to human existence.[21] Slate's concepts suggest a broad application of the vampire-as-drainer metaphor. His warning about global vampirism potentially includes any organization that chooses to act in a "vampiric" manner. Upon closer inspection, an obvious question emerges. What constitutes vampirism in a corporation, and what constitutes plain greed and malfeasance? Those involved in the Bernard Madoff investment scandal and the Enron scandal come to mind. A clearer understanding of psychic vampirism may contribute to society's ability to combat certain crimes.

Literary Sources

Samuel Taylor Coleridge's narrative poem *Christabel* (1797–1800) is about a young woman named Christabel, the daughter of wealthy Sir Leoline, who encounters a beautiful young woman named Geraldine in the woods. Geraldine relates a tale about being kidnapped by wild young men who've left her alone beside a giant oak tree, threatening to return. Bracy the Bard, a poet in Sir Leoline's household, dreams of a snake encircling a white dove, symbolizing the relationship of Christabel and Geraldine.

> Coiled around its wings and neck.
> Green as the herbs on which it couched,
> Close by the dove's its head it crouched;
> And with the dove it heaves and stirs,
> Swelling its neck as she swelled hers.[22]

After she receives a fleeting impression of Geraldine as predatory snake, Christabel begs her father to send the visitor home. But Sir Leoline falls deeply in love with the beautiful Geraldine and appears to choose her love over that of his daughter. Geraldine doesn't prey on Christabel's blood, but she seems to seduce her sexually and plans to absorb and extinguish her life energies.

John Keats' "La Belle Dame Sans Merci" (1819) also depicts a destructive psychic vampire. In his poem, a medieval knight falls victim to a beautiful lady's psychic powers:

> Oh what can ail thee, knight-at-arms,
> Alone and palely loitering?
> The sedge has withered from the lake,
> And no birds sing.

The knight replies that he's become enthralled by a beautiful but terrible woman.

> I met a lady in the meads,
> Full beautiful—a faery's child,
> Her hair was long, her foot was light,
> And her eyes were wild.

Then he spends a rapturous evening with the lady in her "elfin grout," where he comforts her "with kisses four" before falling asleep. He begins to dream, and in his dream many try to warn him of the dangers he faces from the lady:

> I saw pale kings and princes too,
> Pale warriors, death-pale were they all;
> They cried—"La Belle Dame sans Merci
> Hath thee in thrall!"

Then the scene changes and he recalls:

> I saw their starved lips in the gloam,
> With horrid warning gaped wide,
> And I awoke and found me here,
> On the cold hill's side.[23]

Despite these horrific visions, the knight continues to linger in the desolate winter landscape. By what means does she keep him in thrall? Keats' poem implies that the "astral" lady attacks psychically rather than physically—making her a psychic vampire who drains the knight of willpower, energy, and ultimately life itself. This poem, along with Coleridge's, introduced a strange and novel character into literature, one that would reappear over the next two centuries.

In 1897 Rudyard Kipling published "The Vampire" (see Chapter Two), another poem about a beautiful, heartless young woman who plays men for fools—inspired by "Le Belle Dame Sans Merci." In Kipling's poem, the "woman who did not care" functions much like a psychic vampire, although she absorbs victims' emotions and material possessions, not their psychic energy. Kipling's first stanza sketches her character:

> A fool there was and he made his prayer
> (Even as you or I!)
> To a rag and a bone and a hank of hair
> (We called her the woman who did not care),
> But the fool he called her his lady fair
> (Even as you or I!)

Kipling's "woman who did not care" represents psychic vampirism by draining her foolish admirers of wealth, willpower, and vitality. The motion picture made from this poem, *A Fool There Was* (1914), established Theda Bara as a "vamp," a psychic vampire who coldly seduces and then abandons hapless males—like the lady in Keats' "La Belle Dame Sans Merci" who holds the lingering knight in thrall.

Bara made an astonishing forty-four films during her movie career, most during the duration of World War I, 1914–1918. She portrayed Cleopatra, Salomé, Carmen, Sappho, Madame du Barry, and Satan's daughter as well as the "woman who did not care." In these seductive roles she epitomized the vamp style, and her influence extended to other actresses of the era. Pola Negri, Marlene Dietrich, Tallulah Bankhead, Greta Garbo, Stacy Davis, Joan Crawford, and Louise Brooks all established reputations depicting sultry, seductive, ruthless women from the 1910s through the early 1930s. Each character represented a psychic vampire preying on weak and often silly men.

Psychic vampires appeared in American literature at the turn of the twentieth century. One of the first fictional psychic vampire narratives was Mary E. Wilkins-Freeman's short story "Luella Miller" (1902), which depicts a woman who refuses to perform routine housework or any sort of physical or mental labor. Eventually she exhausts and drains everyone she's persuaded or employed to care for her. Shortly after she marries a man named Erasmus Miller, he contracts a blood disease, and he dies within a year. A similar fate awaits her housekeeper. When the housekeeper grows too weak to work,

Luella seeks others to care for her. She has never known any form of work and prides herself that "I never made coffee in all my life." Later she's betrothed to a local physician, who also wastes away and dies. One night, as Luella finally approaches her own death, a neighbor witnesses her dead husbands and housekeepers walking out from her front door as ghosts. When the neighbor knocks on the door she discovers Luella dead.

In 1911 the British writer Algernon Blackwood published "The Transfer," a science fiction story involving a male psychic vampire. On a barren hillside at the end of a rose garden, Mr. Frene absorbs psychic energy from his friends. The hillside itself "needs" the energy to grow plants and trees. Frene tends the hillside and, along with the hill, absorbs energy from others. Blackwood describes him as "a supreme, unconscious artist in the science of taking the fruits of others' work and living—for his own advantage." Frene vampirizes "every one with whom he came in contact; left them exhausted, tired, listless." He draws energy from normal humans. "Others fed him," Blackwood writes, "so that while in a full room he shone," whereas "alone by himself, and with no life to draw upon, he languished and declined." Blackwood's vampire draws vital energy from both men and women. Psychic vampires like Frene constitute a mortal threat to those with whom they come in contact, proving to be just as dangerous and destructive as blood-sucking vampires.[24]

In 1949 Fritz Leiber published "The Girl with the Hungry Eyes." The girl of the title possesses a magical photogenic talent, and people who view her image in advertising are strangely mesmerized. Leiber's photographer/narrator explains why the girl makes him uneasy:

> All right, I'll tell you why the Girl gives me the creeps. Why I can't stand to go downtown and see the mob slavering up at her on the tower, with that pop bottle or pack of cigarettes or whatever it is beside her. Why I hate to look at magazines anymore because I know she'll turn up somewhere in a brassiere or a bubble bath. Why I don't like to think of millions of Americans drinking in that poisonous half-smile.... She's unnatural. She's morbid. She's unholy.

To allay skepticism on the part of readers, the narrator says, "Oh it's 1948, is it, and the sort of thing I'm hinting at went out with witchcraft? But you see I'm not altogether sure myself what I'm hinting at, beyond a certain point. There are vampires and vampires, and not all of them suck blood."[25]

Leiber's haunting psychic vampire feeds with her eyes, "the hungriest eyes in the world." The photographer who sells her image to the advertising world tries to follow her home one night and sees her get into a man's car, and that same man turns up dead later in the evening. Eventually the photographer attempts to kiss his model, but she turns him away. She doesn't want his love, his memories, his life's joys and sorrows. She explains:

I want you. I want your high spots. I want everything that's made you happy and everything that's hurt you bad. I want your first girl. I want that shiny bicycle. I want that licking. I want that pinhole camera. I want Betty's legs. I want the blue sky filled with stars. I want your mother's death. I want your blood on the cobblestones.[26]

Science Fiction

Psychic vampires disappeared from Hollywood after 1934 with the imposition of the Hays Production Code, a standard for regulating movies that disallowed "vamp" and "gold digger" characters. During the 1960s and 1970s, however, enforcement of the code relaxed, and Mario Bava's cult classic *Planet of the Vampires* (1965) brought sci-fi psychic vampires to the cinema. In this film, the spacecraft Argos responds to a false signal from a distant planet and falls into a deadly trap when parasitic beings living off human energy seize control of the ship. After the ship's crew members fall asleep, aliens seize control of their bodies. These aliens, inhabitants of a dying planet, intend to invade and vampirize the Argos' home planet. One crew member exclaims, "Our world invaded by these horrible creatures! Just thinking about it gives me a nightmare!" Captain Mark Markary (Barry Sullivan) and Sanya (Norma Bengell) wage a desperate struggle as the aliens commandeer the crew members' wills, one by one. Eventually aliens control the entire crew. When technological problems develop with the Argos' meteor shield, the aliens scrap their plans to visit the humans' planet, instead charting a course to a closer inhabitable planet—ironically, earth.

The film's dramatic tension between humans and aliens reminds us of contemporary issues far closer to home. Sociologists Dennis D. Loo and Ruth-Ellen Grimes reveal that, according to polls taken in 1963–1964, hot-button civil rights topics concerned Americans far more than any other issue. Street crime and juvenile delinquency concerned only a minority of Americans, while nearly half the population feared racial conflict.[27] A spacecraft full of aliens intent on feeding off human energies symbolized fears fanned by conservative media during the Civil Rights Movement. Union organizers, civil rights demonstrators, and other progressives were demonized as "outside agitators" intent on destroying America.

Interest in psychic vampirism accelerated during the 1960s and 1970s as a result of a fierce culture war that broke out over psychic vampirism. In Roger Vadim's *Barbarella* (1968), the title character (Jane Fonda) encounters the evil Dr. Durand-Durand (Milo O'Shea), who threatens to unleash the Excess Machine—a version of Reich's Orgone Accumulator that kills by intensifying human sexual psychic energy during orgasms. He vows, "I'll do things to you that are beyond all known philosophies! Wait until I get my devices!" However, the intensity of Barbarella's orgasm burns out the machine.

In 1973 Woody Allen included an Orgasmatron machine in *Sleeper,* a movie about a clarinet player/health-food store owner who falls asleep and wakes up in the future. When he disguises himself as a robotic domestic servant he encounters the Orgasmatron, a glass booth in which individuals experience sexual orgasms. This device, like the Excess Machine in *Barbarella,* references Wilhelm Reich's Orgone Accumulator.[28]

Anton LaVey, author of *The Satanic Bible* (1969), publically rejected psychic vampires in "Nine Satanic Statements," charging that "Satan represents responsibility to the responsible instead of concern for psychic vampires!" LaVey felt compelled to speak out against psychic vampires because of their popularity at the time.[29] (But LaVey borrows freely from Reich in his writings, especially in describing "electro power units" that accumulate energy to be absorbed by humans.[30]) Despite LaVey's attacks, the era's sexual revolution fueled interest in Wilhelm Reich's Orgone Box, along with his central concept of "orgone energy" generated by sexual orgasms.

In 1972 the psychic vampire drama "The Girl with the Hungry Eyes" aired as an episode of the popular *Night Gallery* television series, narrated by Rod Serling. Based on the Fritz Leiber short story of the same name (discussed above), the episode features Joanna Pettet as the young fashion model with the "hungry eyes." Her eyes exert such a profound effect that men who see them on a billboard or in a magazine are addicted and lust after her. She serves as a new and nameless "It Girl." After being photographed by fashion photographer David Faulkner (James Farentino), she becomes a superstar, like the original "It Girl" Clara Bow in the 1920s. A beer company selects her as its poster girl, but soon others arrive at the photographer's doorstep demanding to purchase her image. She forbids anyone to follow her or even to know her name, but one night Faulkner trails her to a sleazy neighborhood and sees her walking with a man. Later he finds that man lying dead in a park, apparently drained of his life essence. From that point Faulkner knows the mortal danger posed by this woman. He cries, "Hungry eyes—hungry for my soul!" He exclaims, "You suck the love from us—it's your life force!"

Faulkner vows to "destroy you before you bleed the world dry!" The "It Girl" threatens every man on the planet. Psychic vamps transform in this episode into a far more deadly element than their counterparts in past eras. The "girl with the hungry eyes" poses mortal danger to men and to patriarchy. The danger subsides only after Faulkner sets fire to all her photographic images, thereby destroying a being that's been created by the media. "The

Girl with the Hungry Eyes" features a powerful proto-feminist character who's mysteriously alluring yet deadly as she literally sucks the lives out of male admirers. She may be seen as symbolizing anxieties about the emergence of powerful, feminist women.

In the 1970s, psychic vampires invaded the big screen. Brian Clemens released *Captain Kronos—Vampire Hunter* in 1974, and it quickly became one of the most revered Hammer Film Productions vampire movies. The film stars Horst Janson as Captain Kronos, a master swordsman who battles vampires after surviving a deadly vampire attack on his family. The film's vampires attack humans to sustain their life and youth, but not through blood. They're attracted to "someone young and fair," and their attacks leave victims unnaturally old or dead. They don't leave tiny pinpricks on victims' necks, but they often cause victims to bleed from the mouth. This film features a character with a famous name in vampire lore—Karnstein—although she goes by her married name, Lady Durward. As a psychic vampire, Karnstein/Durward (Wanda Ventham) drains young girls of their youth, not their blood. Kronos slays her in the end and watches as she shrivels into a dry, hideous mummy.

In 1983 Michael Mann released an artistic version of a psychic vampire in *The Keep*. Mann's film revolves around the struggle between a positive psychic vampire, Glaeken Trismegestus (Scott Glenn), known as "the stranger," and a monstrous creature, Radu Molasar (Michael Carter), imprisoned for hundreds of years in a medieval Romanian castle. During World War II, Nazi forces occupy Romania and open the castle, allowing Molasar to escape. Although the Nazis fear a revolt by local partisans, Molasar is their real danger. Suddenly free after centuries of captivity, he immediately murders two Nazi soldiers by draining their energy. Now flush with vitality, he attacks everyone in sight. At this point "the stranger" appears, a supernatural being charged with imprisoning Molasar forever. Molasar's release threatens everyone on earth, and "the stranger" deploys an array of energy-emitting devices against the monster, including a cross from which pulses of plasma energy emanate. A bazooka-like arm that emits plasma energy forces Molasar back to his prison. The band Tangerine Dream provides moody soundscapes, adding to the film's appeal. The two antagonists, both psychic vampires, represent opposite metaphysical positions: Molasar embodies raw, unbridled greed and savagery, while Trismegestus—who relies on futuristic armaments—represents science and technology. Similar tensions between human nature and science resonate throughout pop culture, providing a dynamic source of dramatic energy and intensity.

One Dark Night (1983), directed by Tom McLoughlin, involves three high school students—Julie (Meg Tilly), Carol (Robin Evans), and Kitty (Leslie

Speights)—who are trapped inside a mausoleum after hours. Carol and Kitty are part of a small club called "The Sisters," and Julie is a pledge whom the others frighten with scary props as part of an initiation ceremony. Carol dislikes Julie because she dates Carol's ex-boyfriend Steve (David Mason Daniels), and she hatches a plan to scare her. Steve learns of her plan and enters the mausoleum to assist Julie. Unbeknownst to any of them, Karl "Raymar" Raymarseivich—a supposedly dead Russian psychic—inhabits the mausoleum. He uses young women's life forces to create deadly bolts of psychic energy. To maximize their energy, he frightens the women nearly to death before draining them. Raymar learns to control the energy bolts that stream from his eyes and uses them to reanimate corpses. On this particular night, he reanimates the corpses in the mausoleum and commands them to attack Steve and the women.

Events soon turn violent as the corpses stand ready to destroy all the living characters—until Olivia McKenna (Melissa Newman), Raymar's estranged daughter, enters and confronts her father with the psychic powers she's inherited from him. He proves stronger than Olivia until she uses a mirror to reflect his energy bolts back onto him, causing his death and unanimating the zombie-like corpses. (Director McLoughlin obviously borrowed his ending from the Greek myth of Perseus and the Gorgon, in which the hero uses his highly polished bronze sword to reflect the face of Medusa— the very sight of whom had the power to kill.) Raymar possesses unusually strong psychic vampirism because of his special genetics and because he's honed his psychic skills over a long period of time. But he abuses his powers by attacking unwilling victims. At one point a writer for an occult magazine, Dockstader (Raymond Hotton), interviews Olivia and asks, "Have you ever known anyone who has left you drained of energy?" Dockstader informs Olivia that many psychic vampires exist, with Raymar being the most potent. This leads to her confrontation with her father.

Tobe Hooper's *Lifeforce* was released in 1985, based on Colin Wilson's acclaimed novel *The Space Vampires* (1976). In the movie, a spaceship from earth on a mission to investigate Halley's Comet unexpectedly encounters three aliens in suspended animation. Brought to earth, the three escape government custody and begin vampirizing Londoners. They emerge from their living-death state for two hours each day and absorb life force through physical contact with the living. Their victims become zombie-like psychic vampires, and the transformation process is repeated. Male vampires collect the energy—colored blue, like Wilhelm Reich's orzone—and bring it to the female vampires, who transfer it to a spaceship orbiting earth. Psychic energy, a life force highly prized by space vampires, consists of the victims' souls. Their bodies immediately perish after a beautiful female vampire (Mathilda May) imprisons the souls on her spaceship to feed her people. She also abducts Colonel Tom Carlsen (Steve Railsback), the shuttle commander who originally discovered her hibernating body. It turns out that psychic energy is also a powerful spaceship fuel, and she channels some of it to the craft's engine and blasts off into deep space. The film implies that such visits by aliens have occurred every seventy-five years and will continue into the future, reaping millions of souls each time.

Lifeforce's reception was positive, with some critics expressing pleasure about the introduction of non-blood-sucking vampires. Others panned the film for being uneven and cliché ridden. However, little doubt exists about its originality. Hooper's film, and Wilson's novel, transformed the psychic vampire genre from horror into sci-fi. Instead of focusing on individuals' aberrant behavior—like Count Dracula raping and draining victims of their blood—in *Lifeforce* the soul, a relatively neglected subject in cinema, suddenly has great value, echoing religious views of its sanctity and immortality.

Mick Garris's *Sleepwalkers* (1992)—also discussed in Chapter Three—features psychic "sexual vampires" created by scriptwriter Stephen King. These ancient Egyptian feline/humans drain their victims' life force by sucking their breath away, an act that references the popular myth that domestic house cats will smother infants to death. The life force in this film consists of a glowing green light. The vampires, Charles Brady (Brian Krause) and his mother Mary Brady (Alice Krige), live off the spirits of virginal young women. Like nineteenth-century Byronic vampires, the Brady pair destroy youth and beauty in order to stay alive. Consequently they must move often, as they fall under suspicion for the unexplained deaths left in their wake.

Charles enrolls in a local high school and decides to victimize beautiful Tanya Robertson (Madchen Amick). He attempts to drain her soul on their first date (in a graveyard). However, Tanya proves more than a match for Charles and his mother as she fights back. She faces daunting obstacles, however, because not only can Charles and his mother adopt very charming persona, they can also transform into hideous and powerful felines. On one level Charles and his mother exemplify an unusually dysfunctional family, while on another they symbolize criminal psychosis. As passionate lovers, they violate the incest taboo, a violation considered by some psychologists to be "sexual sadism," a severe personality disorder.[31] As psychic "sexual vampires," they represent a threat to the local community and a cautionary tale. If left unchecked, antisocial behavior undermines community order and stability.

The 1995 comedy *Vampire Vixens from Venus,* directed by Ted Bahus, features shapeshifting aliens. Immediately after exiting their spacecraft, hideous aliens transform not into felines but into sexy, buxom young women named Shampay (Michelle Bauer), Shirley (Theresa Lynn), and Arylai (J.J.

Colonel Tom Carlson (Steve Railsback) receives a deadly kiss from an extraterrestrial psychic vampire (Mathilda May), who kills him by draining his psychic energy in the sci-fi cult classic *Lifeforce* (1985) (Kobal Collection at Art Resource, New York).

North). These space vampires feed on attractive young men. Their disguises as sexy babes who dress and behave like prostitutes and strippers help them coax virile young males into exciting sexual situations. Then they extract the "life force" from their unsuspecting victims at the peak of sexual orgasm. Unfortunately, the men die after the vampires drain them, but they depart with smiles on their faces. This film treats psychic vampirism playfully and makes full use of the psychic vampire metaphor in which sex substitutes for the life force. *Vampire Vixens from Venus* relies on softly pornographic images and wildly improbable plot devices to attract audiences. The aliens in the film act forcefully and aggressively, symbolic feminists. Although the comedy stretches thin, the movie asserts female sexuality and deserves to be considered feminist, despite its obvious low-budget sexploitation.

In 1995 Jon Jacobs released a low-budget movie version of *The Girl with the Hungry Eyes* that many now regard as a classic. Jacob's narrative takes place at an art deco hotel called The Tides (the film was shot in Miami's South Beach). The hotel owner, Louise Balfour (Christina Fulton), committed suicide in 1937 after discovering her husband not only having an affair with another woman but also swindling her. However, during an electrical storm Balfour is resurrected as a vampire in her old hotel room. She approaches Carlos (Isaac Turner), a local photographer experiencing dire financial difficulties, and asks for a modeling job. Because he owes money to the mob, Carlos accepts Balfour's terms of complete anonymity. He snaps one role of film before she departs to attack and drain nearby humans. Each time she drains a fresh victim, the hotel lights rejuvenate and burn brightly. Although Balfour represents the traditional, sanguinary vampire, the hotel itself functions as a psychic vampire. Problems arise after clients view Carlos's photos and fall in love with Balfour's image. They demand that Carlos sell them the photos, agreeing to pay $500. When thugs attempt to murder Carlos for money, Balfour kills them, proving her love for the photographer and demonstrating the futility of attacking any human who has a vampire protector. After the two make love, she decides to renovate the hotel, presumably with blood from fresh victims. Like Franz Leiber's short story and the television version of it, Jacobs's film focuses on blood and energy, while the vampire hotel in the movie symbolizes predatory capitalism.

Psi Comics and the Internet

Selene Gallio, a vampire who gains enormous strength and energy by draining victims of their psychic energy, arrived on the pages of Marvel

Comics in 1985, and she quickly became one of the most popular cartoon characters. Her abundant superpowers include speed (175 mph in short bursts), telekinesis, telepathy, hypnosis, super healing, shapeshifting, and immortality. She also has extensive knowledge of sorcery. In a twist on the Countess Elizabeth Bathory story (see Chapter Two), Selene retains her youthful appearance and vitality not by bathing in the blood of young women but by absorbing their psychic energy.

Selene made numerous appearances in *Marvel* comics, including *X-Men* and *Wolverine*. At one point she was the tremendously powerful Dark Queen. She inspired the character of Selene (Kate Beckinsale) in the *Underworld* movie series (2003–2012). In the films, Selene transforms from a psychic vampire into a more conventional sanguinary vampire, but she retains many of the same superpowers as her comic book counterpart. Both characters symbolize strikingly powerful feminists who are ready and able to combat evil at every turn.

Interest in psychic vampirism is reflected in a growing Internet presence. Michelle Belanger's *The Psychic Vampire Codex* (2004), a compendium of information about psychic vampirism, remains a popular book and blog series. Belanger describes psychic vampires as possessing "a nexus" of "tendrils," or psychic feeding tubes. "The tendrils are varying shades of grey, with a smooth, rope-like appearance," she explains. These can assist psychic vamps in draining donors of their "life force," or psychic energy. Energy donors don't die but may require rest and recuperation after allowing a psychic vampire to feed from their energies.[32]

Michael Mohammed's popular *Hell Horror* website contains the following definition of psychic vampirism:

> These vampires seek out victims whom they can interact with in order to create strong emotions in these victims, sexual intercourse usually being the biggest. At the peak of climax, the vampire will then absorb mental energy from the victims' aura. Some other vampires usually try a more subtle approach. They will attack the victim whilst they sleep. This often causes vivid dreams in which the victim will awake feeling drained and tired.[33]

One writer even labeled former Vice President Hubert Humphrey as a psychic vamp "in that he got energy from the crowd. He drew it in, and he returned it like a transformer processing one level of voltage into another."[34] Anyone may become accused of psychic vampirism because the concept proves difficult to define. Whether you call it psychic energy, prana (India), *élan vital* (Henri Bergson), or orgone (Wilhelm Reich), it defies definition by its very nature. Of what substance does it consist?

According to *the Free Online Dictionary*, "psychic energy" might mean:

psychic energy—an actuating force or factor
mental energy
motivation, motive, need—the psychological feature that arouses an organism to action toward a desired goal; the reason for the action; that which gives purpose and direction to behavior; "we did not understand his motivation"; "he acted with the best of motives"
incitation, provocation, incitement—something that incites or provokes; a means of arousing or stirring to action
libidinal energy—(psychoanalysis) psychic energy produced by the libido[35]

The problem arises when one attempts to measure something as ephemeral as "libidinal energy." Still, psychic vampirism proves useful in terms of metaphor.

Psychic energy closely corresponds to the concept of "aura," or a field of energy extending beyond the physical body. Scientists at the University of Granada in Spain discovered that individuals claiming to perceive human auras often experience a neuropsychological phenomenon known as "emotional synesthesia," in which brain regions devoted to sensations are intensely interconnected. This produces a rare ability to see or taste a sound, feel a taste, or associate people with particular colors.[36] Psychologist Joe H. Slate conducted a systematic study on the human energy system, funded by the U.S. Army Missile Development and Research Command. Using special photographic techniques, he discovered that the physical body's "aura" and what he calls its "central energizing core ... are each influenced by the presence of others." Slate discovered that "the auras of couples whose interactions were positive tended to complement and energize each other, with each aura becoming brighter and more expansive. Conversely, negative interactions tended to constrict the aura and actually induce a state of mental and physical fatigue." In addition, he observed that "when constrictions occurred in the aura, intellectual functions became slower, short-term memory declined, and physical strength decreased by as much as fifty percent."[37]

These phenomena closely approximate the process of psychic vampirism. Some self-proclaimed psychic vampires maintain that the practice remains largely misunderstood and unfairly vilified. "We do not claim to be undead beings like Dracula or Lestat. We don't possess super-human powers," says Michelle Belanger. Instead, "much of our natural abilities can be learned by others skilled in magickal [sic] work. Our hallmark talent is energy manipulation, and that's being taught these days in weekend seminars for Reiki and Qi-Gong."[38]

Concerns about psychic vampires have inspired quizzes that you can take to determine whether or not you qualify as one. The following questions typify this kind of quiz: "Do you feel energized when you are around certain individuals?" Or "Are you most comfortable when you are around one or more people, rather than being alone?" You might feel slightly uncomfortable if you answer yes to "When your telephone conversations end, is it most often the other party who cuts the call short?" Another uncomfortable answer might be "I am my own worst enemy."

Energy Wasters

In the recent drive for greener, less wasteful energy consumption, psychic vampires became associated with electrical appliances—from cell phone rechargers to cable converter boxes—that are left plugged in long after use. Duke Energy Corporation released guidelines to its power customers in North Carolina warning against all the following: cable/satellite boxes, digital TV converters, DVR, VCR, DVD players, cellular devices, MP3 players, video game consoles, standby coffee makers, devices that turn on instantly via remote control, and devices with standby light or clock. The company promised customers a net savings of up to twenty percent if they made a practice of unplugging these "energy vampires when not in use."[39]

In October 2014, the U.S. Department of Energy posed this question in a bulletin: "Are Energy Vampires Sucking You Dry?" A photo shows actor Max Schreck—complete with long, hooked fingernails—in menacing silhouette as Count Orlok in the film *Nosferatu.* The vampire is "presumably climbing the stairs to plug in some unused appliances," the caption says. The article ends by suggesting that power consumers replace inefficient appliances with highly efficient "Energy Star" devices certified by the USDE.[40] Standby power, namely unused appliances with secondary functions like clocks, constitutes significant energy waste in many households, according to the USDE—an example of energy vampirism.[41] Count Dracula never makes his appearance as a contemporary "energy vampire," yet he remains the model for predatory, selfish behavior. Unused appliances sucking up precious electricity are personified as voracious bloodsuckers that attack unsuspecting victims and consume their precious lifeblood (or their money). The vampire metaphor offers a useful way to demonize energy waste and promote conservation.[42]

The Supernatural

Renewed interest in psychic vampires corresponds to the prevalent belief in the existence of supernatural beings. A 2013 Harris Poll revealed that "while a strong majority (seventy four percent) of U.S. adults do believe in God, this belief is in decline when compared to previous years." Slightly more than four in five (eighty-two percent) expressed a belief in God in 2005, 2007, and 2009. By contrast, only four percent expressed belief in vampires.[43]

Psychic vampires stand in silent rebuke of rationalism and logical positivism, the popular philosophies that emphasize reason and scientific knowledge. Contemporary belief in extrasensory energy may also reference a teleological component—belief in God or gods. In some traditions, "psyche" means "soul." Vitalism, the philosophy underlying psychic vampirism, now seems linked to the theory of intelligent design—the idea that the beauty, complexity, and perfection of human beings demands the existence of a creator deity. Adherents to this theory hold that humans exist because God has imbued them with divine "essence."[44]

Psychic Symbols

Psychic vampirism serves as an apt metaphor for hostile corporate takeovers, Ponzi schemes, predatory lending practices, and other objectionable recent enterprises. To some, psychic vampirism goes beyond mere symbolism and describes reality. Psychologist Slate maintains that psychic vampirism actually accounts for many social ills, including racial and ethnic prejudice and discrimination. It exists "in a vicious, collective form," he says, in "organizations that feed on prejudice and hate, or corporations that blatantly vampirize their employees through deception and greed." He believes that some psychic vampires choose to associate with others of their kind for greater efficiency in procuring psychic energy. These are the organizations, according to Slate, that engage in "narcotics trafficking, organized crime, and so-called 'ethnic cleansing.'" Other collectivized vampires practice "discrimination based on age, race, gender, or sexual orientation," he says, sapping entire classes of their dignity and robbing them of their civil rights. In his view, psychic vampires even exist on a global scale and affect the course of wars and economies.[45]

Karl Marx made a similar point by observing that the process of capital accumulation itself amounts to "dead labor which, vampire-like, lives only by sucking living labor, and lives the more, the more labor it sucks."[46] His widely quoted "capitalists as vampires" metaphor equates vampires with greedy capitalists who sap the value of labor's contribution to capitalism. Although Marx probably intended the connection to be metaphorical, Slate believes in its reality. To him and other psychic vampire adherents, real psychic vampires form innocent-appearing organizations that serve as fronts for psychic vampire collectives. These psychic covens may exist largely on an unconscious level, and members may not realize the true nature of the organizations they join and support.

Although nebulous and amorphous psychic vampirism challenges scientific observation and measurement, its qualities make it quite effective as a cultural metaphor. Psychic vamps can represent predatory capitalists, fear of feminism, corrupt government officials, racists, or groups outside society's norms, as well as wasteful appliances sucking electricity from millions of homes. Psychic vampires deliberately rob others of their energy or sexuality to enhance their own existence. They act as psychic sponges, draining victims and casting them aside once they've been depleted. In an individualistic society, psi vamps can represent humanity's violently competitive nature. Who among us has not suffered from the presence of a negative person who seems to drain our energy and weaken our spirit? What about the scam artists, fortune hunters, fair-weather friends, and jealous neighbors we encounter in the "real" world?

Psychic vamps continue to amuse, fascinate, and at times terrify us. As with other vampire subgenres, fans need not believe in their literal existence to appreciate them as metaphors—metaphors that may help us identify and learn how to deal with negative people. As for energy vampires, they can be defeated only by avoiding, unplugging, and empowering ordinary people to act as "vampire slayers."

• Six •

Slayers

In 1992, *Buffy the Vampire Slayer* brought the vampire slayer into contemporary consciousness. Although many already knew about Abraham Van Helsing, Buffy impacted pop culture even more profoundly than Bram Stoker's vampire slayer ever had. Writer Lisa Rosen observes, "Buffy was the first young woman on television who was both empowered and realistically portrayed." Creator Joss Whedon explains that his popular television series and subsequent movie versions tapped into an audience's desire for strong female characters. "People cared for her because she fulfilled a need for a female hero, which is distinctly different from a heroine."[1]

Monster slayers are among the oldest of mythological characters, appearing in the legends of many ancient peoples. Slaying ferocious adversaries played a vital role in establishing societies, regardless of whether the monsters had human, animal, or supernatural origins. Perseus, Heracles, the Navajo's Monster Slayer, and the Mayas' Hero Twins all arose in mythology in response to formidable threats. Western monster slayers descend from St. George, the twelfth-century Christian dragon slayer who relied on the sign of the cross to defeat a fire-breathing monster that preyed on citizens.[2] Medieval Crusaders returning from the Holy Land brought back legends of vampires and slayers, which gradually merged with those of St. George.

In mythology, vampire slayers may emerge from the union between a vampire and a human. Their offspring, called "dhampir" or "hybrid," possess characteristics of both humans and vampires.[3] Often born on a Saturday, a vampire slayer has the ability to see vampires that are invisible to others, amounting at times to clairvoyance or a "sixth sense." Slayers, like the vampires they stalk, inhabit a universe rich in supernatural characters. To locate and kill their quarry, they rely on religious iconography, vampire lore, science, and technology. This blend of Christianity, paganism, science, and war craft offers abundant symbolic possibilities.

In vampire mythology, powerful slayers often appear when humanity seems most threatened. They employ medical science (in the form of blood

Buffy (Kristy Swanson), a high school senior and hereditary vampire slayer, under-goes intensive training to "buff" her slaying skills in *Buffy the Vampire Slayer* (1992). Some feminists revered her as a manifestation of female power, while others found her character too traditionally feminine (Kobal Collection at Art Resource, New York).

transfusions and other technology) and armaments, as well as Christian and Celtic icons, garlic, crucifixes, and holy water. Neither strictly Enlightenment nor Romantic symbols, slayers represent a mélange of both scientific rationalism and Romanticism. Among vampire characters, slayers inhabit both the realistic world of science and technology and a hidden, supernatural world.

Nineteenth-Century Slayer Models

The first slayer characters that appeared in nineteenth-century literature proved too weak to prevail against vampires. Samuel Taylor Coleridge's *Christabel* (1816) features the vampire Geraldine and two victims, the maiden Christabel and her father, Sir Leoline. Coleridge also created a potential slayer named Bracey the Bard, a poet who dreams that a bright green snake encircles and strangles a white dove, a symbol for Christabel. Bracey relates his dream to Sir Leoline, his liege lord:

> But yet for her dear lady's sake
> I stooped, methought, the dove to take,
> When lo! I saw a bright green snake
> Coiled around its wings and neck.
> Green as the herbs on which it couched,
> Close by the dove's its head it crouched;
> And with the dove it heaves and stirs,
> Swelling its neck as she swelled hers!
> I woke; it was the midnight hour,
> The clock was echoing in the tower;
> But though my slumber was gone by,
> This dream it would not pass away—
> It seems to live upon my eye!
> And thence I vowed this self-same day,
> With music strong and saintly song
> To wander through the forest bare,
> Lest aught unholy loiter there.[4]

Although Bracey's poetic spirit allows him to intuit the danger posed by Geraldine, his subsequent search fails to locate the monster, and he lacks the strength and skill to slay a vampire. Without a professional slayer to prevent the impending murders, Coleridge's poem ends on a somber, pessimistic note. Geraldine's hypnotic spell transforms a loving father into a fatally negligent parent who cares more for his childhood friendship and current infatuation than for his only child.

Fifty-six years after Coleridge's poem appeared, novelist Sheridan Le Fanu published *Carmilla* (1872), the first work of fiction to feature a potent vampire slayer. Some argue that Le Fanu based his novel on Coleridge's poem, and that *Carmilla* represents his attempt to complete Coleridge's unfinished work.[5] Like Coleridge's poem, Le Fanu's novel presents an encounter between two beautiful young women who initially appear well suited as friends, springing from similar upper-class origins. Laura, the novel's youthful protagonist, meets Carmilla—seemingly also a young woman—after a minor accident in front of Laura's mountain castle. Carmilla, like Coleridge's Geraldine and all her descendants, asks to be invited in. Both vampires transform into animals at night: Geraldine changes into a bright green snake, while Carmilla assumes the form of a monstrous cat.

Unlike Coleridge, Le Fanu created a dedicated, professional hunter to track down and destroy vampires. His slayer, Baron Vordenburg, is descended from a legendary hero who had rid the region of vampires hundreds of years earlier. Vordenburg is the first aristocratic slayer, predating Bram Stoker's Von Helsing and probably serving as Stoker's model. Like most slayers since then, Vordenburg becomes an authority on vampires. He discovers that his ancestor was romantically involved with Mircalla, Countess Karnstein— whose portrait looks exactly like Carmilla—before she became a vampire. Using his forefather's notes, he locates Carmilla's hidden tomb. Laura's father and Baron Vordenburg summon an imperial commission from the Hapsburg Empire to open the tomb and destroy the vampire inside.

Not handsome or outwardly heroic, Baron Vordenburg appears colorful and rather odd. Le Fanu describes him as "tall, narrow-chested, stooping, with high shoulders, and dressed in black. His face was brown and dried in with deep furrows; he wore an oddly-shaped hat with a broad leaf." His clothing, grooming, and behavior added to his oddball appearance:

> His hair, long and grizzled, hung on his shoulders. He wore a pair of gold spectacles, and walked slowly, with an odd shambling gait, with his face sometimes turned up to the sky, and sometimes bowed down towards the ground, seemed to wear a perpetual smile; his long thin arms were swinging, and his lank hands, in old black gloves ever so much too wide for them, waving and gesticulating in utter abstraction.[6]

In addition to his colorful persona—a trait shared by many subsequent slayers—Vordenburg displays a penchant for researching vampire lore and referencing local history, specifically his ancestor's notes, to locate Carmilla's tomb. Vordenburg's scholarship modeled later nerdy, aristocratic slayers who assimilate vast amounts of scientific, historical, and vampire information. Le Fanu's slayer triumphs not through physical strength and valor but through knowledge and meticulousness.

Vordenburg lacks Carmilla's youth, beauty, and superpowers, but he ultimately destroys her through hard work and determination. The metaphor of an unattractive slayer triumphing over a beautiful seductress pits science against romance, plainness against beauty, and technology and esoteric lore against psychic powers. During the Romantic era, the slayer metaphor presented an opportunity to depict popular themes such as the supremacy of imagination over reason, the healing power of nature, and the evocative power of symbols.[7]

Bram Stoker borrowed heavily from Le Fanu's Baron Vordenburg for his slayer in *Dracula* (1897). Like Vordenburg, Stoker's slayer—Dr. Abraham Van Helsing—has an aristocratic heritage, and both slayers rely on science and reason to defeat their powerful antagonists. Stoker's Van Helsing boasts of a Dutch ancestry and a substantial and varied education; he's a doctor of medicine, a doctor of philosophy, and a doctor of letters, among other accomplishments. An eminent scholar whose expertise encompasses several fields, Van Helsing relies on the latest technology to combat Dracula, including syringes, tubes for blood transfusions, and an early Dictaphone for note-taking.

Van Helsing's appearance expresses his aristocratic lineage and underscores his tenacity and forcefulness, qualities that assist him in his struggles with Dracula. Stoker describes him thus:

> ... a man of medium weight, strongly built, with his shoulders set back over a broad, deep chest and a neck well balanced on the trunk as the head is on the neck. The poise of the head strikes me at once as indicative of thought and power. The head is noble, well-sized, broad, and large behind the ears. The face, clean-shaven, shows a hard, square chin, a large resolute, mobile mouth, a good-sized nose, rather straight, but with quick, sensitive nostrils, that seem to broaden as the big bushy brows come down and the mouth tightens. The forehead is broad and fine, rising at first almost straight and then sloping back above two bumps or ridges wide apart, such a forehead that the reddish hair cannot possibly tumble over it, but falls naturally back and to the sides. Big, dark blue eyes are set widely apart, and are quick and tender or stern with the man's moods.

Although he lacks Dracula's handsome, suave persona, in intellectual attributes Van Helsing appears superior to the monster he eventually defeats. Stoker describes him as possessing a powerful intellect and indomitable willpower:

> He is a philosopher and a metaphysician, and one of the most advanced scientists of his day, and he has, I believe, an absolutely open mind. This, with an iron nerve, a temper of the ice-brook, and indomitable resolution, self-command, and toleration exalted from virtues to blessings, and the kindliest and truest heart that beats, these form his equipment for the noble work that he is doing for mankind, work both in theory and practice, for his views are as wide as his all-embracing sympathy.[8]

With these impressive abilities at work, it comes as no surprise that Van Helsing eventually destroys Count Dracula. Science and technology, along with religion and a dominant will, defeat Dracula's occult powers. The following dialogue illustrates Van Helsing's powerful will and his use of Christian iconography:

Count Dracula: Come here.
[*Dracula raises his hand to hypnotize Van Helsing.*]
Count Dracula: Come here.
[*Van Helsing takes three hypnotized steps towards Dracula but soon steps back, resisting Dracula's power over him.*]
Count Dracula: Your will is strong, Van Helsing.
[*Van Helsing reaches out for his crucifix as Dracula looms toward him.*]
Count Dracula: More wolfbane?
Abraham Van Helsing: More effective than wolfbane, Count.
Count Dracula: Indeed.
[*Dracula lunges towards Van Helsing. Van Helsing holds up the crucifix. Dracula snarls and turns away. Van Helsing, in triumph, puts away the crucifix.*]

Twentieth-Century Slayers

Unlike Bram Stoker, German filmmaker F. W. Murnau weakened and emasculated his vampire slayer in *Nosferatu* (1922). Murnau relegated his slayer, Professor Bulwer (John Gottowt) to a minor role and assigned the honor of killing the vampire to Ellen Hutter (Murnau's substitute for Mina Harker), played by Greta Schroeder. In defiance of an order by her husband (Gustav von Wangenheim) that she not read a book about vampires, Ellen discovers that the only way to destroy one is for someone of pure heart to lure it to remain out of its coffin past daybreak, since sunlight instantly destroys vampires. Murnau's decision to let his heroine slay the monster seems to be a nod to the era's potent feminism. (Women gained voting rights in Germany in 1918 and in the U.S. in 1920.)

In order to destroy the vampire, Ellen flings open her windows and symbolically invites the leering monster—played masterfully by Max Schreck—to feed off her in her bed, immediately after ordering her husband to summon Professor Bulwer, the local vampire slayer. The professor arrives too late to save Ellen, but her act of courageous submission culminates in the vampire's vaporization by pure sunshine. Ellen sacrifices herself by allowing the hideous vampire to ravish her, adding a sexual twist to the Christ-like sacrifice of her body. Professor Bulwer, the would-be slayer, arrives too late to lend assistance and becomes irrelevant.

Audiences first encounter Professor Bulwer as he lectures about vampirism in the plant world, using the Venus flytrap as an example. His most memorable line, appearing as text in this silent film: "Never walk away from your destiny." This applies to Ellen, destined to slay a deadly vampire. By directing his heroine to destroy the vampire, Murnau provided an early example of a strong female character.

Tod Browning's classic movie *Dracula* (1931) returns to Dr. Van Helsing (Edward Van Sloan) as the vampire slayer. Van Helsing tracks Dracula to his casket in daylight when the count is sleeping. He drives a stake through the count's heart, thereby freeing Mina Harker of her vampirism, and she reverts to her former human form. The square, spectacled Dutch scientist outwits and defeats the powers of darkness embodied by Dracula, but not without assistance from vampire lore and potent Catholic icons. Van Helsing says, "I have studied, over and over again since they came into my hands, all the papers relating to this monster."

While others seem confused or oblivious to the dangers posed by Dracula, Van Helsing recognizes them immediately. He explains, "Gentlemen, we are dealing with the undead.... Yes, Nosferatu, the undead, the vampire. The vampire attacks the throat. It leaves two little wounds, white with red centers." Van Helsing uses his extensive knowledge of vampires to identify their presence and plot their annihilation. In London, when he and Dracula finally meet face to face, the vampire takes the measure of Van Helsing in a clash of wills. Dracula warns Van Helsing to return to his home country, leaving Londoners unprotected against him. Van Helsing replies, "I prefer to remain and protect those that you would destroy." Dracula refuses to back down, boasting that he controls Lucy Westenra, now one of his vampire thralls. His stubbornness prompts Van Helsing to vow to have "Carfax Abbey torn down, stone by stone, excavated for a mile around. And I will drive that stake through your heart." This enrages Dracula, who employs all his powers in an attempt to hypnotize and kill Van Helsing. But the count's powers of hypnosis, shapeshifting, and super strength ultimately are no match for Van Helsing's science and religion. This metaphor speaks volumes about the ultimate power of Christianity, assisted by science, to rid the world of evil.

Edward Van Sloan's performance as Dr. Van Helsing is memorable. His forceful delivery and assertive body language make him a potent force against Dracula and his thralls. When viewing Van Sloan's performance, it's natural to believe that he possesses greater perceptive powers and intellect than Dracula. Sloan's Van Helsing epitomizes European post–Enlightenment reliance on science and technology, assisted by insights from religion and folklore.

In 1936 Universal Pictures released *Dracula's Daughter*, a sequel to the

1931 version of *Dracula,* directed by Lambert Hillyer. This film picks up the story after Dracula's death. In the first scene, Professor Abraham Von Helsing (Edward Van Sloan) stands in a crypt next to the bodies of Count Dracula and Renfield, vampires he's recently staked and killed. Two policemen discover him standing over the bodies and question him. Von Helsing calmly and professionally announces, "I did it"—at which time one of the officers decides that "this is a case for Scotland Yard" and arrests him for murder. Soon, however, Countess Marya Zaleska (Gloria Holden), Dracula's daughter, steals her father's body and burns it, hoping to free herself of the curse of vampirism she has inherited from her father. Psychologist Jeffrey Garth (Otto Kruger) arrives to defend his friend Von Helsing against murder charges and meets Countess Zeleska. She begs Garth to help her overcome her "obsession," by which she means her blood addiction. With his assistant and girlfriend Janet Blake (Marguerite Churchill), Garth eventually discovers Zaleska's vampirism, but not soon enough to prevent the countess from abducting Blake to Transylvania to serve as her next meal.

After pursuing Zaleska and Blake halfway across Europe, Von Helsing arrives at the vampire's castle with the police. They destroy Zaleska and release Blake from captivity, thereby closing another vampire cycle. But will it ever end? In this film Von Helsing emerges as an even stronger character than his counterpart in *Dracula,* and Dr. Garth plays the role of assistant slayer. The two work together in the final act as Von Helsing saves Garth from Zaleska's thrall after Garth drives a stake through the countess' heart. The slayers triumph by cooperating with each other. Conquering evil requires teamwork, and Zaleska is too potent to yield to a single individual, even one as powerful as Von Helsing. Garth represents reason and logic pitted against Countess Zaleska's implicit lesbianism, while the slayers Von Helsing and Garth symbolize patriarchy.

In 1958 Abraham Van Helsing returned in *The Horror of Dracula,* by Britain's Hammer Film Productions. Setting his film in 1885 in the remote village of Karlstadt, director Terrance Fisher pits Peter Cushing as Van Helsing against Christopher Lee as Count Dracula. Jonathan Harker (John Van Eyssen) plans to slay Dracula as he lies in a coffin, but he becomes distracted and instead slays a female vampire in a nearby coffin. Dracula escapes and bites Harker, infecting him with vampirism. Dr. Van Helsing, Harker's fellow vampire hunter, receives information about his friend's last whereabouts and scours Karlstadt looking for him. He encounters his first problem when he asks a local innkeeper how to find the castle. When the innkeeper refuses to assist him, Van Helsing says, "If the investigation that Mr. Harker and I are engaged upon is successful, not only you, but the whole will benefit. Castle

Dracula is somewhere here in Klausenberg. Will you tell me how I get there?" The obviously intimidated landlord replies, "You ordered a meal, sir. As an innkeeper, it is my duty to serve you. When you've eaten, I ask you to go and leave us in peace."

Van Helsing eventually discovers Harker, transformed into a vampire at Dracula's castle, and stakes him—but Dracula escapes. The antagonism between Van Helsing and Dracula deepens as Dracula uses his superpowers and initially gains the advantage. In the final scene, however, Van Helsing rips off the window shades and lets in the sunshine, incinerating Dracula. Van Helsing also forms a makeshift cross and points it at the slowly disintegrating Dracula. Van Helsing the scientist defeats Dracula the undead spirit, both by light and by the Christian cross. Sunlight symbolizes Christianity, while darkness symbolizes vampirism. In this film Cushing as Van Helsing appropriately receives top billing, above Lee as Dracula. This astounding reversal marks a turning point. From this time on, vampire slayers increase in power and strength, adding layers of meaning to the vampire-slayer metaphor.

In the 1958 film *The Return of Dracula*, directed by Paul Landres, the narrator establishes a horrific mood in the first scenes:

> It is a known fact that there existed in Central Europe a Count Dracula. Though human in appearance and cultured in manner, he was in truth a thing undead … a force of evil … a vampire. Feeding on the blood of innocent people, he turned them into his own kind, thus spreading his evil dominion ever wider. The attempts to find and destroy this evil were never proven fully successful, and so the search continues to this very day.

Landres' Dracula (Francis Lederer), intent on emigrating to the U.S., murders a man in Transylvania and assumes his identity. He boards a steamer bound for Carleton, California, where he plans to live with the dead man's family. There he seduces and vampirizes the woman of the house, Rachel (Norma Eberhardt), promising her eternal life: "We shall never be touched. The world shall spin and they all, all shall die. But not we." Rachel's lover, Tim Hansen (Ray Stricklyn), finally confronts Dracula in an abandoned mine and causes him to fall into a mine shaft. When he lands, he's impaled on a wooden beam. Like Ellen in *Nosferatu*, Tim assumes a slayer's role previously assigned to professional vampire hunters like Stoker's Van Helsing and Le Fanu's Baron Vordenburg. In order to slay the monsters that plague us, this film implies, we must take up arms ourselves, not rely on outside professionals to do it for us.

In his 1962 cult classic *The Bloody Vampire*, Mexican director Michael Morayta returns to the professional slayer motif by creating an entire family of slayers headed by Count Valsamo Cagliostro (Antonio Rexel). They make it their sacred duty to oppose and destroy a dangerous vampire family headed by Count Siegried Von Frankenhausen (Charles Agosti). *The Bloody Vampire* was the first pop culture creation to replace individual slayers with an organized group. Le Fanu's Baron Vordenburg, who relies on his ancestor's notes, serves as the model for an entire family that has inherited their ancestors' slaying ability—thereby increasing the pressure on vampires and illustrating the wisdom that killing vampires requires close cooperation among all interested parties. This film ranks highly with critics for its dramatic settings, innovative musical score, excellent performances, and idiosyncratic perspectives on vampires.

In the film, Count Cagliostro—a scientist reminiscent of Dr. Frankenstein—is working to develop a substance that will neutralize "vampirina," the blood pathogen that causes vampirism. The Cagliostro mansion happens to lie close to Frankenhausen's castle, which the Cagliostros suspect is a vampire haven. In order to investigate their suspicions, young Anna Cagliostro (Begona Palacios) responds to an advertisement for a maid in the Frankenhausen household. Her fiancé, Dr. Richard Paisser (Raoul Farell), visits the Frankenhausens to check on the ailing Countess Eugena Frankenhausen (Erna Martha Bauman). This enrages Count Frankenhausen and his housekeeper Frau Hildegarde (Bertha Moss), who'd forbidden any visitors to the countess, but they extend a forced courtesy to the doctor. Count Frankenhausen informs Paisser that insanity, not physical illness, affects his wife. Countess Frankenhausen continues to send for Paisser, who's secretly assisted by his fiancée Anna, now the countess' chambermaid.

Anna's willingness to serve as informant for her family makes her an early example of a female vampire slayer. Although she provides Paisser with valuable information, Anna never convinces him of the count's vampirism until the final scene, when he and Count Cagliostro surprise Frankenhausen in his family crypt and engage him in combat. Count Frankenhausen transforms into a gigantic bat and attacks the two men. Although most members of the Frankenhausen family perish, the count escapes—insuring additional outbreaks of vampirism in the surrounding area and laying the groundwork for a potential sequel.

In this film the slayers and the vampires both occupy an elite social class. But although the two families claim the same socio/economic status, they couldn't exhibit greater difference in their feelings for one another and for fellow citizens. The Cagliostros appear to be open-minded, progressive, courageous, and humanistic, while the Frankenhausens display a complete lack of regard for each other or for outsiders. The bitter rivalry between the families reminds us of the rivalry between the Montagues and the Capulets in Shakespeare's *Romeo and Juliet*. The vampires in this film obey a strict ritual code as formal and ancient as that of the Freemasons and the Knights Templar. Their dissimulations and cruelties do little to endear them to viewers. Once again science defeats vampirism, which in this film equates with savagery, coldness, and sadism. Anna plays a significant role on the slayer team, acknowledging female power and foreshadowing the feminist vampire films of the 1970s.

In 1964 *The Last Man on Earth* was released, directed by Ubaldo Ragona and based on the popular 1958 sci-fi novel *I am Legend* by Richard Matheson. In Ragona's film, Dr. Robert Morgan (Vincent Price), battling a virus outbreak, eventually finds no other humans left alive after the virus seemingly transforms everyone else into zombie/vampires who constantly seek to devour him and drink his blood. Morgan begins the movie by saying, "Another day to live through. Better get started." To counter the threat from millions of zombified vampires thirsting for his blood, Morgan transforms himself into a vampire-slaying machine. By night he manages to keep the bloodthirsty crowd of vampires out of his house by ringing it with garlands of garlic, and during the day he impales all the vampires he finds with wooden stakes he's fashioned on his lathe. One day he asks himself, as he fills up a bag with stakes, "How many more of these will I have to make before they're all destroyed? They want my blood. Their lives are mine. I still get squeamish." By daylight Morgan drives to abandoned stores to replenish his supplies, staking any sleeping vampires he encounters along the way. Before nightfall he returns to his home, where he encounters ravenous vampires every night.

Like Van Helsing, Morgan has a medical degree and conducts scientific experiments, keeping detailed notes in his quest to destroy vampires. Ultimately, Morgan destroys vampirism entirely by using his own blood—a powerful anti-vampire antidote—although he sacrifices his life in the process. Vampires in this book and film symbolize the fear of virulent diseases as well as Cold War concerns about Communist fifth columnists working to destroy America from within. Morgan represents science's ultimate mastery over all antagonists. He relies far more on science than on the familiar Christian icons employed to good effect by earlier slayers. In the film and the novel, crosses and holy water prove inadequate to overcome the menace of vampirism, leaving only science to provide the lifesaving serum.

Roman Polanski released his spoof *The Fearless Vampire Killers* in 1962, featuring Jack MacGowran as Professor Abronsius, bat researcher and would-be vampire slayer. Polanski himself plays Alfred, Abronsius's slow-witted assistant. Together they travel to Transylvania in search of vampires. In a village there, Alfred falls in love with Sarah (Sharon Tate), the innkeeper's daughter. However, Sarah also comes to the attention of Count von Krolak (Ferdy Mayne), a vampire who abducts her to his castle. When Abronsius and Alfred visit the count, he and his gay son Herbert (Iain Quarrier) urge them to stay on as guests. The next night the count invites his vampire colleagues to a formal ball honoring Abronsius and Alfred—but he plans to offer them as food and transform Abronsius into his own vampire companion. At the ball, Count von Krolak formally addresses his vampire colleagues in mock religious tones:

> A year ago exactly on this same night we were assembled here in this very room: I your pastor, and you my beloved flock. With hopefulness in my heart I told you then that with Lucifer's aid we might look forward to a more succulent occasion. Cast back your minds. There we were, gathered together, gloomy and despondent, around a single meager woodcutter.

Now, however, Krolak prepares to offer them the two academics, presumably more delicious than a mere woodcutter. Abronsius and Alfred find themselves with few weapons to use against von Krolak and his monstrous friends, having lost their suitcase containing garlic and crucifixes. But Christian icons offer no assistance against the innkeeper Shagal, a Jewish vampire. When a young woman tries to fend Shagal off with a cross he replies, "Oy vey, have you got the wrong vampire!"

Eventually Abronsius and Alfred manage to rescue Sarah, not realizing that she has transformed into a vampire. She promptly bites them both. The narrator points out the irony of the situation: "That night, fleeing from Transylvania, Professor Abronsius never guessed that he was carrying away with him the very evil he had sought to destroy. Thanks to him, this evil would now be able to spread itself across the world."

The Fearless Vampire Slayers received poor reviews—in part because the producer, fearing a restrictive rating, cut twenty minutes and added the subtitle *Pardon Me, But Your Teeth Are in My Neck*. But Polanski's original film, now restored, has the same problems as the butchered version: namely, unfunny jokes. Film critic Roger Ebert, reviewing the truncated version, observed that no one in the audience laughed. "One or two people cried, and a lady behind me dropped a bag of M&Ms which rolled under the seats, and a guy on the center aisle sneezed at forty-three minutes past the hour. But that was about all the action. There wasn't even a dog that ran onto the playing field."[9] A later extended version makes for better viewing but still requires abundant patience.

Despite the film's problems, Polanski succeeded in lampooning many genre conventions while focusing on the consciousness of the slayers. *The Fearless Vampire Killers*—like *The Last Man on Earth*—elevates slayers above vampires. These films mark the evolution of the slayer role from ancillary character to protagonist, a process that began in the 1950s with *The Horror of Dracula*. The role of slayer has metamorphosed over the long history of pop culture vampires, becoming increasingly powerful and metaphorically complex.

In 1974 Hammer Film Productions released its own slayer movie, *Captain Kronos: Vampire Slayer*. Directed by Brian Clemens, the British film borrowed heavily from Polanski's *The Fearless Vampire Killers*. Horst Janson stars as Captain Kronos, a skillful swordsman and vampire slayer. Kronos travels to a small village with fellow slayer Professor Hieronymous Grost (John Cater), a hunchback, to learn what has caused several young women to suddenly age and appear to be on the brink of death. Along the way they pick up Carla (Caroline Munro), who functions as an apprentice slayer. Grost gives the village doctor a lesson about vampire diversity: "You see, doctor, there are as many species of vampire as there are beasts of prey. Their methods and their motive for attack can vary in a hundred different ways." Kronos adds, "As are the methods of their destruction!" Captain Kronos introduced the idea that vampires come in a wide variety of types. The first step to ridding an area of vampires, Kronos believes, is to capture one of them and experiment on it until it dies. Then slayers must tailor their remedies to match the exact vampire menace they seek to eradicate. This suggests that society's problems are multiplying, demanding a variety of slayer approaches.

Joel Schumacher's cult classic *The Lost Boys* (1987) features some memorable vampire slayers. After their parents divorce, brothers Michael (Jason Patric) and Sam (Corey Haim) Emerson move with their mother Lucy (Dianne Wiest) to Santa Carla, California to live with her father (Barnard Hughes). Once in town, they learn that the seemingly quiet beach community has the country's highest murder rate. Sam soon meets the Frog brothers— Edgar (Corey Feldman) and Alan (Jamison Newlander)—who inform him of Santa Carla's status as a vampire haven. Michael meets Star (Jami Gertz), the girlfriend of local vampire leader David (Keifer Sutherland). He gets picked up by David's vampire gang, finds himself at a party at an abandoned hotel, and inadvertently drinks some of David's blood. Soon afterward he begins to show signs of physiological transformation, raising Sam's anxieties about his brother becoming a vampire.

At this point Michael sleeps with Star, prompting Sam to seek advice from the Frog brothers, who had revealed their interest in slaying vampires. Michael, Sam, and the Frog brothers attempt to stake David, hoping to save Michael from vampirism, but the raid goes awry when they accidentally awaken David and his gang. Michael grabs Star and the group escapes into the daylight, prompting David to threaten vengeance "tonight!" They spend the day preparing for a raid from the gang by filling a bathtub with garlic, loading squirt guns with holy water, and gathering a stockpile of wooden stakes. A fierce fight ensues when the gang arrives, and Michael ends up shoving David into a pair of mounted deer antlers, killing him.

Despite David's death, Michael continues to show signs of impending vampirism, so the slayers renew their search for the "master vampire." They chance upon his identity when they secretly observe Max (Edward Herrmann) and Lucy returning home from a date. Max sees David's body and reacts so strongly that the slayers realize he's the master vampire. Says Max, "It was all going to be so perfect, Lucy. Just like one big, happy family. Your boys ... and my boys." At this point, Edgar Frog exclaims, "Great! The Bloodsucking Brady Bunch!"

After they confront Max, he grabs Sam and threatens to kill him unless Lucy agrees to their union. At this point Lucy's father smashes his car through the wall and emerges with wooden stakes. In the ensuing melee Max dies, along with all vampirism in the community. In this film all the family members are vampire slayers, from grandfather to mother to sons. The Emersons, like the Cagliosto family in *The Bloody Vampire*, learn the necessity of family solidarity. A single individual—like Robert Morgan in *The Last Man on Earth*—may lack the necessary strength to defeat a vampire guarded by many thralls, but when families stick together they can defeat any and all vampires.

Female Slayers

In 1992, Buffy Summers (Kristy Swanson) became the first full-fledged female vampire slayer, in *Buffy the Vampire Slayer*. A high school cheerleader, Buffy may not seem like an appropriate instrument for destroying superpowerful vampires, but this film transformed the entire idea of vampire-slaying away from masculine tests of strength. Buffy receives her lore from a crash course provided by Merrick (Donald Sutherland), the scion of an ancient family of vampire-slayer trainers known as "Watchers." When he first meets Buffy, Merrick explains to the startled and dubious schoolgirl that only a few females may become slayers. "Since the dawn of man, the vampires have walked among us, killing and feeding. The only one with the strength or skill to stop their heinous evil is the slayer, she who bears the birthmark, the mark of the coven." When a slayer dies, the coven selects a successor; each of these comes with a Watcher who functions as both trainer and information source. Buffy, of course, possesses the "slayer's mark," an unusual birthmark.

After witnessing vampires rising from their graves at midnight, Buffy reluctantly agrees to undergo Merrick's training and become "the Chosen." She studies vampire lore and hones her martial arts and gymnastic skills in preparation for attacking and destroying the master vampire currently causing havoc in the community. After vampire king Lothos (Rutger Hauer) kills Merrick, Buffy teams up with her boyfriend Pike (Luke Perry) to destroy him. Lothos and his thug-like gang of thralls crash the senior prom seeking to find and destroy Buffy, the new slayer they all fear. But Buffy, assisted by Pike, manages to defeat them.

Later Lothos approaches Buffy and demands that she become his vampire bride, exclaiming, "You and I are one." Buffy replies, "One what, cute couple? I don't think so!" During their fight she attempts to stake him, and he responds mockingly, "Now I'm really pissed off!" When Buffy brandishes a cross he says scornfully, "This is your defense? Puh-lease! Your puny faith?" She ignites the cross and pulls the cap off a hairspray can. "My keen fashion sense," she says before spraying the burning cross with hairspray, engulfing his face and killing him. Thus Buffy the teenage cheerleader defeats Lothos, a throwback to Eastern European vampire machismo, through creative use of hairspray.

Buffy illustrates the feminist message that men with superpowers are ineffective against well-trained, agile young female slayers. Lothos epitomizes patriarchal attitudes toward women, while Buffy symbolizes women's innate powers that—when properly nurtured—can defeat even the most ardent patriarchs. Lothos, who appears as a middle-aged man, demonstrates his deviancy by attempting to force Buffy, a high school girl, to become his bride. That would violate the sanctity of childhood and brand Lothos a pedophile; even by suggesting it, Lothos qualifies as a social deviant.

This film marks a milestone in slayer metaphors by giving the slayer not only top billing but also title rights. Although female vampires populate pop culture, before Buffy no female slayer had achieved this level of distinction. The film was popular with teenage audiences, and a television series also starring Kristy Swanson was launched in 1997. It lasted until 2003, signaling the coming of age of female vampire slayers and a renewed interest in vampire slayers, both male and female.

Robert Rodriguez's *From Dusk Till Dawn* (1996) stars George Clooney and Quentin Tarantino as Seth and Ritchie Gecko, bank robbers trying to avoid capture by escaping to Mexico. To ensure their safety, they take the vacationing Fuller family as hostages, including Reverend Jacob Fuller (Harvey Keitel), his daughter Kate (Juliette Lewis), and adopted son Scott (Ernest Liu). The Geckos cross the Mexican border with their hostages and head for the notoriously rowdy Titty Twister Bar, open "from dusk till dawn." They experience some trouble with the bouncer, played by Cheech Marin, but once inside they enjoy the party atmosphere, including a sexually graphic dance by Satanico Pandemonium (Salma Hayek). But Ritchie gets in a fight with a vampire who stabs him in his hand, and when Pandemonium sees the blood she transforms into a hideous vampire. She bites Ritchie in the neck, at which point Seth shoots her off his brother's back. Seth assumes leadership of the remaining humans in the bar, even cheering them on as if engaged in a normal barroom brawl: "All right, vampire killers…. Let's kill some fucking vampires!"

Seth and the few remaining humans—including Jacob Fuller, Kate Fuller, Scott Fuller, and a bar patron named Sex Machine (Tom Savini)—frantically discuss tactics to use in their war against vampires. After Reverend Fuller reveals that he has no crosses, his son Scott interjects, "What are you talking about? We got crosses all over the place. All you gotta do is put two sticks together and you got a cross!" Sex Machine adds, "He's right. Peter Cushing does it all the time." Seth says, "Okay, I'll buy that." Then Jacob asks, "Has anybody here read a real book about vampires, or are we just remembering what a movie said? I mean a real book." Sex Machine asks, "You mean like a Time-Life book?"

The movie's dialogue, bizarre plot twists, and exotic settings mark it as an ironic spoof of vampire films. One reviewer labeled it "a grisly, quasi-comedy."[10] The comedic intent is most apparent during the film's second half, when the slayer metaphor clarifies. In order to survive vampire attacks, humans must fight fiercely as a team and pool their knowledge of vampire lore. The criminal-like vampires die only when human criminals like the Gecko brothers unite with non-criminals, including a clergyman and a youthful, Buffy-inspired Kate. This common narrative demands that ordinary and extraordinary people survive only when they unite, discard any remaining inhibitions, and are willing to stop at nothing to destroy their enemies. They must toughen up and forget about propriety and the rule of law. No vampire slayers ever read vampires their rights before locking them in jail to await trial. Instead, they all qualify as vigilantes.

Blade (1998) further advanced the macho slayer metaphor through its title character, played by Wesley Snipes. Director Stephen Norrington cast Kris Kristofferson as Abraham Whistler, Blade's weapons technician and backup slayer. Whistler's first name evokes the famous slayer Abraham Van Helsing of *Dracula* fame. Whistler invents weapons such as "vampire mace" and a special flashlight to wield against vampires. After Blade rescues Dr. Karen Jenson (N'Bushe Wright) from vampire Quinn (Donal Logue), she joins the others as an apprentice slayer. Blade, a vampire/human hybrid, relies on a serum to keep his vampirism in check and allow him to be a "Day Walker." Dr. Jenson, a blood specialist, creates a serum that will make him completely human, but he rejects it because it would eliminate the super-powers he needs to destroy vampires. Instead, he asks her to make another batch of the serum that lets him retain his superpowers but avoid some of the drawbacks of vampirism, especially the inability to withstand sunlight.

Meanwhile, a "made" vampire named Deacon Frost (Stephen Dorff) hatches a plot to resurrect master vampire La Magra (Frankie Ray), the "Blood God," and unleash a deadly reign of terror against humans. To defeat La Magra, Blade must first destroy all of Deacon Frost's vampires and Frost himself. One of Frost's thralls, Quinn (Donal Logue), snatches the slayer's legendary vampire-killing knife and exclaims, "I got his pig sticker"—at which point the booby-trapped handle explodes, taking off his hand. Ultimately Blade destroys La Magra with exploding capsules and then travels to a Russian-speaking country, where he attacks a male vampire preying on a young woman. The implication seems clear—to stamp out crime, we must forget about bringing criminals to justice and simply assassinate all suspects.

John Carpenter's *Vampires* (1998) relies on another macho male to slay vampires. Carpenter's film, considered a classic today, stars James Woods as Jack Crow, master vampire hunter working for the Vatican, and Daniel Baldwin as Anthony Montoya, Crow's fellow slayer. In the opening scene the two men lead a tough-looking squad of slayers into an abandoned house in the New Mexico desert, where they destroy all the vampires inside except for master vampire Jan Valek (Thomas Ian Griffith). Valek tracks the hunters to a sleazy motel where a wild "victory" party is taking place, involving much booze and several prostitutes. As soon as he enters, Valek seduces and bites a hooker named Katrina (Sheryl Lee). Then he kills all the vampire slayers except Crow and Montoya, who manage a last-minute escape with Katrina.

Crow burns the bodies of his dead comrades to prevent them from transforming into vampires, then visits Cardinal Alba (Maximilian Schell), who informs him that Valek became a vampire during the fourteenth century in Europe after being burned at the stake for heresy against the Church. Father Adam Guiteau (Tim Guinee) joins Crow as an apprentice vampire slayer. Meanwhile, Montoya waits in a hotel room with Katrina, who is telepathically connected with Valek. Hoping she will lead them to their target, Montoya and Crow bring her along on their search. Eventually they locate Valek and his thralls lurking inside an abandoned building. Crow exclaims, "What the fuck do you want, Valek?" Replies the vampire, "Oh, you hate me so, don't ya? But you made me, Crusader. You hate what you made. You fear it because it is superior to you. For six hundred years, I've fed on your kind at will!"

Crow, Montoya, and Father Guiteau destroy the vampires one by one until only Valek remains. Finally they also slay him. Male slayers prevail this time, not females, although Katrina plays a good supporting role. She presents an opposite gender perspective from that depicted in *Buffy*—patriarchal and definitely not feminist. The film's vampire slayers resemble action heroes in combat with their use of weaponry. The message is clear: vampires must be tracked down and summarily executed with firearms, crossbows, and knives.

Dracula 2000 features another imaginative version of the conflict between Van Helsing (Christopher Plummer) and Dracula (Gerard Butler). In this film, directed by Joel Lussier, thieves break into a vault and steal a fancy casket, believing it contains treasure. Unable to open the casket, they load it onto a cargo plane. During the flight one of the thieves, Nightshade (Danny Masterson), cuts his hand while attempting to break the casket open. It seems to devour his blood, resurrecting Dracula—who then attacks the rest of the thieves and the flight crew, causing the plane to crash.

Dracula survives the crash and heads to New Orleans, where he plans to attack Mary Heller (Justine Waddell), the daughter of Abraham Van Helsing, and turn her into a vampire to enact vengeance against Van Helsing. This Dracula reveals his true origin as Judas Iscariot, the disciple who betrayed Jesus for thirty pieces of silver (hence vampires' abhorrence of silver). Because of this betrayal, supposedly God cursed Judas with vampirism, and only the Christian pure in heart can destroy him. Dracula cannot be killed by normal means—such as holy water, staking, and decapitation—so Van Helsing needs extra time to discover a method for killing him. Therefore he keeps Dracula's body locked in a casket full of leeches, occasionally removing one of them and injecting himself with the blood of Dracula contained in its body. Like other recent slayers, Van Helsing must transform partially into a vampire in order to kill Dracula—but by living off the vampire's blood for one hundred years, his human identity begins to transform into a vampire identity. After Dracula attacks his daughter Mary, Van Helsing warns him:

Abraham Van Helsing: You—you can't have her ... ever!
Dracula: Can't I?
Van Helsing: If you harm my daughter, I swear to the Lord Christ....
Dracula: Shh! He doesn't care. In that you can trust. You stole life from my blood and passed it to another. She's my Mary now.
Van Helsing: No. Never! You want revenge? Take it! Right here, right now!
Dracula: You know not the depths of my vengeance.

Like Van Helsing, many successful vampire slayers transform into vampire/human hybrids in order to acquire the superpowers of their antagonists. In this film Van Helsing slays by ingesting vampire blood from leeches. This reminds viewers of medical practices employing these creatures for treating a variety of human illnesses. In ancient times, in fact, "leeches" became a synonym for physicians. Van Helsing's use of them clearly symbolizes medical science, but not in a positive way. Today leech therapy survives only as a fringe movement, and its appearance in this film discredits the tactic of using medical science to combat vampirism. Only heroic, concerted, violent action can break Dracula's strength—as in the final scene, in which Mary Van Helsing beheads a vampire with a sword while Van Helsing's assistant Simon (Jonny Lee Miller) beheads another. In the end, Dracula incinerates in the morning sunlight. His slayers rely on community violence plus sunlight. Depending on science and reason alone is inadequate to defeat this potent monster, and he ultimately dies at the hands of the young woman he attacked.

Post–9/11 Slayers

In 2001 an indie slayer film that turned into an underground cult hit moved the vampire slayer metaphor into new territory. *Jesus Christ Vampire Hunter* brings the Christian Son of God into the business of slaying vampires. In addition, it reinvents the slayer film as a full-blown musical. Directed by Canadian Lee Demarbre, this film stars Phil Caracas as Jesus Christ and Maria Moulton as Mary Magnum, Christ's assistant slayer. Christ gets involved in slaying vampires after Father Eustice (Jim Devries), concerned about the disappearance of some of his parishioners, prays to God to stop the killing of lesbians in Ottawa. Vampires there had learned to prey exclusively on lesbians because few would miss these "deviants." In addition to feeding from them, vampire physician Dr. Pretorius (Josh Grace) grafts their skin onto nocturnal vampires, curing their sunlight allergies and allowing them to walk freely during the day. Of course, this renders them even more dangerous to humans. Christ, preparing for the Second Coming, must first rid the earth of these nuisances. At one point he proclaims in a song, "I was born in a manger/ doomed to live in danger."

Vampires Maxine Schreck (Murielle Varhelyi), named after *Nosferatu* actor Max Schreck, and Johnny Golgotha (Ian Driscroll), named for the place where the Romans crucified Jesus, operate a ring that supplies vampires with lesbian victims. They capture and bite Mary Magnum, transforming her into a vampire. To replace her and to help Jesus combat vampires, God sends champion masked wrestler Santo Enmascarado de Plata (Jeff Moffet) to assist his Son. The pair, possessed of formidable martial arts skills, slay dozens of vampires. When Schreck, Golgotha, and Magnum (now a vampire) attempt to capture Christ and bind him with ropes, de Plata bites through the ropes, releasing Jesus and allowing the slayers to destroy even more vampires. Then Father Eustice—now a vampire—stakes Christ through the heart, but the wound allows bright light to escape and shine on the vampires, destroying them all. In the end, Christ heals Magnum, who then begs Jesus to heal Schreck, making it possible for the lovers to reunite.

In this film Christ refuses to discriminate against lesbians or classify them as deviants. He says instead that "there's nothing deviant about love." His views, anathema to many Evangelicals, go beyond tolerance of differences and embrace violence for the sake of a good cause. Lesbianism here equates with feminism and progressivism. Reviewer Maryann Johanson labeled the film "a pro–Jesus, anti–Church screed against hypocrisy and bigotry" and "bizarre and funny and full of the good Jesus stuff that no one could argue with. The charmingly low production values and creative use of entrails are just bonuses."[11] As a metaphor, this film makes full use of Jesus as a pop culture artifact, as did previous works such as *Jesus Christ Superstar* (1973).

In 2004 the most famous vampire slayer finally wound up in a movie title. *Van Helsing*, directed by Stephen Sommers, features Hugh Jackman as Gabriel Van Helsing, a descendent of the slayer made famous by Bram Stoker. Gabriel Van Helsing works for the Vatican to eradicate European vampires. David Wendham plays Friar Carl, Van Helsing's faithful assistant on loan from the Vatican. They receive orders to journey to Transylvania to help the Valerious family kill Count Vladislaus Dracula (Richard Roxburgh). There they meet Anna Valerious (Kate Beckinsale), a princess from a once-powerful family of vampire slayers, now represented only by herself and her brother Velkin (Will Kemp). They also encounter three harpies, Aleera (*Elena Anaya*), Marishka (*Josie Maran*), and Verona (*Silvia Colloca*), brides of Count Dracula. When the harpies swoop down from the sky to attack Valerious, Van Helsing barely manages to save her, but the harpies promise to return.

Van Helsing borrows heavily from the 1962 film *The Bloody Vampire*. Like the earlier film, Sommers' movie combines vampire mythology with Frankenstein lore. It includes the Frankenstein monster (Shuler Hensley), Dr. Victor Frankenstein (Samuel West) and his faithful servant Igor (Kevin J. O'Conner), and even Dr. Jekyll (Stephen Fisher), Mr. Hyde (Robbie Coltrane), and an uncredited Wolfman. A Catholic cardinal (Alun Armstrong) serves as the Vatican's contact with Van Helsing. These disparate characters and plot twists render *Van Helsing* rather confusing. Like *The*

Bloody Vampire, the film features two rival families—one vampire and the other slayer—and Princess Anna shares the same first name as *The Bloody Vampire's* Anna Cagliostro, also a member of a slayer family. But unlike Cagliostro, the princess actively slays vampires, placing her on a par with Buffy and other female slayers.

Slayer, a 2006 TV movie, further updates the vampire slayer mythology by equating vampirism with radical environmentalism and vampire slayers with more mainstream attitudes. The main action occurs in the Peruvian rainforest and the town of Aqua Caliente following a deadly vampire attack on an American military platoon. After the survivors return to the U.S., Colonel Jessica Weaver (Lynda Carter) sends Captain Tom "Hawk" Hawkins (Casper Van Dien) and his men, including Sergeant Alex Juarez (Alexis Cruz), back to Aqua Caliente to join Grieves (Kevin Grevioux) and a platoon to reconnoiter the situation. By strange coincidence, Hawk's ex-wife, Dr. Laurie Williams (Jennifer O'Dell), is in the same area heading a small group of jungle guides who are there to identify exotic insects.

The vampires begin attacking locals and transforming them into vampires. Much of the film consists of fights between the troops and the vampires—who bear a striking resemblance to the region's native population. Grieves is vampirized and assumes a leadership role among the vampires, but he dies at Hawk's hands after a lengthy fight. Head vampire Javier Vasquez (Tony Plana), a former conquistador from the court of Queen Isabella I, confronts Hawk and offers him Grieves' old position as vampire military commander. He plans to expand vampire rule throughout the entire countryside, envisioning a vampire empire with himself in charge.

The film's perspective on environmental issues becomes clear. "They [vampires] lived for centuries on wild animals," Dr. Williams explains, "that is, until men came into the jungle." Amplifying that, Vasquez says, "Countless millions of acres of rainforest were cleared by corporations and governments too greedy to realize what they were doing, or care." He threatens, "If we cannot live in peace here, in the jungle, then it is time to grow our numbers onward and upward, on our terms." Exploitation of the environment brought about the current plague of vampires, which threatens to grow much worse as the vampires retaliate against deforestation. Vampirism represents a form of retribution for environmental crimes.

Vast segments of Americans agree with at least some of Vasquez's charges. In a 2011 Gallup poll, sixty-three percent expressed fears about loss of tropical rain forests, while seventy-nine percent had deep concerns about the deterioration of water and land. By contrast, only fifty-one percent felt fearful about global warming.[12] But *Slayer's* vampire killers, Hawk and Dr.

Williams, oppose extreme environmentalism, as represented by the vampires. In the final scene, Col. Weaver arrives with military reinforcements and deftly stakes one vampire with a special bullet fired from a pistol. In this case, vampire slayers symbolize the American military, while vampires symbolize radical environmentalism and armed guerrilla movements.

In *I Am Legend* (2007), Francis Lawrence's spin on Richard Matheson's 1954 sci-fi novel that inspired *The Last Man on Earth* (1964), Dr. Krippen (Emma Thompson) modifies a measles virus to target cancer cells invading a human body. A television anchorperson proudly proclaims, "The world of medicine has seen its share of miracle cures, from the polio vaccine to heart transplants. But all past achievements may pale in comparison to the work of Dr. Alice Krippin." But Krippin's virus soon mutates into a deadly pathogen that transforms people and animals into zombie-like vampires that shun sunlight and feed off human blood. Seemingly everyone dies except for Dr. Robert Neville (Will Smith), who concentrates on killing New York City vampires by day and surviving nighttime assaults on his fortress-like home. In this version of the Matheson classic, New York becomes an apocalyptic landscape in which herds of deer and even a pride of African lions run wild through vegetation-choked streets.

One day Neville captures a female vampire (Joanna Numata) and brings her home to test his recently developed anti-vampire vaccine. When the vaccine appears to fail, Neville revives the woman but keeps her in captivity for future tests. Soon he's ensnared in a trap similar to the one he designed for catching a vampire, and when he regains consciousness he finds himself hanging upside down. He manages to free himself, but vampires and vampire dogs attack him. His dog Sam fights off the vampires to save Neville's life, but Sam's injuries are so severe that Neville must put him out of his misery. Enraged, Neville drives off into the night to run down as many vampires as he can, only to crash and be surrounded by vampires. Suddenly he's rescued by two humans, Anna (Alice Braga) and her son Ethan (Charlie Tahan). The three go to Neville's home, where they face a massive assault by vampires. Just before they break through his defenses, Neville realizes that the female vampire he'd inoculated a day earlier has completely reverted to her human form. As the vampires storm the house, Neville gives Anna a vile of the transformed vampire's blood—now a potent anti-vampire serum—and helps her and her son escape through a tiny passage before he himself succumbs to the vampire onslaught.

The final scene depicts a rural setting in which a castle-like wall and an iron gate protect a tiny community of human survivors sealed off from the outside world like a colony of survivalists. Anna gives the life-saving vaccine to the leader as she proclaims:

In 2009, a deadly virus burned through our civilization, pushing humankind to the edge of extinction. Dr. Robert Neville dedicated his life to the discovery of a cure and the restoration of humanity. On September 9th, 2012, at approximately 8:49 p.m., he discovered that cure. And at 8:52, he gave his life to defend it. We are his legacy. This is his legend. Light up the darkness.

The plight of a tiny band of humans isolating itself from a hostile society may resonate with survivalists who perceive themselves as the besieged victims of a corrupt and tyrannical government. In fact, a vast majority of Americans express profound distrust of the role of government in contemporary society. A 2014 poll by the Pew Research Center revealed that only twenty four percent of Americans trusted their government, down from over seventy percent in 1960.[13]

I Am Legend symbolizes survivalist groups that expect to defend themselves from plagues, attacks by a corrupt U.S. government, or foreign invasion. During the Ebola epidemic of 2014, "survivalists" began preparations for pandemonium breaking out as the epidemic deepened. Their concerns were not only about contracting the disease but mostly about surviving attacks by desperate neighbors if government breaks down.[14] *Doomsday Preppers,* a television documentary series that has aired on National Geographic Channel since 2011, joins survivalist television shows *Doomsday Bunkers, Destination America's Armageddon Arsenals,* and *Animal Planet's Meet the Preppers.* Of these, *Doomsday Preppers* enjoys the greatest popularity, making it National Geographic's most successful series. One episode depicts survivalists building underground bunkers and stockpiling 5,000 pounds of food. To date, some three million Americans are said to qualify as "doomsday preppers." One prepper explained that "even if you're cosmically conscious, you'll still need to prepare for what it'll be like with no food or water."[15]

In the *Twilight* novels by Stephenie Meyer and the films by Catherine Hardwicke, vampires themselves transform into slayers. In the 2008 film that begins the series, the Cullen "family" of "good vampires" takes on the role of vampire slayer, killing rogue vampire James, part of a band of killer vampires that live off human blood. Seventeen-year-old Bella Swan has uniquely fragrant blood that inflames James, who also seems sexually obsessed with Edward Cullen. James captures Bella to force Edward to rescue her. In the ensuing fight, the entire Cullen family—working as a combat unit—dismembers and burns James, killing him and neutralizing his threat to Bella and Edward.

Daybreakers (2009), directed by Michael and Peter Spierig, also features "good" and "bad" vampires, while it depict slayers as a small, secretive, separatist guerrilla band. The movie is set in 2019, when vampires constitute ninety-five percent of all humans and unturned humans are a fragile, besieged minority on the verge of extinction. Vampires control society—but only at night. Ethan Hawke plays Dr. Edward Dalton, vampire hematologist at the Bromley Marks Corporation, who works tirelessly to invent a synthetic source of human blood to feed the vampires. In the meantime, Bromley Marks relies on a huge blood-harvesting chamber in which captive humans lie attached to tubes that drain their blood as soon as their bodies produce it. As the number of humans continues to dwindle and the world is populated with more and more vampires, food shortages force the vampires to feed on each other, and even on themselves. Those that feed on other vampires transform into "sub-siders"—degraded, monstrous creatures that threaten "normal" vampires and humans alike.

After an experimental synthetic blood substitute causes a vampire to explode at the Bromley lab, Dalton begins to doubt the wisdom and effectiveness of synthetic blood. He also realizes that with so few humans remaining, the species will soon go extinct. As he drives through the countryside he's distracted when he sees a reflection of his ear in the rearview mirror—though vampires like him cast no reflection. His momentary distraction causes him to crash into another car, and when he investigates a crossbow-wielding human emerges from the other vehicle and fires an arrow, cutting Dalton's wrist. Sirens sound in the distance, and Dalton gathers the humans from the other car into his own car and switches on a daytime protective device that renders them invisible from the outside. When the police arrive he misdirects them, and the humans thank him as they depart.

Later Audrey (Claudia Karvan), one of the humans he'd saved, surprises Dalton at his office when she jumps in front of him with a crossbow pointed at his heart. She tells him of a cure for vampirism developed by humans and offers to help him transform back to human form. He accepts, and she drives him deep into the woods to meet Elvis (Willem Dafoe), the leader of a small, intensely hunted group of humans. Elvis and Audrey drive Dalton to a secluded mountain cabin. Using the method Elvis had accidentally discovered to cure his own vampirism, little by little Dalton exposes himself to sunlight, transforming himself back into a human.

Elvis, Dalton, and Audrey return to Bromley Mark Corporation, where they encounter vampire Charles Bromley (Sam Neill). After Bromley is goaded into biting Dalton, he immediately transforms into a human. It turns out that cured human blood cures vampirism. The slayers shove Bromley outside, where hungry vampires, sensing his humanity, quickly bite and drain his body. But they, too, transform into humans, and other vampires bite them—and so on. The entire population experiences a rapid, dramatic transformation from vampire to human. Medical science, in this film, solves humanity's most vexing problems.

The vampire hunters in *Daybreakers* are rogues and rebels unwilling to conform to the surrounding vampire culture. In order to survive, they form a small, cooperative community reminiscent of a 1960s commune. But unlike 1960s commune dwellers, humans in this film appear strong, determined, and skillful with weapons. They also resemble contemporary survivalists who live in seclusion, rejecting society. The vampires these slayers encounter, like Charles Bromley, appear normal in public but act monstrously in private, as when Bromley vampirizes his own daughter, Alison (Isabel Lucas). These vampires symbolize society's corruption, and the slayers represent rugged individualists attempting to survive. This film pleased audiences, earning combined foreign and domestic ticket sales of $51 million with a production budget of only $20 million.[16]

In 2010 Marvel Comics redirected their popular X-Men franchise toward mutants versus vampires. In 2011 Marvel anthologized their vampire-slaying *Curse of the Mutants* episodes in a hardback edition. These episodes chronicle a war waged between vampires and mutants in San Francisco. Xarus, son of Dracula, vampirizes an army of thralls to conquer the X-Men and create a new breed of vampires. The X-Men battle various vampires, including a vampiric whale. Their science team works feverishly to find a cure for the blood-borne virus spread by Xarus. They enlist the aid of vampire slayer Blade and ask the unthinkable: can they resurrect Dracula himself, slain by Xarus, to combat his own son? Do they dare?

Timur Bekmambetov released *Abraham Lincoln: Vampire Hunter* in 2012, and his film became popular, especially overseas, where it garnered $79 million. The American box office revenue was nearly $38 million, giving the film combined earnings of $109 million on a production budget of $69 million.[17] The film arrived to mixed reviews, due in part to the slightly ludicrous plot featuring President Abraham Lincoln (Bryan Walker) as a young clerk and lawyer who becomes an axe-wielding vampire slayer at night. Lincoln turns to slaying after a failed attempt to kill vampire Jack Barts (Marton Csokas), who had murdered his parents. Vampire slayer Henry Sturges (Dominic Cooper) trains Lincoln in vampire-killing martial arts for a decade and then offers Lincoln the time-honored role of slayer in a world grown increasingly vulnerable to vampire attacks. Sturges tells Lincoln that vampires are on the verge of overwhelming humans and that humans alone possess the ability to destroy them, because "only the living can kill the dead."

After Lincoln becomes president in 1860, Confederate President Jefferson Davis (John Rothman) enlists vampires—controlled by master vampire

Adam (Rufus Sewell)—to combat the Union army. Vampires defend slavery because it provides easy access to human blood. Presumably, vampires find approval in the Confederacy if they limit their victims to slaves. Sturges urges Lincoln to fight the Civil War not for revenge but to end slavery and vampirism. "If vengeance is all you seek you will never be able to save mankind. Fight this war with me not for one man but for the whole world!" Ultimately Lincoln slays Adam and ends the vampire epidemic, but he refuses Sturges' offer to transform himself into a vampire so he can wage war against vampires forever. The following day he falls victim to John Wilkes Booth's attack at Ford's Theatre.

By depicting the Civil War as simply a struggle over slavery, *Abraham Lincoln: Vampire Hunter* oversimplifies the war's actual causes—including the differences and resulting competition between North and the South, the development of one-crop agriculture in the South, and the increasing wealth and power of Northern factories.[18] The film depicts Lincoln as a vehement lifelong opponent of slavery, yet prior to his presidency he was a more cautious critic. During one of his debates against Senator Stephen Douglass, Lincoln said, "I will say then that I am not, nor have I ever been in the favor of bringing about in any way the social and political equality of the white and black races.... There must be a position of superior and inferior, and I ... am in favor of having the superior position assigned to the white race."[19] The necessities of war helped persuade Lincoln to sign the Emancipation Proclamation.

Seth Grahame-Smith, scriptwriter for *Abraham Lincoln: Vampire Slayer*, noted that he decided on Abraham Lincoln as his slayer because of the power of his personal story. "The man's life is a nineteenth-century superhero story. He comes from nothing, has no education, no money, lives in the middle of nowhere on the frontier. And despite the fact that he suffers one tragedy and one setback after another, through sheer force of will, he becomes something extraordinary: not only the president but the person who almost single-handedly united the country."[20] This story of rising from obscurity and overcoming formidable obstacles along the way is a variation on the popular "rags to riches" master narrative.

Slaying vampires currently enjoys renewed popularity, and a number of websites and books instruct novices in the fine art of killing vampires. The *Darkstalkers* series of video games (1994–2013) trains humans to fight against vampire antagonists. *The Vampire Combat Club* website lists several defenses against attacks, including shotguns, knives, swords, stakes, garlic, and teaming up with other human slayers to destroy vampires. In 2012 the website began offering a book—*The Vampire Combat Manual*—for serious vampire slayers. This book is also available in bookstores and directly from the publisher.[21]

Effective vampire slayers first appeared in literature in 1872, in *Carmilla*, and today their popularity seems destined to grow even more. By the mid-twentieth century, slayers had gradually transformed from aristocratic European males to professionals like psychologist Dr. Jeffrey Garth in *Dracula's Daughter*, 1936 and physician Dr. Robert Morgan in *The Last Man on Earth* (1964). These slayers seem more realistic than the Romantic era's aristocrats. By 1992 pop culture had abandoned upper-class male slayers, substituting middle-class females like Buffy. Before this, a high school cheerleader wouldn't have come to mind as an ideal slayer, but Buffy's strength as a character derives from her humble origins and the fact that she's female. Writer Josh Whedon created Buffy explicitly to counter the stereotyped female virgin as victim.

Like many contemporary vampire slayers, Buffy functions as a highly trained team member. This development began with *Dracula's Daughter* (1936) and includes *The Lost Boys* (1987), *From Dusk Till Dawn* (1996), *Daybreakers* (2009), and *X-Men* (2010–2011). These films symbolize the value of human cooperation in solving seemingly intractable problems. Slayers like Buffy, Blade, Robert Neville, and Blood come in a variety of ethnicities and genders, reflecting an increasingly diverse world. Finally, they represent all age categories, from grandparents to schoolgirls. The 2012 inauguration of Abraham Lincoln as a lifelong vampire slayer brought the slayer metaphor full circle, from white European aristocrat to an American president. *Abraham Lincoln: Vampire Slayer* marks a turning point in vampire slayers and allows a more aggressive, contemporary action-hero image for our sixteenth president, who tops the list of most popular American presidents alongside Ronald Reagan and John F. Kennedy.[22]

At one level, slayers symbolize rites of passage from adolescence to adulthood, and a growing number spring from the ranks of teenagers. Although youthful audiences, which identify with both vampires and slayers, have been purchasing fewer movie tickets since 2013, they have increased movie viewing on other formats.[23] Slayers provide metaphoric remedies against the hazing and bullying often experienced by today's young people. In 2008 researchers found that at least twenty percent of Americans between the ages of two and eighteen have reported at least one instance of bullying.[24] A 2001 Kaiser Foundation survey found that a significant majority of adolescents identified bullying as the most serious problem they faced—far more than the dangers of drugs, alcohol, racism, or concerns about sex.[25] Teenage vampire slayers strike back against their oppressors, symbolic substitutes for human bullies. To today's audiences, vampire slayers right contemporary injustices along with ancient wrongs.

Vampire slayers also epitomize vigilantes fighting crime directly, without assistance from established police or military forces. The standard dictionary definition of a vigilante is "a person who is not a police officer but who tries to catch and punish criminals." A vigilante may be "a member of a volunteer committee organized to suppress and punish crime summarily (as when the processes of law are viewed as inadequate); *broadly*: a self-appointed doer of justice."[26] Slayers have all of the attributes of vigilantes, including the often-unstated idea that traditional law enforcement is valueless in the face of a super-powerful vampire. Criminologist David Weisburd notes the powerful role vigilantism often plays in pop culture and American justice, including vigilantism in the Old West, nativist and racist outbreaks in the American South, and armed neighborhood watch groups in large cities.[27] Freed from the legal constraints that restrict all law enforcement agencies, vampire slayers become pure "outlaw heroes."

Folklore professor Graham Seal says, "Outlaw heroes arise in historical circumstances in which one or more social, cultural, ethnic, or religious groups believe themselves to be oppressed and unjustly treated by one or more other groups who wield greater power." He also observes, "The oppressed group often has a fear—not necessarily made explicit—that its sense of identity, as coded into its traditions, customs, and worldview, is being outraged, ignored, or otherwise threatened."[28] Vampire slayers represent outlaw heroes by definition, forced to take the law into their own hands in order to save themselves and/or the rest of humanity. Slayers represent the fears of citizens that the government's administration of the law codes has failed to keep them safe, so they must avail themselves of outlaw slayers willing to take extralegal action to secure society.

Ultimately, slayers merge their roles as saviors with the roles of the vampires they oppose. That often means undergoing vampirization—voluntarily or involuntarily—to assume the superpowers necessary to defeat and kill vampires. The danger lies in identifying too closely with their antagonists, so that "good" and "evil" blur. As nineteenth-century philosopher Friedrich Nietzsche observed, "Whoever fights monsters should see to it that in the process he does not become a monster. And if you gaze long enough into an abyss, the abyss will gaze back into you."[29] Today, fighting monsters may involve everything from modern warfare to psychoanalysis. Victory often goes to those who adapt the wisdom, strategy, and power of the terrors confronting them. Slayers merge with their prey, just as victims invite their own fate.

SEVEN

Narratives

Vampire characters function as complex and varied metaphors. In pop culture, these metaphors serve as "master narratives" that provide guidance and information about society's most sensitive and controversial cultural issues. The vampire trope may symbolically reference everything from sexuality and gender issues to authority and aggression.

Lexicographers define metaphors as figures of speech comparing two different but somehow related words. The word "metaphor" derives from a Greek word meaning to "transfer."[1] Metaphors often become so commonplace that we fail to recognize them, as in this United Airlines advertisement: "Life is a journey, travel it well." This metaphor is so familiar that it has become a trite cliché. Other examples of the "life is a journey" metaphor include having "arrived" at a particular certain stage in life, life taking a particular "direction," "setting out" on an adventure, arriving at a "crossroads," finding one's "destination," "crossing a bridge" between careers, events taking an "unexpected direction," having to "move on" in life, and someone "passing away" at death.[2]

Metaphors safely code such sensitive issues as drug abuse, crime, paternalism, and life crises. Vampire metaphors also code messages about racism, sexuality, gender, aggression, immigration, crime, combat, disease, energy, and law enforcement. In addition to providing escapist entertainment, vampires invite us to explore symbolic responses to real-world problems. Author Sara Libby Robinson observes that through the nineteenth and early twentieth centuries, "Western culture frequently expressed its political ideologies through blood-related metaphors," including vampire metaphors. "In order to demonize Jews," she writes, "the Church had associated them with vampire-like acts such as the blood libel accusation. Later, anti-clericals depicted the Church itself as a vampire in order to characterize it as ignorant, backwards, and superstitious." Robinson further notes that anti-capitalists associate profit-making businesses with blood-draining vampires, while pro-capitalists label anarchists and labor organizers as vampires. In response to the female emancipation movement, "journalists and novelists frequently invoked a selfish, vampiric woman that kills men and children instead of nurturing them."[3] English professor Teresa Goddu notes that today's vampires embody "the shift from the nineteenth century's ghostly intimate to the twentieth century's power hungry predator."[4]

Vampires inhabit a hybridized, symbolic zone affording a wealth of metaphoric possibilities and inspiring an infinite variety of fictional characters. As supernatural beings, they evoke gods, goddesses, ghosts, demons, and other spirits. When human-like, they embody the entire range of human behavior, including positive and negative emotions, sexuality, gender roles, family, love, violence, and aggression. They also represent controversial issues and events. *Newsweek* writer Jennie Yabroff observes, "Depending on whom you ask, vampire stories can be read as symbols of venereal disease, capitalism, immigration, industrialization, colonialism, AIDS, homosexuality, mental illness, and anti–Semitism, technology or class warfare."[5] Vampire metaphors never remain stable in pop culture but transform over time, reflecting changing socio/political concerns, issues, and fads. When they appeared in nineteenth-century popular culture, they evoked that era's anxieties (immigration, feminism, sexual predation). The vampire is capable of embodying so many complex issues because it is one of the classic figures of the menacing, foreign "Other" in Western culture. Says author Anne Rice, "I always thought of the vampire as being a metaphor for the outsider in each of us, the criminal, the predator. I was writing about a mythical being that represented our own dark sides."[6] Today, the "Other" includes rapists, corporate raiders, corrupt politicians, psychopathic criminals, rogue intelligence agents, foreign and domestic terrorists, atheists, Communists, and undocumented aliens.

Mythological Origins

Turkish mythology is what originally inspired our vampire obsession. Though rare in other parts of Europe and Asia, reports of vampirism arose in the Ottoman Empire in the late seventeenth century and remain common in some regions even today. In Ottoman mythology, "cadi" were revenants who preyed on the living. They functioned as vampires and served as prototypes for later Euopean and American vampire characters. However, cadi include not only vampires but also ghosts and witches, whereas in other parts of Europe and in the U.S., mythological demons were classified as vampires based solely on their proclivity to prey on humans for their blood.[7]

The Ottoman wars in Eastern Europe—from the fourteenth century until World War I—resulted in European lands being absorbed by the Empire. Vampire myths began to spread into Europe. In 1872 author Sheridan Le Fanu noted in *Carmilla*, "You have heard, no doubt, of the appalling superstition that prevails in Upper and Lower Syria, in Moravia, Silesia, in Turkish Serbia, in Poland, even in Russia; the superstition, so we must call it, of the vampire."[8] The lands indicated by Le Fanu formed the borders of the Ottoman Empire at that time.

Human Origins

Surprisingly, the lives of just three extraordinary human beings from the sixteenth through the nineteenth centuries provided the inspiration for today's vampires. Their dramatic, often shocking actions scandalized contemporaries and gave rise to an ever-evolving array of fictional vampire characters and paranormal narratives.

Prince Vlad Dracul (1393–1447)—also known as Vlad the Impaler and Vlad Tepes—was the inspiration for countless vampire characters. Prince of Wallachia, a province of modern Romania, Vlad the Impaler is considered by scholars to be Bram Stoker's chief model for Count Dracula. Dracul battled Ottoman armies and spent his early years as a captive in what is now Turkey, where he probably encountered vampire mythology. Ottoman lore provides a key to his controversial behavior in war and peace. Tepes was a "viovode," or prince, of the House of Basarab in Wallachia.[9] Stoker's fictional count shares the name Dracula with him, and Stoker's description of his vampire approximates historical descriptions of Prince Vlad Tepes. Many details in Stoker's novel stem from Tepes legends, including drinking human blood (Vlad dipped his bread in blood). Staking vampires through the heart may originate with Tepes' infamous terror tactic of impaling victims on large wooden stakes; thousands died slow and agonizing deaths this way. Tepes' remarkable penchant for torturing small insects and animals inspired Stoker's Renfield character, who tortures and swallows flies, spiders, and rats.[10]

Hungarian Countess Elizabeth Bathory (1560–1614) reputedly murdered more than six hundred young women in order to bathe in their blood. The countess, like her distant kinsman Vlad Dracul, fought Ottoman forces intent on conquering her lands. However, her blood fixation and sadism took a different form than Dracul's. For her violent crimes, Countess Bathory earned the title "Blood Countess," and she served as the inspiration for Le Fanu's

Carmilla (1872) featuring vampiric Countess Carmilla. The similarities between Countess Bathory and Countess Carmilla begin with their physical description. Both stood tall and presented an elegant appearance, "their hair exquisitely long and black, eyes large and full of mystery, sensual and small mouths, hands long as needles and white skin." Carmilla's governess Darvulia seems strikingly similar to Countess Bathory's assistant Dorottya Szentes. The real Countess Bathory and the fictional Countess Carmilla illustrate the ironic connections between reality and fiction.

Lord George Gordon Byron (1788–1824), the gifted and flamboyant Romantic poet, inspired and co-created the first handsome, aristocratic "rake" vampire, the template for a long line of seductive vampires that followed. In real life Lord Byron achieved fame as one of the most active seducers of both men and women in history. Like Tepes and Bathory, Byron waged war against the Ottoman Turks, where he first encountered vampire mythology. His military training began in 1823 when he joined with Greek patriots fighting for independence from the Ottoman Empire. Lord Byron contracted a virus and died after only three months as a combatant.[11]

Each of these vampire-like humans has become associated with a distinctive subgenre. Vlad Tepes inspires tales of monstrous Nosferatu-type vampires, while Countess Bathory models female vamp characters. Lord Byron provides inspiration for suave, wealthy, seemingly youthful "Byronic" vampires who entice victims with promises of pleasure, then drain and eventually destroy them.

Sixteenth-century Hungarian Countess Elizabeth Bathory (Anna Friel) relaxes in a bath of blood drawn from virginal females in *Bathory* (2008). The real Countess Bathory was convicted of murdering and torturing hundreds of young women and bathing in their blood in search of eternal youth (Kobal Collection at Art Resource, New York).

Psychological Origins

According to psychologists, mythology originates in the unconscious and springs from humanity's "dark side." Sigmund Freud postulated a "censorship role" for the unconscious that systematically transforms disturbing images into "dream images." Dream images symbolize sensitive, taboo materials rather than depict them realistically. Freud notes, "In consequence of the severity of the censorship of dreams, the latent dream-thoughts are obliged to submit to being altered and softened so as to make the forbidden meaning of the dream unrecognizable." He identified "taboos" as explosive or politically incorrect issues and postulated that the "magical power that is attributed to taboo is based on the capacity for arousing temptation." Vampires, with their aura of mystery and subliminal sexual allure, arise from the unconscious and epitomize Freud's "monsters from the id."[12]

Writer Nancy Dougherty explains pop culture's attraction to vampires by evoking materialism. "Our already exploitative materialism has the power to trick us into seeing everyone and everybody as 'other.'" She adds that "vampire motifs challenge us to "come to terms with these energies."[13] Since vampires prey on individuals they can easily symbolize capitalists preying on humanity. German philosopher Karl Marx famously observed: "Capital is dead labour, that, vampire-like, only lives by sucking living labour, and lives the more, the more labour it sucks. The time during which the labourer works, is the time during which the capitalist consumes the labour-power he has purchased of him."[14]

Dartmouth psychologist Paul Whalen observes that vivid pop culture narratives, including vampire stories, serve as coded references to traumatic events such as the 9/11 terrorist attacks, recessions, and natural disasters. Such disturbing events continuously stimulate the amygdala—a region of the brain associated with emotions—to seek out and discover new coping strategies. Pop culture creates standard "master narratives" that assist us in managing our fears and anxieties as we feature ourselves engaged in fictionalized behavior.[15]

Master Narratives

Pop culture weaves vampire metaphors into standard plots or "master narratives"—fictional stories that audiences experience imaginatively. Audiences perceive themselves in similar experiences and settings, coping with similar problems and identifying with the characters. Heroes engage in epic journeys, experience adrenaline-saturated adventures, overcome obstacles and challenges, find true love, and obtain enlightenment—each of these a master narrative. They are often seen as "formulas" or "scripts" that we use when we tell stories. They embody our expectations about how things work. Typically, they're based on actual experience.

These "metanarratives" present a series of interrelated stories that form a pattern or model.[16] Vampire mythology references narratives of struggle, seduction, sin, violence, predation, and salvation. French philosopher Jean-François Lyotard observed that master narratives allow individuals to code their own experiences into coherent stories that help explain and interpret disturbing events.[17] These narratives are ubiquitous and often appear patently true. Violent conflicts between individuals and groups constitute one of the most prevalent master narratives. People tend to assume the truth of master narratives because their many exposures in pop culture render them seemingly obvious and fundamental.[18]

The Garden of Eden story in the third chapter of the Bible's book of Genesis serves as a familiar master narrative depicting seduction, betrayal, guilt, and retribution. Like Coleridge's Christabel, Le Fanu's Laura, Stoker's Lucy and Mina, and Rice's Lestat, humanity fails to resist the allure of the dark side and is seduced, abandoned, and evicted from a lush garden home. This master narrative—sometimes coded as a tale of vampire seduction— remains a staple of pop culture. Often called "the Fall," or "the fall from grace," it speaks to humanity's corruption and eventual redemption. In Anne Rice's *Interview with the Vampire* the vampire Armand tells the vampire Lestat, "You are the spirit of the age." Exclaims Lestat, "I'm not the spirit of any age. I have never belonged with anyone at any time." Armand retorts, "But Louis … this is the very spirit of your age. Don't you see that? Everyone feels as you do. Your fall from grace and faith has been the fall of the century."[19]

Seduction

Vampire seducers of both sexes challenged Victorian "family values," and they continue to challenge neo-Victorianism. The sexuality they symbolize often proves too sensitive for more direct depiction. Male seducers of females remain one of the most popular narratives. Lord Byron's romantic and extravagant life—alternating creative bursts of productivity with numerous seductions and jealousies—influences contemporary vampire characters, including *Twilight*'s romantic hero Edward Cullen (Robert Pattinson) and *True Blood*'s Bill Compton (Stephen Moyer). Brooding, misunderstood protagonists like these, possessed of superpowers and immortality, are titillating and provocative. The five movies in the *Twilight* series cost just $418 million to produce, yet they grossed an astonishing $4.7 billion worldwide.[20] The extraordinary profitability of these films, earning more than eight hundred percent of production budgets, testifies to the continuing popularity of seductive vampires.

Younger audiences especially seem to enjoy sexual vampires. Chris Noland's musical *I Kissed a Vampire* (2012) developed from a series of YouTube videos into a popular low-budget motion picture. It stars Lucas Graybeel as Dylan, an emotional, moody teenager who's vampirized by an attractive exchange student named Sara (Adrian Slade). After his slow transformation into being a vampire, his initial love for Sara turns to bloodlust—and whenever he attempts to kiss her, his fangs protrude like two erect penises. At this point an older vampire with a coven of sexy females, Trey Sylvania (Drew Seeley), appears to instruct Dylan on vampire lifestyle while also seducing Sara. Dr. Dan Helsing (Chris Coppola), a scientist working on a cure for vampirism, attempts to cure Dylan, but Trey whisks them all to his remote castle, where his female thralls keep Dylan busy while Trey seduces Sara. This narrative resonates with that of Byronic seducers who also bond with other males, providing undertones of homosexuality. *I Kissed a Vampire* glorifies Goth culture, demonizes mainstream society as boring and ineffectual, and supports LGBT gender identity.

Female vampires—vamps—project personas that are charming, cultivated, and seductive. Vamps may seduce men as well as women; in either case, they exhibit assertiveness and independence from paternalism. Unlike human females, who face social pressures to present asexual facades, female vampires routinely display ravenous appetites for both blood and sex, thereby violating the taboo that renders women submissive, subservient sex partners. Author and educator Pamela Madsen finds female enjoyment of sexuality still so taboo that most women focus exclusively on satisfying male sexual appetites while minimizing or ignoring their own desires. As a result, "We have created a culture of women 'doers' as opposed to giving permission for women to simply receive."[21] Licentious, aggressive, self-confident female vampires, however, model a more feminist lifestyle, and the growing popularity of these characters reflects deep changes in public opinion regarding gender roles. Despite growing acceptance in pop culture, however, a recent study showed that a majority of females—regardless of their own sexual histories—reject friendship with "promiscuous" women who admit to having had twenty or more sexual partners. By contrast, men are more accepting of promiscuous males.[22]

Gender

Vampires symbolize a wide variety of gender roles, including heterosexual patriarchs, feminists, and LGBTs. By their very nature, vampires conform to the definition of "Byronic" or "outlaw" heroes. English professor Atara Stein explains, "The Byronic hero is a figure of autonomy, self-reliance, defiance, and power, and he is an outlaw who lives by his own moral code." Byronic vampires "successfully act on their desires to defy authority and can successfully confront obstacles in their path. They do not have to bow to institutional power or to oppressive forces, for they have both the supernatural abilities and the attitude required to fight them. At the same time, they validate their audience's own doubts and fears and sorrows."[23]

LGBT sexual orientations figure prominently, though symbolically, in vampire narratives, mirroring today's pan-gendered society. Some pop culture vampires continue to reflect heterosexism, patriarchy, and homophobia, however, and LGBT orientations remain controversial. Psychologists Phillip L. Hammack and Bertram J. Cohler examine two competing master narratives:

> Once relegated to hidden gathering places, demonized as deviants, pathologized as mentally ill, and even considered threats to national security in the USA, same-sex attracted individuals can now live beyond the shadows of shame and stigma. In some countries, such as Canada and Spain, same-sex attracted individuals are accorded the full rights of citizenship and may even receive full legal recognition through the right to marry someone of the same sex.[24]

In the United States, the right to marry someone of the same gender became the law of the land after the U.S. Supreme Court decision in 2015. Both modalities in the gender wars appear in recent vampire pop culture. The British film *Lesbian Vampire Killers* (2009) demonizes lesbians, in the view of feminist Milly Shaw.[25] But we must acknowledge that other recent lesbian vampire films—*Life Blood* (2009) and *Byzantium* (2012), for example—clearly project powerful females and strong feminist perspectives. Even in campy spoofs such as *Lesbian Vampire Killers*, Carmilla-type vampires, by the threats they pose to men, exemplify feminist master narratives.

Discrepancies in how pop culture treats gender reflect what many consider a contemporary crisis in feminism. Historian Stephanie Coontz observed in 2013, "The gender revolution is not in a stall. It has hit a wall."[26] But there's evidence of a gradual loosening of the past's strict gender expectations. Gender stereotypes for America's youth currently appear less rigid than in the past, though they remain powerful and pervasive in popular culture. And the changes in recent decades seem more dramatic for women than for men.[27]

Even when vampire metaphors avoid LGBT issues, they often appear within a patriarchal, heterosexist zeitgeist. English scholar Jolene Zigarovich observes that today's pop culture narratives "often revolve around male crusaders 'saving' females from the sexual liberation and corruption the vampire invites, and conclude with the reassertion of traditional gender roles through the violent destruction of the threat."[28] In popular series like *Twilight* and *True Blood,* these male crusaders transform into "good vampires" saving humans and hybrids from narcissistic "bad vampires."

Today patriarchy comingles with feminism in pop culture. Early episodes of *Twilight* feature male vampires protecting a frail human schoolgirl, with Edward Cullen and his "uncle" Carlyle Cullen re-enacting traditional paternal roles. But Bella Swan, heroine of Stephenie Meyer's novels and the film adaptations, appeals to many feminists. In later episodes she transforms into a full-fledged vampire, able to best werewolves and vampires in hand-to-hand combat—even possessing the ability to shatter solid rock with her fists. Reviewer Kate Muir found herself impressed with Swan's new power in the 2012 installment, *The Twilight Saga: Breaking Dawn–Part 2.* "Bella slams werewolves into trees, arm-wrestles the Cullen clan into submission, karate chops rocks, and bites the throat of a mountain lion without staining her blue silk dress," she says. "At this point, the final film in five, Stewart's character Bella has become an unlikely feminine, even feminist icon, a depressed teen that turns action heroine by the end of the series." Muir speculates, "Clearly the action adventuress torn between two lovers is the ultimate formula for the new female franchise."[29]

Along with other LGBT identities, male homosexuality frequently appears symbolically in vampire literature and films, as writer Amanda M. Podonsky observes. Mirroring societal fears and distaste toward homosexuality, "the count embodies the concept of the 'abnormal' mingling among a 'normal' society."[30] When Dracula's wives attempt to seduce Jonathan Harker in Stoker's novel, the count flies into a rage and snarls jealously, "How dare you touch him, any of you? How dare you cast eyes on him when I have forbidden it! Back, I tell you all! This man belongs to me! Beware how you meddle with him, or you'll have to deal with me!"[31] Harker faints and then awakens in his bed, having been bitten, drained of some blood, undressed, and put to bed by Count Dracula. The obvious homosexual references, occurring metaphorically, escaped Victorian censors. Homosexuality threatened Victorian society. Anti-homosexuality laws resulted in the imprisonment of playwright Oscar Wilde in 1896, one year before Stoker published *Dracula.*

Eventually pop culture's vampires displayed a more permissive perspective on LGBT. Decades ago, Joel Schumacher's cult classic *The Lost Boys* (1987) was one of the first mainstream films to reflect a strongly homoerotic element. Pop culture now depicts many positive, symbolic LGBT vampires. *The Brotherhood* (2001–2008), a made-for-television series of six films, relies on a barely concealed homoerotic plot. In the films, "pretty boy" fraternity men practice a form of sadomasochistic vampirism that goes beyond drinking each other's blood and emphasizes male bonding.

Critic Stephen Marche believes the current vampire craze symbolizes something much larger than homosexuality, namely "a quiet but profound sexual revolution and a new acceptance of freakiness in mainstream American life." Positive LGBT vampires "have appeared to help America process its newfound acceptance of what so many once thought strange or abnormal."[32] This acceptance of diversity also shows in recent dramatic changes in public opinion regarding same-sex marriage. While only thirty-five percent of Americans said they supported it in 2003, by 2013 fifty percent expressed a favorable opinion of same-sex marriage. That ranks as one of the most rapid changes on any social issue in history.[33] And in today's pop culture, both women and men may play victim, aggressor, and slayer roles. Their genders no longer place limits on their actions.[34]

Ethnic Narratives

Dracula, an aristocrat, springs from the Caucasian race. Classic vampires were members of the aristocracy, belonging to close-knit, powerful organizations and conforming to upper-class social and ethnic roles. They are fallen aristocrats, likened by some to fallen angels like the Bible's Satan.[35] By contrast, today's vampires and slayers derive from diverse racial, ethnic, and socio/economic groups. Theater arts professor Kevin Wetmore notes, "Despite the vampire renaissance of the past thirty years, the romantic aristocrat is gone."[36] Today's diverse vampires reflect the racial, ethnic, and gender mixes currently seen in the United States. The white, European, upper-class vampires of Victorian England have evolved into male and female Asians, African Americans, Jewish, Hispanics, and adolescents, more accurately reflecting contemporary audience demographics.

During the Civil Rights era in the U.S., the film *Blacula* (1972) replaced European Count Dracula with the African prince Manuwalde (William Marshall). This "superhero with an attitude" reflected the era's acceptance of African Americans in leading movie roles, though continuing to show negative racial stereotypes. A racist Dracula himself dooms Blacula to eternity for daring to fight back against the count's fang attack: "You shall pay, black prince. I shall place a curse of suffering on you that will doom you to a living hell. I curse you with my name. You shall be … Blacula!" As a vampire, Blacula proves especially deadly, attacking and killing a growing number of California citizens. Because of the "superstud" stereotypical behavior depicted, critics labeled *Blacula* and its successor *Scream, Blacula, Scream* (1973) as "Blaxploitation." However exploitive it may have been at the time, *Blacula* proved popular enough to pioneer the way for later roles such as Wesley Snipes as the title character in the *Blade* series (1998–2004) and Will Smith's interpretation of vampire slayer Robert Neville in *I Am Legend* (2007).[37] African Americans also play other prominent roles as vampires, including Grace Jones as a sexy vampire in *Vamp* (1986); Eddie Murphy as Maxmillian, a vampire searching for his soulmate in *Vampire in Brooklyn* (1995); and Akasha (Aaliya), the original vampire queen in *Queen of the Damned* (2003).

Chris Nahon's *Blood: The Last Vampire* (2009) exemplifies contemporary vampire diversity. Nahon's film stars Gianna Jun as Saya, who seems to be a sixteen-year-old Asian girl but actually is four hundred years old, a human/vampire hybrid called a "Halfling." She sits on the Council, a centuries-old covert organization that identifies and then destroys vampires threatening military as well as civilian authorities in contemporary Japan. Like Buffy, Saya employs martial arts, including her finely honed samurai skills, to slay dangerous, out-of-control vampires. She may be the most unlikely of a host of diverse vampire hunters and slayers, with her girlish looks and clothing, yet no one matches her samurai skills—even Onigen (Koyuki), the original maternal vampire. In a Buffy-like reversal from what many in the audience expect, the frail-looking Saya overpowers and kills the muscular Onigen, underscoring female power.

Religious Narratives

While vampires and their slayers once reflected a strictly Christian, predominately Catholic perspective, often symbolizing Biblical characters such as Satan and Jesus Christ, more recent creations channel Buddha, bodhisattvas, and even Mormon presidential candidate Mitt Romney. Fictional vampires now include Jews, to whom Christian symbols like crucifixes pose little threat, while Buddhist vampires wield advanced martial arts skills. In a 2008 survey, American Christians expressed increased tolerance for Jews, Muslims, and Buddhists.[38] Since then, however, Pew Research Center opinion polls have revealed rising religious intolerance.[39] As society secularizes, it appears to grow less religiously tolerant. And although vampires no longer become weak and powerless in the face of a Christian crucifix, they increasingly suffer from existentialist angst, focusing inwardly on their own salvation instead of mere blood consumption.

Although modern vampires exist in a secularized world, they bear remnants of their former religious connections. In fact, vampire mythology owes a huge debt to Christianity. The "Vampire Trinity" of vampire/victim/slayer parodies the Father/Son/Holy Spirit Trinity of Christianity. Vampires retain the structure of Christianity in their ceremonial blood-drinking (*Blade, True Blood, and Twilight*). By symbolically drinking Jesus' blood and eating his flesh during the sacrament of Communion, many Christians believe they die and are reborn as immortals. Like God, vampires bestow the gift of eternal life upon their followers. And finally, blood is a prominent symbol in many Christian hymns, such as "Are You Washed in the Blood?," "Jesus Thy Blood and Righteousness," "Nothing but the Blood," "Saved by the Blood," "The Blood-Washed Throng," "The Blood-Washed Pilgrim," "There Is a Fountain Filled with Blood," and "There Is Power in the Blood."

It should come as little surprise that vampires, drenched in religious iconography, often assume godlike powers. For an increasing number of cultists, vampires comprise the only real gods in existence. Today there are Goth-oriented churches that transform Christian Communion ceremonies into celebrations of vampirism.[40] Contemporary vampires possess immortality and other godlike qualities, while at the same time they exude sin and epitomize evil. Their perennial popularity reflects continued interest in those attributes, which often fall within the religious domain.

Family Narratives

Pop culture's vampires provide potent family narratives, until recently featuring aberrant, dysfunctional families. Sheridan Le Fanu's *Carmilla* demonstrates the fragility of family values. The lesbianism of Carmilla and Laura became associated with the Victorian New Woman—independent-minded suffragettes much feared by conservative Victorians. Despite or because of this fear, Carmilla was unsettling, and her sexuality and symbolic vampirism threatened Victorian family structure and solidarity, sexualizing the normal process of youth differentiating from their parents. Carmilla's contemporary descendants also reflect rapidly evolving postmodern family structures. As critic Trudi Van Dyke observes, "The New-Woman-like vampires in Carmilla and Dracula embody the most notorious traits associated with the Victorian New Woman, alleged sexual aggression or deviancy, and a quest for autonomy that signaled the usurpation of male power."[41]

Popular culture vampires often inhabit postmodern families that deviate sharply from the traditional "family values" model popularized in mid to late twentieth-century America. In the decades following World War II, American families transformed from large extended families into smaller units that usually included only one adult generation. Recent decades have witnessed the reversal of this trend. More families now consist of two adult generations plus children, as many adult children are still living with their parents. This has happened because of the economic pressures caused by the Great Recession as well as increased longevity.[42]

Currently a minority of Americans cling to the traditional nuclear family model, whereas the fastest-growing sector of society consists of singles, cohabitating adults, gay and lesbian couples, transgender couples, mixed-race couples, and countless other relationships that some label "postmodern." By 2012, households consisting of single individuals had risen to forty percent or higher in Atlanta, Denver, Seattle, San Francisco, and Minneapolis. In Manhattan and Washington, D.C., singles constituted nearly half of all households.[43]

Current vampire families deviate from traditional family patterns while symbolically violating social taboos. In the *Twilight* series, individual vampire family members aren't actually related to each other but choose to live in an amalgamated "blended family" under the leadership of Dr. Carlyle Cullen (Stregone Benefico), who assumes a traditional patriarchal role. This household more closely reflects today's blended, postmodern families than the toxic predatory vampire family depicted in Stephen King's *Sleepwalkers* (1992), and it further paved the way for today's heroic lesbian vampires (*Byzantium*, 2012). *Twilight's* rogue vampires, James and Victoria, behave far differently than the "humanitarian" Cullen family. "Rogue vampires" symbolize the predatory, nomadic lifestyles associated with biker gangs, white supremacist organizations, survivalists, and other fringe groups. The superpowers wielded by these vampires symbolize the seriousness of the threats they pose to humanity.

Invasion Narratives

Dracula and many of his imitators originate in Europe, emigrate to England or the U.S., and attack the local inhabitants—sometimes planning humanity's total annihilation. They represent widespread fears of immigration. Creators of vampire metaphors symbolically appeal to popular prejudices by depicting vampires as aggressive, devious, alien agents threatening to inundate humanity. Bram Stoker's *Dracula* (1897) references concerns about massive legal immigration to England at the end of the nineteenth century. Dracula and his minions threaten the destruction of British civilization, while at this same time the British Empire was expanding and colonizing many other regions. The novel plays on anxieties about Britain competing against other colonial empires—the Japanese, Americans, Germans, and Spanish. H.G. Wells' classic science-fiction novel *War of the Worlds* arrived the same year as *Dracula* and also presents a cautionary tale about foreign threats to Great Britain. While Stoker saw the threat as emanating from personal relationships, Wells viewed it as a military conflict between Martians and the British. In Wells' novel, the aliens symbolize unwanted Eastern European immigration. Both novels, still popular more than a century later, are testament to the emotional power of immigration.

In 2011 Vincent Lannoo released *Vampires*, a low-budget documentary about a supposedly real vampire family in Belgium, the Saint-Germains. The family vampirizes illegal immigrants to Belgium that are delivered to their door by a local business. When Grace Saint-Germaine's father commands her to eat, she says, "No, we've been eating Blacks for three weeks now!" In the United States, real vampires are said to feed on illegal immigrants crossing the border from Mexico. Individuals attempting to enter New Mexico have related stories of vampire attacks, and Border Patrol officers noted that immigrants were terrified after supposedly witnessing a vampire drag two people into the surrounding hills. The attacks are said to have occurred in eastern Otero County, an area known as the *Journado del Muerto*, or "Journey of Death," because of its harsh terrain.[44]

Violence Narratives

Nosferatu-type violent vampires resonate in today's society. In 2013 sixty-six percent of Americans reported a lack of trust in others, up from fifty percent in 1972.[45] Vampires reference master narratives of personal violence as survival strategies, symbolizing humanity's "dark side" of raw aggression, greed, and lust. Murderous, voracious vampires threaten humanity with complete annihilation—Armand Tesla in *The Return of the Vampire* (1944); Jan Valek in *Vampires* (1998); Marlow in *30 Days of Night* (2007); James and Victoria in *Twilight* (2008–2012); and Adam in *Abraham Lincoln: Vampire Hunter* (2012). These characters prey voraciously on humanity and practice sadistic cruelty to achieve their ends. Armand Tesla relies on potent hypnotic abilities that override victims' wills and force them to sacrifice themselves to Tesla and his thralls, while Valek uses super strength to mutilate and destroy a seasoned band of vampire hunters. In *Twilight,* James and Victoria brazenly attack and kill humans, while Marlow in *30 Days of Night* leads a band of voracious vampires who hunt down and murder nearly all of the citizens in Barrow, Alaska. Adam in *Abraham Lincoln: Vampire Hunter* even recruits vampires to defend slavery by serving in the Confederate Army during the Battle of Gettysburg, where thousands of Union soldiers are slaughtered. These characters represent fears about human cruelty, duplicity, and predation, and they reflect a growing sense that we may not be able to trust our fellow humans.

Pop culture vampires often function as metaphoric criminal gangs and syndicates, closely resembling public images of organized crime. They appear during periods of high anxiety about violence. From 1994 through 1998, Americans pointed to crime as the nation's most serious and pressing problem, and from 1999 through 2001 they identified it as the second or third most serious issue.[46] During the 1990s, *Buffy the Vampire Slayer* (1992) battled vampire cells, *Innocent Blood* (1992) depicted vampires as mobsters, *Bordello of Blood* (1998) showed vampires operating prostitution rings, and *Vampires* (1998) presented them as clandestine terrorists. Despite public perception about the threat posed by criminals, actual violent crimes declined significantly during the decade, a trend that continues today. The violent crime rates for 2012 had declined significantly (twelve percent) from those of 2003.[47]

Organized crime, with its strict code of loyalty and its hierarchical structure, bears a striking resemblance to vampire "families" and "broods." These organizations behave with astonishing unity, controlled by a cruel and dictatorial master vampire functioning much like a mob boss. Today's vampires may symbolize drug cartels, motorcycle gangs, and ethnic-based mobs. In *Innocent Blood,* gangster/vampire characters merge as vampires take over an urban crime mob in a comedy film. In the *Blade* series (1998–2002), the scenario is less comedic as the Dragonetti mob symbolizes an old-style Mafia-type organization. Franchises such as *Twilight* and *True Blood* depict vampire families as gangs. Pop culture instantly demonizes gangs and other criminal syndicates. According to communications professor John M. Sloop, media typically depict accused criminals as "animalistic and senseless" and possessing "warped personalities," ignoring mitigating factors of poverty, race, and family.[48] Many of popular culture's vampires symbolize these personality stereotypes. A few, including those in *Daybreakers* (2009), *Twilight* (2008–2012), and *True Blood* (2008–2013), reflect diversity, individuality, and a degree of humanity—thereby enriching their metaphoric potential.

Dangerous, savage Nosferatu-type vampires also symbolize domestic terrorists. Vampire king Russell Edgington (Denis Ohare) of *True Blood* brutally slays a television news anchor, prompting American Vampire Association spokesperson Nan Flanagan (Jessica Ines Tuck) to blast him as "an extremist and a terrorist." But Flanagan reminds viewers "that's not because he is a vampire. It is because he's an extremist and a terrorist." Simply being a vampire does not automatically qualify one as a terrorist.

Until recently vampires died at narrative's end, only to be reborn through their thralls. Their tenacity underlines deep-seated pessimism about society's ability to eradicate terrorism and other forms of violence. When vampires behave like criminals and terrorists, killing them on sight becomes the only possible solution. Their pursuit, capture, and summary execution by slayers parallels the current U.S. policy of assassinating suspected international terrorists with unmanned Predator drones and black op raids. Approval of direct assassination of suspected terrorists—such as Osama bin Laden in 2011—finds expression in the savage, brutal slaying of vampires by slayers.

Law Enforcement Narratives

Slayers protect humans and often enforce an ancient code of justice. Vampire slayers symbolize social justice, and as law enforcers they refuse to abide by any legal or moral restrictions on their actions. The slayer narrative contrasts with the established law enforcement model in which police officers investigate crime scenes, identify suspects, and jail them, leaving the criminal justice system to either convict or acquit. Vampire slayers function as vigilante enforcers, empowered to attack on sight and murder vampires by decapitating them, driving wooden stakes through their hearts, or exposing them to sunlight. *Dracula* slayer Abraham Van Helsing attacks Count Dracula and his thrall Lucy Westenra with vampire-hunter tools.

The vigilante metaphor applies to all vampire slayers, from Van Helsing to Abraham Lincoln to Buffy. They all function like outlaw heroes from other genres, such as Robin Hood, Dirty Harry, John Rambo, Batman, Superman, and X-Men. They confront and destroy terroristic threats to domestic security while reaffirming conventional values of honor, justice, patriotism, strength, heroism, shrewdness, cunning, and fierceness in battle. Philosopher and author Scott LaBarge explains, "We need heroes first and foremost because our heroes help define the limits of our aspirations. We largely define our ideals by the heroes we choose, and our ideals—things like courage, honor, and justice—largely define us."[49]

Like the earliest models for vampires—Prince Vlad the Impaler, Countess Elizabeth Bathory, and Lord Byron—the earliest slayers claim an elite lineage, with titles like Baron, General, doctor, and professor. They frequently possess scientific and technological expertise. Slayers amass vast knowledge of vampire lore to use against the undead. They symbolize a blend of Romanticism and scientific thinking, as if the Enlightenment had joined forces with the Romantic Movement. In the twentieth century, vampire slaying evolved into a specialized craft open to physicians, psychiatrists, martial artists, military commandos, vampire/human hybrids, and even high school cheerleaders, many of them having superpowers as well as humanistic values. Modern slayers come from every social strata, ethnicity, and age. Slayers like Buffy, Blade, and recent versions of Van Helsing rely on a blend of technology, physical abilities, and inherited superpowers.

When vampire hunters succeed in getting rid of dangerous criminals—saving humanity in the process—vicarious relief may be experienced by audiences deeply concerned about economic recession, global terrorism, nuclear meltdowns, global climate change, catastrophic storms, earthquakes, and pandemics. Slayers reflect a deep desire to suspend civil and human rights and simply hunt down and assassinate suspected criminals. No slayer thinks of reading vampires their Miranda rights, nor does he or she challenge an antagonist to a duel at high noon on Main Street. Instead, slayers use every trick in the book—including dirty ones—to outwit and eliminate their prey.

Vampire slayers form part of a larger group of mythological heroes who slay dragons and other monsters. Monster-slayers rid a community of threats to its existence while reinforcing values like courage, strength, intelligence, and advanced knowledge. Van Helsing and his successors (Buffy, Blood, Blade, and so on) reference a mythology of godlike beings assigned to protect humanity. Sometimes referred to as guardians, or guardian angels, these beings provide divine assistance to humans under attack by supernatural forces. In vampire mythology, ancient orders combat each other, in the process symbolizing the main components of the human psyche—including the id, from which vampires originate, and superego, the protector/controller that confronts lawless elements.

Warrior Narratives

By their very nature, vampires often evoke warrior narratives. Battles pitting vampires and their thralls against an array of slayers symbolize military forces engaged in deadly combat. Recent films and videos adapt vampire mythology to World War II-era themes. In movies such as *Blood-*

rayne: The Third Reich (2010), *Fangs of War* (2014), and *The Bloody* (2014), Nazis transform into vampires, and vice versa, to threaten the U.S. and its World War II allies. In 2011 the popular comic book series *American Vampires* issued a five-volume miniseries titled *American Vampire: Survival of the Fittest.* The series features vampire hunters operating behind Nazi lines in Romania, where they work with a secret organization seeking a cure for vampirism.

War functions as a common cultural metaphor—as in the war on poverty, war on drugs, war on gangs, gender wars, and class warfare. Vampire wars against humans began in Bram Stoker's *Dracula* with Count Dracula threatening Abraham Van Helsing and his slayer assistants: "Your girls that you all love are mine already; and through them you and others shall yet be mine." Later Dracula flees England on the ship *Czarina Catherine* (Catherine the Great), named after the Russian noblewoman notorious for her promiscuity. Dracula's threat and his choice of getaway ships implies a fear that female sexuality, if allowed to run amok, will result in humanity's destruction.

In pop culture, vampires wage war against werewolves or lycans in the *Underworld* and *Twilight* series and against rival vampire groups in the *True Blood* TV series; the *Twilight, Daybreakers, Live Evil, The Dead Undead,* and *Blade 2* movies; and the novel *The Saga of Darren Shan* by Darren O'Shaughnessy. They combat witches in season four of *True Blood*, and a vampire organization known as the Red Council combats the White Council of Witches in *The Dresden Files* novels. Teenage Mutant Ninja Turtles combat vampires in their television show *Ninja Turtles: The Next Mutation* (the "Unchain My Heart" episode, 1998) as well as the comic book.

The "vampires as warriors" metaphor calls to mind the role of combat in the legends and deeds of Vlad the Impaler, Countess Elizabeth Bathory, and Lord Byron. At different times in history, each battled the forces of the Ottoman Empire—the most important source of vampire mythology. While Bathory and Byron were famous (or infamous) in part as seducers, Vlad remains better known for his savage but effective combat roles. Warrior vampires embody humanity's aggressive and warlike traits, providing pop culture consumers with abundant martial narratives. Although a few vampire narratives depict war between vampires and werewolves, vampires and zombies, or vampires and humans (*Daybreakers, Twilight, Abraham Lincoln: Vampire Hunter, Vampires vs. Zombies*), most portray smaller battles between vampires and slayers. Smaller battles distance audiences from mass warfare, paralleling U.S. unmanned drone attacks on foreign terrorists.

Disease Narratives

Vampires can symbolize disease, epidemics, and plagues. Writer Katherine Ramsland coined the term "Renfield Syndrome" after one of Dracula's thralls in Bram Stoker's *Dracula,* referring to a compulsion to drink blood. This malady is also called "clinical vampirism."[50] In seventeenth and eighteenth-century Poland, the fear of vampires grew overwhelming as people began dying of cholera, a previously unknown disease. To prevent the deceased from reanimating in their graves, Poles sometimes buried them with sickles across their necks so they'd be decapitated if they moved in their coffins.[51]

Stoker's *Dracula* references Victorian fears of venereal disease, especially syphilis. At that time many believed that blood, like semen, transmitted human genetic material, so any blood mixing indirectly referenced sexuality, emphasizing the risks involved. In Stoker's novel, vampires are associated with rats, symbolic of plague. The deadly plague known as the Black Death infected and killed an estimated 50 million people in Europe, 1.5 million of them in England alone, between 1348 and 1350.[52] More recently, fear of pandemics rose in 1918 when influenza swept through Europe and the United States. Few today realize the destructive power of this outbreak. Whereas World War I resulted in 16 million deaths, the 1918 flu pandemic killed upwards of 50 million in Europe and the U.S., dwarfing World War I casualties.[53]

In F. W. Murnau's *Nosferatu* (1922), Count Orlok (Max Schreck) sleeps in a coffin filled with dirt infected with bubonic plague. Murnau's classic—the first true vampire film—connected anxiety about paranormal characters such as vampires with the fear of pandemics. Vampirism continued to symbolize plagues well into the twentieth century. In her short story "Master of Rampling Gate" (1984), Anne Rice blames the fourteenth-century bubonic plague pandemic on vampirization.

Films in the apocalyptic genre include *The Last Man on Earth* (1964), *The Andromeda Strain* (1971), *Outbreak* (1995), *Twelve Monkeys* (1995), *I Am Legend* (2007), *28 Days Later* (2002), and *28 Weeks Later* (2007). Both *The Last Man on Earth* and *I Am Legend* are based on Robert Matheson's 1954 novel *I Am Legend,* about a pandemic that turns humans into vampires who drink human blood and act like mindless zombies. The zombified vampires serve as metaphors for fears about both drug addiction and pandemics. These two movies share many elements with *28 Days Later* and *28 Weeks Later.* Each depicts a world under siege by biological agents that threaten the entire earth. All these films speak to fears such as the polio outbreaks in the 1950s and 1960s, HIV, H1N1 (swine flu), and the use of chemical and biological weapons by terrorist groups.

Addiction Narratives

One popular master narrative concerns "people who do not have control over their substance abuse" and for whom substance abuse becomes "the organized principle of their lives," as described by Norwegian social sciences professor Hanne Thommesen.[54] This cautionary narrative blames substance abuse on the victims' immoral, lax, and undisciplined lives. Many pop culture vampires qualify as symbolic substance abusers, due to their intense craving for human blood. This blood lust corresponds to drug, alcohol, sex, or power addiction. Films such as *The Hunger* (1983), *The Addiction* (1995), and *The Thirst* (2006) revolve around addiction metaphors, prompting *Time* critic Richard Corliss to coin the term "junkie vampires."[55]

Energy Narratives

Energy wasters—"energy vampires"—today find themselves besieged by power companies and the U.S. Department of Energy. The use of vampires to symbolize energy-wasting electrical appliances illustrates the remarkable utility of the vampire metaphor. Once associated with perceived threats from mass immigration or sexual predators, vampires now symbolize everything from high-watt conventional light bulbs and appliances left plugged in to tiresome acquaintances who drain vital energy—*i.e.*, the psychic vampire. The latter is said to employ invisible tendrils to extract human energy and/or sexuality. In such narratives, people produce powerful, supernatural energy within their bodies, and psychic vampires feed from this energy. Initially they may charm their victims. Only later, when victims feel drained, tired, and irritable, do some begin to suspect their friends or neighbors of vampirism. Psychic vampires prey on invisible, sexual, orgiastic energy that closely resembles the philosophical concepts of life force, *joie de vivre*, soul, and psyche. Psychologist Joe H. Slate warns, "Psychic vampirism is a widespread yet often unrecognized human energy phenomenon that can interrupt and impede progress." He advises that "steps need to be taken to avoid psychic vampire predation," including "mastering the empowerment strategies" needed to overcome it.[56]

Do humans possess invisible energy fields? Theorists posit a seven-layered aura or invisible energy field surrounding every human body and brain. This field may extend for a few feet from the physical body, much like the earth's layered atmosphere.[57] Some label this "New Age" hyperbole and doubt its validity. Author Robert Todd Carroll maintains in *The Skeptic's Dic-*

tionary, "New Age energy isn't measurable by any validated scientific instrument. Instead, quack New Age energy machines claim to do everything from aligning your cell vibrations to reading the digital frequencies of allergens to curing your cancer."[58] We need not commit to a belief in the physical existence of human energy fields to understand them as metaphors. Anything or anyone sapping one's energies may receive a vampire label, even if the victim doesn't believe in vampires. Energy vampires speak to ongoing concerns about the availability and cost of energy supplies—from gas and oil to electricity and solar power—as well as, metaphorically, physical and spiritual health and vitality.

Psychic or "psi" vampires effectively reduce vampire metaphors to their simplest terms. They don't need to seduce, attack, and drain victims, relying instead on subtle invisible mechanisms to rob them of their vitality. They become almost pure symbols for a wide variety of contemporary issues, from energy supplies to physical, mental, sexual, and psychological health and well-being. In fact, anything that's in high demand, especially if it's one of life's necessities, is subject to ethereal forms of vampirism.

Lifestyle Narratives

During the recent Great Recession, pop culture favored metaphors of loss. Humans drained of blood by vampires are ideal symbols for economic misery and hardships. Science writer David DiSalvo observes that the horror we appreciate most tends to mirror what's going on in our lives. "But the vampire is the monster for all seasons. When we're hurting they offer a way out, and when we're feeling good they offer excitement. They're the ultimate manifestation of power and terror, a combination that's as enduring as emotion itself."[59]

Vampires created by writers Anne Rice, Stephenie Meyer, and Charlaine Harris display the human emotions of protectiveness, compassion, and even love. Harris chose to change vampire feeding habits. She hit on the idea of having them drink synthetic blood. Vampires would say, "Oh no, we're not dangerous. We drink synthetic blood. We don't want to grab you and bite you. And people could believe that because people are gullible."[60] Rice's Louis de Ponte du Lac and Lestat de Lioncourt, along with more recent vampires like Edward Cullen in *Twilight*, exude sensitivity and emotionalism. Rice self-identifies with Lestat, who enjoys seducing human victims and reinvents himself when circumstances demand. "I was never a domesticator of the vampire," she says.[61] Other complex vampire characters include Spike from *Buffy the Vampire Slayer* and Stefan from *The Vampire Diaries*. Sensitive, emotional, and increasingly human vampires inspired Grady Hendrix of *Slate* magazine to complain, "Vampires suck. Actually, they don't, and that's the problem."[62] Many, like Hendrix, prefer the traditional narratives of warring, aggressive vampires.

The current explosion of interest in expanding human longevity and curing humanity's most vexatious afflictions forms part of the appeal of immortal vampires. Interest in immortality soared after scholars revealed that the average human lifespan had doubled during the past century. At the same time, interest in vampires has never been greater. The growing popularity of vampires and other immortals may stem in part from the allure of medical science's efforts to expand the human lifespan. Media coverage of such endeavors spiked after Google—one of the world's richest and most technologically innovative corporations—announced the formation of a new company named Calico dedicated to human lifespan expansion. CEO Arthur Levinson—also chairman of Apple's board of directors and former chairman and CEO for biotech giant Genentech—announced an ambitious company mandate: "to try to cheat death."[63]

Ironically, it now turns out that transfusions of blood from the young into the bodies of the old actually may reverse some of the physical and mental effects of aging. Two scientific studies published in 2014 revealed that when young mouse blood was injected into old mice, the aged mice appeared to become young again. They developed darker hair, more supple muscle tissues, and increased blood circulation to the brain. In addition, their senses—including their olfactory organs—were rejuvenated and became more youthful.[64] No study currently exists to show the effects of ingesting youthful blood orally, but the miraculous effects of youthful blood transfused into older subjects gives vampire metaphors greater scientific cogency. It also suggests that Countess Bathory's attempts to derive youth from the blood of youth may have had a scientific basis!

The vampires that have inspired the current craze represent a dramatic shift from previous undead characters. No longer strictly carnivores, today's vampires often control their diet by using synthetic or animal blood, the way many humans do by eating local, organic foods. Researchers have learned through study of South American vampire bats that a blood-based diet changes animals' taste buds. Vampire bats no longer have the ability to distinguish sweet, sour, and other non-blood foods. Their own taste buds demand a blood-only diet.[65]

Contemporary pop culture vampires increasingly live openly with humans and "come out of the coffin"—like those in *True Blood*—to walk about in daylight, immune to garlic and crosses. As vampires' powers have increased, their slayers' powers also have expanded. Today both slayers and vampires are represented as supernatural, godlike beings.

Vampires provide the stimulus for "Goth culture," a recent cultural movement emphasizing black clothing, Christian symbolism, the occult, death obsession, alienation, and depression. Traits of today's Goth movement include facial hair for men, tattoos, and self-mutilization. Goth devotees have included mass murderers Eric Harris and Dylan Klebold (Columbine High School massacre) and Adam Lanza (Sandy Hook School shooting), along with rock stars Marilyn Manson, Van Halen, and Ozzy Osbourne. Violent song lyrics often seem designed as much to shock outsiders as to titillate Goth adherents.[66] By the early 1970s, Gothic had become a distinctive subgenre of rock music, and a distinctive vampire subculture had developed. Members "generally dress in exotic vampire-like attire, decorate their homes in a dark Victorian gloom, and even wear prosthetic fangs and colored contacts. Some … will don white face makeup, dark eye shadows, and black nail polish to create a more gothic appearance," according to the Vampire Underworld website.[67]

The pairing of Gothic with vampires first occurred during the Romantic era (late eighteenth to mid-nineteenth centuries). The Romantics' penchant for gloomy atmosphere, darkly mysterious clothing, and violent lifestyles virtually demanded the creation of vampires. In the subterranean, subconscious world of the imagination, vampires reign like dark princes of human fears and anxieties. Armed with superpowers and immortality, they pose existential threats to humans while offering eternal life and other rewards. Their complexities evoke nature, Romanticism, and the generative power of the human unconscious.

Romantic Narratives

As children of the Romantic era, rapacious and monstrous vampires inhabit deliciously dark subterranean worlds of forests, caves, tunnels, dungeons, and cellars, complete with spiders, bats, and rats. These icy-cold, dripping, and foggy domains provide suitably Romantic backdrops for the clash between reason and emotion. Vampires inhabit mythological lands that bear a surprising resemblance to Greece's Tartarus, Rome's Hades, and the Maya's Xibalba—shadow-filled dystopias deep beneath the earth, representing the dark side of existence. Such places symbolize human unconsciousness, populated by phantasmagoric creatures engaged in bizarre, often violent or erotic behavior. These creatures represent raw human emotions, and the atmospheric settings for their actions seem far more appropriate than sunnier, more sterile, modernist environments.

Vampires inhabit a distinctly anti-rational domain as embodiments of the libido, not the superego. But they coexist with slayers and other inhabitants of the rational world of science, mathematics, and logical reasoning. In fact, vampires and their slayers constitute a metaphorical dyad, a continuum between supernaturalism and science. Stoker's Dr. Van Helsing and a host of slayer knock-offs combat vampires through a combination of pseudoscience and esoteric vampire lore. Van Helsing relies on medical instruments to give Mina Harker a blood transfusion, and he also relies on a prototype of the Dictaphone to record his notes and thoughts. However, his use of mirrors to ascertain if an individual casts a shadow (no shadow indicates vampirism), as well as his reliance on sunlight, holy water, Communion wafers, garlic, and wolfsbane, reveals the extra-scientific nature of vampire slaying.

Recent scholarship suggests that the dichotomy between Romanticism and science may have been over-imagined and overstated. Observes English professor Jennifer J. Baker, "Though scientific methods threatened to demystify nature, to reduce it to mere matter, they also promised to reveal the handiwork of a divine intelligence and the universal laws at work in the natural world." Baker says that a science/Romanticism hybrid became popular during the first half of the nineteenth century, only to dissipate during the latter half of the century. She suggests that during the Romantic era, science and mythology merged into a Romantic science that functioned well enough during this period, with inchoate scientific methods and incomplete understanding of scientific rationalism.[68]

In the twenty-first century, new scientific discoveries are finding their way into vampire narratives. Dr. Christine Knight, a nutrition researcher at Edinburgh University, explains, "Technological changes such as stem cell derived blood or in vitro meat, created in the lab, have influenced the representation of vampires."[69]

By the time Bram Stoker wrote *Dracula*, on the eve of the twentieth century, Romantic science was no longer dominant; science and emotion represented two very different approaches to reality. Stoker's Van Helsing laments, "Ah, it is the fault of our science that it wants to explain all; and if it explains not, then it says there is nothing to explain."[70] The issue of primacy between science/logic and mythology/emotions continues to vex researchers. In 2012, scientists Glenn Begley and Lee Ellis reported that they were able to replicate only six out of fifty-three "landmark" cancer studies. Presumably, the forty-seven studies that couldn't be replicated suffered from significant theoretical and methodological errors. Political scientist Michael Suk-Young Chwe postulates, "A major root of the crisis is selective use of data.... Psychologists refer to this as 'confirmation bias.' We seek out information that confirms what we already believe."[71] Does this mean that the majority of recently published cancer scholarship is invalid? At least this shocking study should raise skepticism about the validity of some scientific studies.

Climate Narratives

Since vampires exist by draining humans of blood, they make excellent metaphors for fears about flooding, drought, and other climatic and geological catastrophes. Since blood and water are both vital to human life, one liquid easily symbolizes the other. Sucking blood can represent draining water from the land. Belief in vampires' effect on climate dates back at least to the end of the nineteenth century, and in 1898 many people believed that vampires actively produced drought conditions by "milking" the clouds dry of water.[72] Throughout history, vampires have been blamed for crop blights as well as droughts.[73]

Vampires also symbolize floods—as in floods of human blood spilled. In 2001 the fourth television season of *Buffy the Vampire Slayer* was titled "Flooded." As Buffy attempts to repair a broken water pipe in her bathroom, it breaks, causing a flood and a high repair bill. Like a flood, demons seem to flow throughout the season as Buffy survives relentless attacks. Author Stephenie Meyer set her *Twilight* series in the nation's rainiest town—Forks, Washington. The rain falls perennially in Forks (population 3,221), totaling more than 120 inches per year. Residents of the real town of Forks report that tourists who flock to the Cullen House restaurant in search of *Twilight* settings love the frequent rain, because it provides just the right atmosphere for their beloved fictional vampires.[74]

Rain and other forms of precipitation frequently appear in film noir, forming a recognizable dark, moody aura. As in film noir, rain is a powerful symbol in vampire mythology, literally dampening any mood, spewing forth from dark, nimbus clouds. Standing water reflects human faces and bodies, symbolizing self-reflection. As if nature is mimicking vampires, atmospheric disturbances coincide with vampire appearances. When Count Dracula's driverless carriage arrives to pick up Jonathan Harker, it is accompanied by thunderclaps and fierce winds. In religious mythologies, Zeus sent a flood to destroy the men of the Bronze Age, and the rain that brought about the Biblical flood symbolized God's wrath. The Hopi creator god Sotuknang caused a great flood with torrential rain and high waves, which the Hopi people survived by floating on reeds.[75]

Conclusion

Kevin Wetmore, author of *Post-9/11 Horror in American Cinema*, observes that after the terrorist attacks of 2001, vampire pop culture divided into two major streams. The first is a continuation of an older cultural model, often called "Byronic vampires." Vampires in this tradition, including recent examples Edward Cullen in *Twilight* and Bill Compton in *True Blood*, symbolize "the sensitive, lonely lost outsider, still romanticized but updated to contemporary culture." They represent "the children of Anne Rice, descended through Buffy and her boyfriend Angel, coping with teen angst by occasionally draining blood. These vampires are simply trying to survive in a world that occasionally tries to kill them." Another, more threatening stream is typified by "the angry, violent vampire who is obviously a different being." Wetmore concludes, "These vampires have no intention of fitting in."[76] The two dramatically different perspectives remind us of the current striking bifurcation in American society around a variety of social and political issues.

Vampires symbolize a variety of social classes, from lower-class, back-alley midnight assailants to upper-class "illuminati" that secretly rule the earth. Today's vampires and slayers no longer spring exclusively from the ranks of the aristocracy. Instead, they rise from mostly middle-class or upper-middle-class origins, like Dr. Carlyle Cullen and the Cullen family in *Twilight*; research scientist Edward Dalton in *Daybreakers*; and Civil War major Bill Compton in *True Blood*. Few of today's vampires have aristocratic titles or speak with foreign accents.

Over time, vampires and slayers have become younger and more diverse—in both gender and ethnicity—widening their symbolic appeal. Pop culture's vampires now include African Americans, Asians, Europeans, Hispanics, Jews, gays, lesbians, bisexuals, and transgenders. The older European/American male vampire has largely disappeared. Today's vampires include youthful-looking examples such as Blade (*Blade*), Selene (*Underworld*), and the characters of *True Blood*. This diversity led writer Nicole Myoshi Rabin to conclude that today's pop culture vampires represent "a symbol of multiracial identity as it is seen within the multicultural discourse that pervades American popular consciousness."[77]

In comparison with earlier eras, today's pop culture consumers demand that vampires and slayers become superheroes while combating and defeating supervillains in brutal conflicts, with humanity's survival often hanging precariously in the balance. The post–9/11 "world of fear" created what critics now call "a cinema of terror," resulting in graphic violence that depicts bleeding, stabbing, piercing, and dismembering. In their book *Horror after 9/11*, Aviva Briefel and Sam J. Miller suggest that after the terrorist attacks of 2001 and during the war on terror that followed, the horror genre became a "rare protected space" in which to decode the hidden dimensions of public discourse. Vampire mythology creates "universes where the fundamental rules of our own reality no longer apply—the dead do not stay dead, skyscraper-sized monsters crawl out of the Hudson River, vampires fall in love with humans—these products of popular culture allow us to examine ... the entire Western way of life."[78]

Threats from terrorists, both foreign and domestic, increasingly become coded as vampire attacks. Writers Travis Sutton and Terry M. Benshoff speculate that post–9/11 vampires like *Twilight's* Edward Cullen not only reference fears of terrorism but also the rebirth of fundamentalist religious values. Pop culture responded to the events of 9/11 and the war on terror with protector vampires possessed of immortality and superpowers.[79] As vampires became more threatening to the social order, slayers became more resourceful and ruthless. The growing polarization in pop culture vampires reflects an increasingly polarized populace, and a deeply divided electorate. Political scientist Alan I. Abramowitz argues that "the roots of polarization are in our changing society—and above all the growing racial and ethnic diversity of the American population." Rapidly increasing racial diversity alarms white Americans, who may view minorities with fear and suspicion, he says. When whites react by attempting to suppress minority rights, minorities also become polarized.[80]

As Americans focus on terrorist attacks and struggle to recover from the most severe economic crisis since the Great Depression, they also face pandemics, identity theft, a growing LGBT population, gay marriage, and other significant social changes. To cope with the anxieties and fears generated by these changes, many are seeking comfort and distraction in vampires. Writer Erin Collopy says that vampires enjoy great popularity today "because they are such an effective metaphor for our own anxieties and desires." He concludes, "We often try to work things out about ourselves through them."[81]

Gender continues to drive many vampire narratives. Charlaine Harris, author of the Sookie Stackhouse novels that inspired the *True Blood* series, reveals that she intended her novels to evoke the struggle for gay rights. "When I began framing how I was going to represent the vampires, it suddenly occurred to me that it would be interesting if they were a minority that was trying to get equal rights."[82] Vampires, with their propensity to suck blood from members of diverse genders, serve as natural and popular vehicles for symbolic LGBT characters.

Vampires also showcase shifting sexual boundaries and sexual mores. While human men and women with robust sexual appetites may be labeled as deviants, vampires allow pop culture to depict seducers and nontraditional sexuality relatively free of censorship. Vampires can symbolize recreational sex, sexual predation, and sex addiction, in addition to alcohol and drug addiction. On the other hand, they illustrate the enduring role of violence and bloodshed and the predatory nature of contemporary society. In a world where "violence is as American as apple pie," as 1960s activist H. Rap Brown put it, the reasons for the enduring popularity of vampires become clear. Vampires embody our obsession with sex, violence, power, and material consumption as well as our growing distrust of fellow humans.

Psychologist Carl Jung postulated that humans possess a "shadow side," a hidden aspect of personality consisting of primitive, negative, and socially or religiously deprecated human emotions and impulses such as sexual lust, power striving, selfishness, greed, envy, anger, or rage. He wrote, "It is a frightening thought that man also has a shadow side to him, consisting not just of little weaknesses and foibles, but of a positively demonic dynamism."[83]

The power of vampire metaphors resides in their ability to illumine the dark and mysterious reaches of the unconscious mind, the source of all creativity. In one hidden corner we encounter vampires as alluring and attractive seducers that tempt and lure not-so-innocent victims. Human literary characters continue inviting these seducers into their homes, like Coleridge's Christabel, Le Fanu's Laura, Stoker's Mina Harker, and Meyer's Bella. These victims suffer from vampire attacks, yet each secretly craves the deep intimacy promised by vampires. In another mental corner, we encounter diverse gender roles rendered symbolically through vampire metaphors. Contemporary vampires challenge paternalistic gender stereotypes, including aggressive, assertive males and passive, submissive females within traditional nuclear families.

In yet another corner of the mind we meet savage vampires symbolizing not love but violence and aggression. Sigmund Freud theorized about two basic human drives in conflict with each other. Eros represents humanity's sexual nature, its tendency toward survival, propagation, creativity, and "life instincts." Ego, the reverse of Eros, also goes by the name of Thantos. Its purpose is "to lead organic life back into the inanimate state."[84] Freud viewed life as "opposition between the ego or death instincts and the sexual or life instincts."[85] Vampires symbolize both of these instincts. When needs arise, humans may commit unspeakable acts of violence against each other and against harmless creatures crossing their paths. The same drives that let humans slaughter and consume animals for food and clothing come into play at times of danger, when the emphasis shifts to self-defense and survival. Then we may transform imaginatively into savage, Nosferatu vampires—or into equally bloodthirsty vampire slayers.

Through pop culture's vampires, humanity retains and reinvents legends of vivid historical personages such as Vlad the Impaler, Countess Elizabeth Bathory, and Lord Byron. These real people exemplify the extremes of human behavior regarding sex, gender, and aggression. When we encounter the vampires they have inspired, we may experience a twinge of recognition as well as guilt. As the cartoon hero Pogo once reported, "We have met the enemy … and he is us."[86]

Chapter Notes

Preface

1. Percy Shelley, "A Defence of Poetry," written 1821, first published 1840; Charles W. Eliot, *The Harvard Classics*. New York: P.F. Collier & Son, 1909–14.

2. Tim Delaney, "Pop Culture: An Overview," *Philosophy Now,* Issue 64, November/December 2007.

3. Morton W. Bloomfield, *The Seven Deadly Sins: An Introduction to the History of a Religious Concept*. East Lansing: Michigan State College Press, 1952, 214–215.

Chapter One

1. *The American Heritage Dictionary of the English Language*, Fourth Edition. Boston: Houghton Mifflin, 2009.

2. Friedrich Nietzsche, *Thus Spake Zarathustra*, 1885. Project Guttenberg translation by Thomas Common, 1998, University of Adelaide, *Ebooks@Adelaide*, Dec. 12, 2014.

3. Ewen Callaway, "How Vampires Evolved to Live on Blood Alone," *New Scientist,* Oct. 2008.

4. Paul P. Jesep, *The Vampire Benning Wentworth and the End of Times*. Createspace 2013.

5. Jeff Wise, *Extreme Fear: The Science of Your Mind in Danger*. Basingstoke, UK: Palgrave Macmillan Trade, 2009.

6. Sigmund Freud, *The Ego and the Id,* ed. James Strachey. New York: Norton, 1962.

7. Anne Stuart, "Legends of Seductive Elegance" in *Dangerous Men and Adventurous Women*, ed. Jayne Ann Krentz. Philadelphia: University of Pennsylvania Press, 1992.

8. James Weaver and Ronald Tamborini, "Frightening Entertainment: A Historical Perspective of Fictional Horror," in *Horror Films: Current Research on Audience Preferences and Reactions,* ed. J. Weaver and R. Tamborini. Mahwah, NJ: Lawrence Erlbaum Associates, 1996, 1–13.

9. H. P. Lovecraft, "Supernatural Horror in Literature," *The Recluse,* 1927, in E. F. Bleirer, ed., *Supernatural Horror in Literature*. New York: Dover, 1973, 11–106.

10. Stephen King, "Why We Crave Horror Movies," *Playboy,* Jan. 1981.

11. Devendra Varma, *The Gothic Flame: Being a History of the Gothic Novel in England: Its Origins, Efflorescence, Disintegration, and Residuary Influences*. London: Arthur Barker, Ltd., 1957.

12. Aristotle, *The Basic Works of Aristotle*, ed. Richard McKeon. New York: Modern Library, 2001, 1458.

13. Angela Connolly, "Psychoanalytic Theory in Times of Terror," *Journal of Analytic Psychology* 48, no. 4, Sept. 2003, 407.

14. Peter S. Goodman, "Economists Say Movie Violence Might Temper the Real Thing," *New York Times,* Jan. 7, 2008.

15. Hal MacDermot, "Top Horror Movie Directors Discuss Art and Impact of Their Movies," *QuietEarth.Us,* March 8, 2009. http://www.quietearth.us/articles/2009/03/08/Top-horror-movie-directors-discuss-art-and-impact-of-their-movies.

16. Douglas S. Winnail, "How the Media Mold the World," *Tomorrow's World* 5, no. 1, Jan-Feb 2003.

17. Alain Silver and James Ursini, *The Vampire Film: From Nosferatu to Bram Stoker's Dracula*. New York: Limelight Editions, 1993, 18.

18. Benjamin Radford, "The Real Science and History of Vampires," *Live Science*, Nov. 30, 2009. http://www.livescience.com/5924-real-science-history-vampires.html.

19. Beverley Richardson, "Eighteenth Century Vampire Controversy," *Vampires in Myth and History*, 2014. www.thingsthatgoboo.com/monsters/vamphistory18thcentury.htm.

20. Allan Johnson, "Modernity and Anxiety in Bram Stoker's *Dracula*," in *Critical Insights: Dracula*, ed. Jack Lynch. Hackensack, NJ: Salem Press, 2009.

21. Nina Auerbach and David Skal, eds., *Dracula*, Norton Critical Editions. New York: Norton, 1996, Preface.

22. Sarah L. Peters, "Repulsive to Romantic: The Evolution of Bram Stoker's *Dracula*," *Academic Forum*, 2002–2003, no. 20, Henderson State University. http://www.hsu.edu/academicforum/2002–2003/2002–3AFRepulsive%20to%20Romantic.pdf.

23. Aristotle, *Rhetoric*, trans. by George A. Kennedy. Cedar Lake, MI: ReadaClassic.com, 2010.

24. José Ortega y Gasset, "Taboo and Metaphor," in *The Dehumanization of Art and Notes on the Novel*. Princeton: Princeton University Press, 1948.

25. Lindsay Bradshaw, "Blood Thirsty: Why Are Vampires Ruling Pop Culture Today?" *Texas Tech Today*, July 2, 2012.

26. Simon Pascal Klein, "A Critical Examination of Gender Roles Within Goth Subculture," *Kle·Pis*, Aug. 11, 2009, klepas.org. http://klepas.org/a-critical-examination-of-gender-relations-within-goth-subculture/.

27. Michael Quirk, "Vampire Fangs Dentistry Is a Real Thing, Apparently," *Dental Products Report*, July 30, 2013. http://www.dentalproductsreport.com/dental/article/vampire-fang-dentistry-real-thing-apparently.

28. George Lakoff and Mark Johnson, *Metaphors We Live By*. Chicago: University of Chicago Press, 2003, 4.

29. Stephen T. Asma, *On Monsters: An Unnatural History of Our Worst Fears*. New York: Oxford University Press, 2009, 14.

30. Margot Adler, "For Love of Do-Good Vampires: A Bloody Booklist," National Public Radio, Feb. 18, 2010. www.npr.org/templates/story/story.php?storyId=123115545.

31. Peter Day, ed., *Vampires: Myths and Metaphors of Enduring Evil*. Amsterdam: Rodopi, 2006, xiv.

32. Nina Auerbach, *Our Vampires: Ourselves*. Chicago: University of Chicago Press, 1997, 4.

33. Jennie Yabroff, "Vampires Everywhere," *Newsweek*, December 5, 2008. http://www.newsweek.com/vampires-everywhere-83275.

34. Barbara Ehrenreich, *Blood Rites: Origins and History of the Passions of War*. New York: Henry Holt, 1997, 61.

35. Joan Gordon and Veronica Hollinger, "Introduction: The Shape of Vampires," in *Blood Read: The Vampire as Metaphor in Contemporary Culture*, ed. Joan Gordon and Veronica Hollinger. Philadelphia: University of Pennsylvania Press, 1997.

36. David Starr Jordan, "The Blood of the Nation: A Study of the Decay of Races," *Popular Science Monthly*, May 1901, in Angela Lahr, "Preaching Eugenics: Religious Leaders and the American Eugenics Movement," *Indiana Magazine of History* 102, No. 1, March 2006.

37. "Red Cross to Use Blood of Negroes," *New York Times*, Jan. 29, 1942. http://www.defensemedianetwork.com/stories/the-american-red-cross-african-american-blood-ban-scandal/. *Also See http://qz.com/344343/during-world-war-ii-the-red-cross-refused-to-accept-blood-from-black-donors/*.

38. Laura Piatti-Farnell, *The Vampire in Contemporary Popular Literature*. New York: Routledge, 2013.

39. John Roach, "Cannibalism Normal for Early Humans?" *National Geographic News*, April 10, 2003. http://news.nationalgeographic.com/news/2003/04/0410_030410_cannibal.html.

40. Anna Salleh, "Human Bite Stronger than Thought," *ABC Science Online*, Nov. 27, 2012. http://news.discovery.com/human/evolution/human-bite.htm.

41. Lauren I. Labrecque and George R. Milne, "Exciting Red and Competent Blue: The Importance of Color in Marketing," *Journal of the Academy of Marketing Science* 40, no. 5, Sept. 2012, 711–727.

42. John L. Flynn, *Cinematic Vampires: The Living Dead on Film and Television, from the Devil's Castle (1896) To Bram Stoker's*

Dracula (1992). Jefferson, NC: McFarland, 1992, 3.

43. "John Polidori and the Vampyre Byron," *Bloodstone: The Magazine for Vampires*, Issue 1, Sept. 1998. www.angelfire.com/jazz/louxsie/bel.html.

44. Margaret L. Carter, *Dracula: The Vampire and the Critics*. Ann Arbor, MI: UMI Research Press, 1988.

45. Radicalesbians, "The Woman-Identified Woman," *Know, Inc.* 1970 pamphlet. http://library.duke.edu/digitalcollections/wlmpc_wlmms01011/.

46. Claire Johnston, "Women's Cinema as Counter-Cinema," in *Sexual Stratagems: The World of Women in Film*, Patricia Erens. New York: Horizon Press, 1979, 133–143.

47. Kimberly A. Frohreich, "Sullied Blood, Semen and Skin: Vampires and the Specter of Miscegenation," *Gothic Studies* 15, no. 1, May 2013.

48. Albert J. Bernstein, *Emotional Vampires: Dealing with People Who Drain You Dry*. New York: McGraw-Hill, 2000.

49. Meryl Quinn, Borderline Personality Disorder: Breeding Psychic Vampires, *Yahoo Voices*, Jan. 14, 2008.

50. Peter.K. Jonason and Gregory D. Webster, "The Dirty Dozen: A Concise Measure of the Dark Triad," *Psychological Assessment* 22, no. 2: 420–432.

51. Dawn Dorey, *From Evil to Love: As Channeled by My Spirit Guides*. Bloomington, IN: AuthorHouse Publishing, 2014, 8.

Chapter Two

1. Matthew Beresford, *From Demons to Dracula: The Creation of the Modern Vampire Myth*. London: Reaktion Books, 2008, 41.

2. David Keyworth, "The Socio-Religious Beliefs and Nature of the Contemporary Vampire Subculture," *Journal of Contemporary Religion* 17, no. 3, Oct. 2002, 355–370.

3. bylightunseen.net/fetishists.htm.

4. Emma Gray, "Vampires and Sexuality: What Are 'Twilight' and 'True Blood' Saying About Sex?" *HuffPost*, Oct. 28, 2011.

5. Fergus Linnane, *The Lives of the English Rakes*. London: Portrait, 2006, 19–20.

6. Graham Parry, "Minds and Manners 1660–1688," in *Stuart England*, ed. Blair

Worden. London: Guild Publishing, 1986, 176–8.

7. Sophie Harland, "Sex, Booze and 18th-Century Britain," smarthistory.khanacademy.org/hogarths-a-rakes-progress.html.

8. www.praxxis.co.uk/credebyron/vampyre.htm.

9. Leslie A. Marchand, *Byron: A Biography*. New York: Alfred A. Knopf, 1957, 442.

10. Mark Keenan, "Ireland: Poetic Justice at Home of Byron's Exiled Lover," *The Sunday Times*, Nov. 17, 2002. http://www.thesundaytimes.co.uk/sto/style/homes_and_gardens/article219740.ece.

11. Paul Douglass, *Lady Caroline Lamb: A Biography*. New York: Palgrave Macmillan, 2004, 360.

12. Heinz Insu Fenkl, "The Literary Vampire," *Realms of Fantasy* 45, Feb. 2002. heinzinsufenkl.net/docs/litvamp.html.

13. D. L. Mcdonald, *Poor Polidori: A Critical Biography of the Author of the Vampire*. Toronto: University of Toronto Press, 1991, 333.

14. Robert Morrison and Chris Baldick, eds., *The Vampyre and Other Tales of the Macabre*. Oxford: Oxford University Press, 2001.

15. William Michael Rossetti, ed., *The Diary of Dr. John William Polidori, 1816*. Ithaca: Cornell University Press, 2009.

16. Jerome Christensen, *Lord Byron's Strength: Romantic Writing and Commercial Society*. Baltimore: John Hopkins University Press, 1993, 59–61.

17. http://study.com/academy/lesson/byronic-hero-definition-characteristics-examples.html.

18. Nina Auerbach, *Our Vampires, Ourselves*. Chicago: University of Chicago Press, 1997, 14.

19. J. Gordon Melton, *The Vampire Book: The Encyclopedia of the Undead*. Canton, MI: Visible Ink Press, 1999.

20. "John Polidori & the Vampyre Byron," www.angelfire.com/jazz/louxsie/polidori.html.

21. Cyprien Berard, *Lord Ruthwin Ou Les Vampires*. Paris: Lavocat, 1820.

22. Cyprien Berard, *The Vampire Lord Ruthwin*. Tarzana, CA: Black Coat Press, 2012.

23. Katharina Mewald, "The Emancipation of Mina? The Portrayal of Mina in Stoker's *Dracula and* Coppola's *Bram Stoker's Dracula*," *Journal of Dracula Studies* 10, 2008.

24. Tom Pollard, *Sex and Violence: The Hollywood Censorship Wars*. Boulder, CO: Paradigm Publishers, 2009.

25. www.imdb.com/title/tt0050280/business.

26. www.imdb.com/title/tt0065073/.

27. J. Gordon Melton, *The Vampire Book: The Encyclopedia of the Undead*. Canton, MI: Visible Ink Press, 1999, 414.

28. Dennis Hensley, *"Schaech's Appeal," The Advocate*, May 22, 2001.

29. Steven D. Greydanus, *"Twilight Appeal: The Cult of Edward Cullen and Vampire Love in Stephenie Meyer's Novels and the New Film,"* 2008. http://decentfilms.com/new/articles/twilight.

30. Nancy Cardos, "Twilight Attracts Unexpected Audience," CBS News, Nov. 22, 2009. www.cbsnews.com/2100–18563_162–5739857.html.

31. Ashley Hayes, "Study: Interracial Marriage, Acceptance Growing," CNN, Feb. 16, 2012. www.cnn.com/2012/02/16/us/interracial-marriage.

32. Emma Gray, "Vampires and Sexuality: What Are 'Twilight' and 'True Blood' Saying About Sex?" www.huffingtonpost.com/emma-gray/vampires-sexuality_b_1063907.html.

33. "FoxSexpert: Why We're Obsessed with Vampire Sex," Fox News.com, Nov. 16, 2009. www.foxnews.com/story/2009/11/16/foxsexpert-why-were-obsessed-with-vampire-sex.html.

34. Alexander Pope, "Epistle II: To a Lady, of the Characters of Women."

35. Janet Howe Gaines, "Lilith, Seducer, Heroine, or Murderer?" *Bible History Daily*, Aug. 11, 2014. biblicalarchaeology.org/daily/people-cultures-in-the-bible/people-in-the-bible/Lilith/.

36. Flavius Philostratus, *The Life of Apollonius*, second/third centuries BCE.

37. Natalie Wilson, "On Seduction: Seducers, Seductresses, Angels in the House, and Vampires in Shining Armor…." https://seducedbytwilight.wordpress.com/2009/08/14/.

38. "Sirens and Seducers," in *Sex and Society*, Vol. 3, Marshall Cavendish Corp., 2010.

39. Katherine Ramsland, "Lady of Blood: Countess Bathory," *Crime Library*.

40. Margaret Nicholas, *The World's Wickedest Women*. London: Octopus Press, 1984, 152–154.

41. Tony Thorne, *Countess Dracula: The Life and Times of Elizabeth Bathory, the Blood Countess*. London: Bloomsbury Publishing, 1997.

42. Catherine Lavender, "The Cult of Domesticity and True Womanhood," 1998. https://csivc.csi.cuny.edu/history/files/lavender/386/truewoman.pdf.

43. Trudi Van Dyke, "At Midnight Drain the Stream of Life: Vampires and the New Woman." slayageonline.com/SCBtVS_Archive/Talks/Van_Dyke.pdf.

44. Elizabeth Signorotti, "Repossessing the Body: Transgressive Desire in Carmilla and Dracula," *Criticism* 38, no. 4, Sept. 1996, 607.

45. Trudi Van Dyke, "At Midnight Drain the Stream of Life: Vampires and the New Woman." slayageonline.com/SCBtVS_Archive/Talks/Van_Dyke.pdf.

46. Carol A. Senf, "Dracula: Stoker's Response to the New Woman," *Victorian Studies* 26, no. 1, Autumn 1982.

47. Israel Regardie, *The Complete Golden Dawn System of Magic*. Tempe, AZ: New Falcon Publications, 1984.

48. Leta W. Clark, *Women, Women, Women: Quips, Quotes, and Commentaries*. New York: Drake Publishers, 1977, 16.

49. Alain Silver and James Ursini, *The Vampire Film: From Nosferatu to Bram Stoker's Dracula*. New York: Limelight Editions, 1993.

50. Andrew Perez, "Horror as Metaphor: *Dracula's Daughter*: Homosexuality and Vampirism," *Sound on Sight*, Aug. 19, 2013. http://www.soundonsight.org/horror-as-metaphor-draculas-daughter-homosexuality-and-vampirism/.

51. *See* Eddie Muller, *The Art of Noir: The Posters and Graphics from the Classic Era of Film Noir*. New York: The Overlook Press, 2004.

52. Scott Snyder, "Personality Disorders and the Film Noir Femme Fatale," *Journal of Criminal Justice and Popular Culture* 8, No. 3, 2001, 155.

53. Tom Fallows, "More Sex and Violence Please, We're British: The Story of Hammer Horror," *What Culture,* Nov. 6, 2009. whatculture.com/film/more-sex-and-violence-please-were-british-the-story-of-hammer-horror-2-php.

54. "History of Sex in Cinema: The Greatest and Most Influential Sexual Films and Scenes," AMC Filmsite. www.filmsite.org/sexinfilms21a.html.

55. D.J.R. Bruckner, "Stage: Vampire Lesbians of Sodom," *The New York Times,* June 20, 1985.

56. Elissa Hunt, "Satanic Lesbian Vampire Killer Tracey Wigginton Terrified Australians in Gruesome 1990s Trial," *Melbourne Herald Sun,* March 5, 2013.

57. James Mottram, "Director Neil Jordon and Actor Gemma Arterton Talk Vampire Feminism in Byzantium," The List, May 17, 2013. https://film.list.co.uk/article/51106.

58. *The American Heritage Medical Dictionary.* Boston: Houghton Mifflin, 2007.

59. Jonathan P. Rosman and Philip J. Resnick, "Sexual Attraction to Corpses: A Psychiatric Review of Necrophilia," *Bulletin of the American Academy of Psychiatry and Law* 17, no. 2, June 1989. http://www.jaapl.org/content/17/2/153.full.pdf+html.

60. Maia Szabvitz, "Q & A: Author Dan Bergner on What Women Want," *Time,* June 6, 2013. http://healthland.time.com/2013/06/06/qa-author-dan-bergner-on-what-women-want-hint-not-monogamy/.

61. Elaine Blair, "I'll Have What She's Having—'what Do Women Want?' by Daniel Bergner," *New York Times,* June 13, 2013. http://www.nytimes.com/2013/06/16/books/review/what-do-women-want-by-daniel-bergner.html?_r=0.

62. Anne Billson, "Vampires: There Will Always Be Blood," *The Telegraph,* Oct. 31, 2012. http://www.Telegraph.Co.Uk/Culture/Film/9635998/Vampires-There-Will-Always-Be-Blood.Html.

63. Nico Lang, "Trampire: Why the Public Slut Shaming of Kristen Stewart Matters for Young Women," *HuffPost,* Nov. 4, 2012. http://www.huffingtonpost.com/news/kristen-stewart-trampire/.

Chapter Three

1. Genesis 2:33.

2. Sandra Litsitz Bem, "Gender Schema Theory: A Cognitive Account of Sex Typing," *Psychological Review* 88, no. 4, 1981.

3. "Boi or Grrl? Pop Culture Redefining Gender," *NBC News,* Oct. 1, 2005.

4. Shannon Winnubst, "Vampires, Anxieties, and Dreams: Race and Sex in the Contemporary United States," *Hypatia* 18, no. 3, Autumn 2003.

5. Bram Stoker, *Dracula,* 1897, Chapter 3.

6. SparkNotes Editors, "Sparknote on Dracula, Analysis: Chapters XIX–XXI." SparkNotes LLC. 2003. http://www.sparknotes.com/lit/dracula/.

7. Candace R. Benefiel, "Blood Relations: the Gothic Perversion of the Nuclear Family in Anne Rice's Interview with the Vampire," *The Journal of Popular Culture* 38, no. 2, 2004, 268.

8. www.transalliancesociety.org/education/documents/03transyouth.pdf.

9. George E. Haggerty, "Anne Rice and the Queering of Culture," *Novel: A Forum on Fiction* 32, no. 1, 5–18.

10. www.feministseventies.net/demandsx.html.

11. www.femagination.com/3559/the-female-vampire-a-model-for-feminists/.

12. jungian.info/library.cfm?idsLibrary=9.

13. www.urbandictionary.com/define.php?term=Blaxploitation.

14. Mia Mask, "Pam Grier: Part Foxy, Part Feminist, All Sexy," *NPR Divas on Screen,* March 2, 2007.

15. www.malleusmaleficarum.org/.

16. Ariel Levy, "Lesbian Nation: When Gay Women Took to the Road," *The New Yorker,* March 2, 2009.

17. Anne Rice, *Queen of the Damned.* New York: Alfred A. Knopf, 1988, 36.

18. Jennifer Baumgardner and Amy Richards, *Manifesta: Young Women, Feminism, and the Future.* New York: Farrar, Straus and Giroux, 2000.

19. Nina Auerbach, *Our Vampires, Ourselves.* Chicago: University of Chicago Press, 1997, 198.

20. boxofficemojo.com/movies/?id=buffy thevampireslayer.htm.

21. ilona Gaul, "Women's Sexual Liberation from Victorian Patriarchy in Sheridan Le Fanu's Carmilla." Munich: GRIN Verlag, 2004. http://www.grin.com/en/e-book/79 669/women-s-sexual-liberation-from-victorian-patriarchy-in-sheridan-le-fanu-s.

22. Suzanne Dixon, "Dracula and the New Woman: The Underlying Threat in Bram Stoker's Classic," Cross-Sections 2, 2006.

23. Trudi Van Dyke, "'At Midnight Drain the Stream of Life: Vampires and the New Woman." slayageonline.com/SCBtVS_Arch ive/Talks/Van_Dyke.pdf.

24. Megan Karius, "Kicking Butt in a Mini-Skirt: The Complicated Feminism of Buffy the Vampire Slayer," MK Feminist, 2011.

25. Jennifer Fountain, "The Vampire in Modern American Media: 1975–2000," Dartmouth College BA Thesis, 2000.

26. Kevin J. Wetmore, Jr, Post-9/11 Horror in American Cinema. New York: Continuum International Publishing Group, 2012, 14–15.

27. Susan Faludi, The Terror Dream: Fear and Fantasy in Post-9/11 America. New York: Henry Holt, 2007.

28. Graeme McMillan, "Buffy Comes Out, as Scifi and Bi," IO9, March 6, 2008.

29. Kurt Conklin, "Adolescent Sexual Behavior: Demographicss," Advocates for Youth, Feb. 2012.

30. David Badash, "Study Shows How Many Americans Are Gay, Lesbian, Bisexual, and Transgender," Gay Agenda News, April 7, 2011.

31. Chillicoathe Encyclopedia of Arcane Knowledge, 1st edition, 1884.

32. Albert Rolls, Stephen King: A Biography. Westport, CT: Greenwood Press, 2008, 107.

33. www.horrorexpress.com/moviere view/vampires-vs.-zombies.

34. Bonnie Mann, "Vampire Love: The Second Sex Negotiates the Twenty-First Century," in Twilight and Philosophy: Vampires, Vegetarians, and the Pursuit of Immortality, ed. William Irwin, Rebecca Housel, and J. Jeremy Wisnewski. Hoboken, NJ: John Wiley & Sons, 2009.

35. Joseph Laycock, "Vampires, Gay Rights, and the Political Underpinnings of Hbo's True Blood," Religion & Politics, Aug. 27, 2012.

36. Leslie Goldberg, "Alan Ball Talks Gay and Lesbian Undertones and Sex on 'True Blood,'" Shewired, Oct. 29, 2009.

37. Eve Dufour, "Lesbian Desires in the Vampire Subgenre: True Blood as a Platform for a Lesbian Discourse." Prandium—The Journal of Historical Studies 1, no. 1, Spring 2012.

38. Margaret Hartmann, "Feminist Reviewer Says Lesbian Vampire Killers Sucks," Jezebel, March 24, 2009.

39. Helen Lewis, "Feminism's Biggest Challenge for 2012: Justifying Its Existence," New Statesman, Dec. 29, 2011.

40. Stephen Marche, "What's Really Going on with All Those Vampires?" Esquire, Oct. 13, 2009.

Mike Szymanski, "Vampires and Bisexuality in Pop Culture, Twilight, True Blood, and More," Examiner.com, Oct. 31, 2009.

Chapter Four

1. Felipe de Brigard, "What Does the Hippocampus Do?" Scientific American Mind 25, no. 3.

2. Sigmund Freud, Beyond the Pleasure Principle and Other Writings, trans. John Reddick. London: Penguin Books, 2003.

3. William Berry, "How Recognizing Your Death Drive May Save Your Life," Psychology Today, Oct. 26, 2011. https://www.psychologytoday.com/blog/the-second-noble-truth.

4. Sigmund Freud, The Interpretation of Dreams, 1900.

5. Anne Rice, The Vampire Lestat. New York: Alfred A. Knopf, 1985.

6. Amanda Podonsky, "Bram Stoker's Dracula: A Reflection and Rebuke of Victorian Society," Student Pulse 2, no. 2, 2010.

7. Gary Gygax and Dave Arneson, Dungeons & Dragons Basic Set (1974), ed. J. Eric Holmes. TSR, edition, 1977.

8. Peter Day, ed., Vampires: Myths and Metaphors of Enduring Evil. New York: Rodopi, 2006.

9. Ani, "The Jewish Vampire: Gothic Antisemitism," Writinghood, March 27,

2008. http://writinghood.com/literature/the-jewish-vampire-gothic-antisemitism/.

10. Amanda Hobson, "Review of Director: F.W. Murnau, *Nosteratu, Eine Symphonie Des Grauens*. H-Net Reviews, H-German, Oct. 2009.

11. A.O. Scott, "Film Review; Son of 'Nosteratu' with a Real-Life Vampire," *New York Times*, December 29, 2000.

12. Denny Phillips, "Good Vampire, Bad Vampire," *Ezine Articles* Feb. 13, 2012.

13. J. Gordon Melton, *The Vampire Book: An Encyclopedia of the Undead*. Canton, MI: Visible Ink Press, 2010.

14. Philip M. Boffey, "Rare Disease Proposed as Cause for 'Vampires,'" *New York Times,* May 31, 1985.

15. Jennifer Sellman, "Dr. Jennifer's House Call: The Vampire Disease," *The Daily Dunklin Democrat*, Oct. 26, 2013.

16. Jason Beaubien, "Wiping Out Polio: How the U.S. Snuffed Out a Killer," *NPR,* October 15, 2012.

17. Susan Zieger, *Inventing the Addict: Drugs, Race, and Sexuality in Nineteenth Century British and American Literature*. Amherst: University of Massachusetts Press, 2008.

18. www.gallup.com/poll/6352/decades-drug-use-80s-90s.aspx.

19. Jodi Lane and James W. Meeker, "Subcultural Diversity and the Fear of Crime and Gangs," *Crime & Delinquency* 46, no. 4, Oct. 2000.

20. James C. Howell and Scott H. Decker, "The Youth Gangs, Drugs, and Violence Connection," *Juvenile Justice Bulletin*, Jan. 1999.

21. Frank Newport, "Americans More Likely to Believe in God than the Devil, Heaven More than Hell," Gallup News Service, June 13, 2007.

22. Tom Pollard, *Hollywood 9/11: Superheroes, Supervillains, and Super Disasters.* Boulder, CO: Paradigm Publishers, 2011.

23. Dana Blanton, "More Believe in Heaven than Hell," Fox News Poll, Oct. 28, 2005. http://www.foxnews.com/story/2005/10/28/102805-fox-poll-more-believe-in-heaven-than-hell.html.

24. "Vampire Fan Base Runs Thicker than Blood Online," Nielson.com. July 22, 2009.

25. https://www.stormfront.org/forum/t770074/.

26. *"True Blood*—100% Anti-White Propaganda," Stormfront.org, Jan. 6, 2011.

27. Alison Herman, "Why Do We Keep Coming Back to '*True Blood'?*," *Flavorwire,* June 17, 2013.

28. Carol J. Williams, "Column One: Dracula Is No Villain in Romania," *Los Angeles Times*, Oct. 25, 1994.

29. Joanne Viviano, "Vampires and Religion in Popular Culture," *The Columbus Dispatch*, Oct. 28, 2012.

30. David DiSalvo, "Vampires Vs Zombies: Who's Winning the War for the Recession Psyche?" *Psychology Today,* Oct. 28, 2010. https://www.psychologytoday.com/blog/neuronarrative/201010/vampires-vs-zombies-whos-winning-the-war-the-recession-psyche.View shared post

31. Carl Boggs and Tom Pollard, *A World in Chaos: Social Crisis and the Rise of Postmodern Cinema*. Lanham, MD: Rowman and Littlefield Publishers, Inc., 2003.

Chapter Five

1. Mario Varvoglis, "What Is Psi, What Isn't?" *Parapsychological Association.*

2. Joe H. Slate, *Psychic Vampires: Protection from Energy Predators and Parasites,* Saint Paul, MN: Llewellyn Publications, 2002, 20.

3. J. Gordon Melton, *The Vampire Book: The Encyclopedia of the Undead*. Canton, MI: Visible Ink Press, 1999, 619.

4. Henry. S. Olcott, "The Vampire," *The Theosophist* XII, 1891. www.austheos.org.au/clibrary/bindex-olcott.html.

5. vampires.monstrous.com/psychic_vampires.htm.

6. http://www.bbc.co.uk/dna/hub/.../A2173088.

7. Marjaana Lindeman and Marieke Saher, "Vitalism, Purpose and Superstition," *British Journal of Psychology* 98, no. 1, Feb. 2007, 33–44.

8. www.religionfacts.com/chinese-religion/beliefs/ch.

9. www.reiki.org/faq/whatisreiki.html.

10. Kaleah LaRoche, "Cutting the Psychic Energy Chords, "*Ezine Articles,* March 10, 2009.

11. Michelle Belanger, "The Vampire and the Reiki Master." https://starlightskundaliniblog.wordpress.com/tag/energy-vampire/.

12. Kaleah LaRoche, "Spiritual Recovery from Emotional Abuse," *Ezine Articles*, March 22, 2007.

13. Judith Orloff, *Positive Energy*. New York: Harmony Books, 2004.

14. Sigmund Freud, *The Interpretation of Dreams*, 1900.

15. Sigmund Freud, *The Ego and the Id*, 1923.

16. http://www.orgonite.info/what-is-orgonite.html.

17. Myron R. Sharaf, *Fury on Earth: A Biography of Wilhelm Reich*. New York: St. Martin's Press, 1983.

18. www.wilhelmreichtrust.org/function_of_the_orgasm.pdf.

19. http://www.monstropedia.org/index.php?title=Sexual_vampire#ixzz2pptej6Fa.

20. www.vampiricstudies.com/sexual.html.

21. Joe H. Slate, *Psychic Vampires: Protection from Energy Predators and Parasites*. St Paul, MN: Llewellyn Publications, 2002.

22. Samuel Taylor Coleridge, *Christabel*, first published in *Christabel; Kubla Khan, a Vision; the Pains of Sleep*, London, 1816.

23. John Keats, *La Belle Dame Sans Merci*. London: The Indicator, May 10, 1820.

24. Leonard Wolf, "The Transfer," in Leonard Wolf, ed., *Blood Thirst: 100 Years of Vampire Fiction*. Oxford: Oxford University Press, 1997.

25. Fritz Leiber, "The Girl with the Hungry Eyes," in Leonard Wolf, ed., *Blood Thirst: 100 Years of Vampire Fiction*, Oxford: Oxford University Press, 1997.

26. Fritz Leiber, "The Girl with the Hungry Eyes," 1949. www.berkleyschools.org/NorthstarMedia/download/112947?token.

27. Dennis D. Loo and Ruth-Ellen Grimes, "Polls, Politicians, and Crime, the Law and Order Issue of the 1960s," *Western Criminology Review* vol. 5 no. 1, 2004.

28. Peter D. Kramer, "The Great Proselytizer of Orgasm,,"*slate*, June 27, 2011.

29. www.churchofsatan.com/Pages/Nine Statements.html.

30. Anton LaVey, *The Satanic Bible*. New York: Avon, 1969.

31. Robert R. Hazlewood, Park Elliott Dietz, and Janet Warren, "The Criminal Sexual Sadist," *FBI Law Enforcement Bulletin* 61, no. 2, Feb. 1992.

32. Michelle Belanger, *The Vampire Codex*. New York: Weiser Books, 2004.

33. www.hellhorror.com /vampires/vampire-types/.

34. www.llewellyn.com/journal/article/1061.

35. http://www.thefreedictionary.com/psychic+energy

36. Enrico de Lazaro, "Study Unveils Why Healers See Human Aura," Sci-New.com, May 7, 2012. http://www.sci-news.com/medicine/article00298.html.

See Also "Synesthesia May Explain Healers Claims of Seeing People's 'Aura,'" *Science Daily*, May 4, 2012. http://www.sciencedaily.com/releases/2012/05/120504110024.htm.

37. Joe H. Slate, "Psychic Vampires," Rense.com, Oct. 14, 2003. www.rense.com/general43/psychic.htm.

38. https://twilightpath.wordpress.com/tag/psychic-vampires/.

39. "Take a Stake to Energy Vampires," Duke Energy, Oct. 22, 2013. http://www.duke-energy.com/news/releases/2013102202.asp.

40. "Are Energy Vampires Sucking You Dry?" *Energy.Gov*, Oct. 30, 2014. energy.gov/articles/are-energy-vampires-sucking-you-dry.

41. standby.lbl.gov/faq.html.

42. energy.gov/.../are-energy-vampires-s...

43. http://www.harrisinteractive.com/NewsRoom/HarrisPolls/tabid/447/ctl/ReadCustom%20Default/mid/1508/ArticleId/1353/Default.aspx.

44. Alberto R. Kornbihtt, "On Intelligent Design, Cognitive Relativism, Vitalism and the Mystery of the Real World," *Wiley Online Library* 59, no. 4–5, Jan. 3, 2008. onlinelibrary.wiley.com/doi/10.1080/15216540701194907/pdf.

45. Joe H. Slate, "Psychic Vampires," *The Llewellyn Journal*, Oct. 10, 2003. www.Llewellyn.Com/Journal/Article/513.

46. Karl Marx, *Das Kapital, Vol. 1*, 1867. www.philosophyparadise.com/quotes/marx.html.

Chapter Six

1. Lisa Rosen, "R.I.P Buffy: You Drove a Stake Through Convention," *Los Angeles Times,* May 20, 2003.

2. Jacobus de Voragine, *The Golden Legend, or Lives of the Saints by William Caxton, Vol. III,* ed. F.S. Ellis. London: J.M. Dent, 1900, 123–45.

3. Bruce A. McClelland, *Slayers and Their Vampires: A Cultural History of Killing the Dead.* Ann Arbor: University of Michigan Press, 2006, 62–79.

4. Samuel Taylor Coleridge, *Cristabel; Kubla Khan, a Vision; the Pains of Sleep.* London: John Murray, 1816.

5. Arthur H. Nethercot, "Coleridge's 'Christabel' and Le Fanu's 'Carmilla,'" *Modern Philology* 47, no.1, Aug. 1949, 32–38. www.jstor.org/stable/435571.

6. Sheridan Le Fanu, *Carmilla,* 1872, Chapter XV.

7. Romanticism: Academic Home Page, Feb. 12, 2009. academic.brooklyn.cuny.edu/english/melani/cs6/rom.html.

8. Bram Stoker, *Dracula,* 1897, Chapter 9.

9. Roger Ebert, "The Fearless Vampire Killers, or Pardon Me but Your Teeth Are in My Neck," RogerEbert.com, Jan. 22, 1968.

10. Desson Howe, "Quentin's 'Dusk': Hurry Up Dawn," *the Washington Post,* Jan. 19, 1996.

11. Maryann Johanson, "Near Dark: Buffy the Vampire Hunter, Once Bitten, Blacula, Love at First Bite, and Jesus Christ, Vampire Hunter (Review)," FlickFilosopher.com, Nov. 2, 2004.

12. wattsupwiththat.com/2011/03/28/gallups-public-opinion-on-global-warming-dead-last/.

13. "Public Trust in Government," *Pugh Research Center: 1958–2014,* Nov. 13, 2014. www.people-press.org/2014/11/13/public-trust-in-government/.

14. Justin Wm. Moyer, "How 'Survivalists' in America Are Planning Their Escape from Ebola Apocalypse—Right Now," *The Washington Post,* Oct. 6, 2014.

15. Alan Feuer, "The Preppers Next Door," *New York Times,* Jan. 26, 2013.

16. www.boxofficemojo.com/movies/?id=daybreakers.htm.

17. boxofficemojo.com/movies/?id=abrahamlincolnvampirehunter.htm.

18. americanhistory.about.com/od/civilwarmenu/a/cause_civil_war.

19. Jamie Schaeffer, "Lincoln's Changing Views on Slavery," *Illinois History,* Feb. 1997. http://www.lib.niu.edu/1997/ihy970225.html.

20. Chris Lee, "*Abraham Lincoln: Vampire Hunter,* Seth Grahame Smith on Its Real-Life Origins," *The Daily Beast,* June 22, 2012.

21. Roger Ma, *The Vampire Combat Manual.* New York: Berkley Publishing Group, 2012.

22. Lydia Saad, "Best President? Lincoln on Par with Reagan, Kennedy," Gallup, Feb. 11, 2009. http://www.gallup.com/poll/114292/Best-President-Lincoln-Par-Reagan-Kennedy.aspx.

23. Andrew Stewart, "Number of Frequent Young Moviegoers Plummets in 2013," *Variety,* March 25, 2014.http://Blogs.Indiewire.Com/Thompsononhollywood/Global-Box-Office-Climb-Continues-In-2011

24. "Talking with Kids About Tough Issues: A National Survey of Parents and Kids," Nickelodean, Kaiser Family Foundation, and International Communications Research, March 8, 2001.

25. https://kaiserfamilyfoundation.files.wordpress.com/2013/01/talking-with-kids-about-tough-issues-a-national-survey-of-parents-and-kids-chart-pack-2.pdf.

26. www.merriam-webster.com/.

27. David Weisburd, "Vigilantism as Community Social Control: Developing a Quantitative Criminological Model," *Journal of Quantitative Criminology* 4, no. 2, June 1988.

28. Graham Seal, *Outlaw Heroes in Myth and History.* London: Anthem Press, 2011.

29. Friedrich Nietzsche, *Beyond Good and Evil,* 1886.

Chapter Seven

1. www.merriam-webster.com/dictionary/metaphor.

2. www.onestopenglish.com/grammar/pdf-content/vocabulary-metaphors/meta

phors-life-is-a-journey-worksheet-and-teachers-notes/147517.article.

3. Sara Libby Robinson, *Blood Will Tell: Vampires as Political Metaphors Before World War I*. Brighton, MA: Academic Studies Press, 2011.

4. Tersea A. Goddu, "Vampire Gothic," *American Literary History* 11, no. 1, 1999, 125–141.

5. Jennie Yabroff, "Vampires Everywhere," *Newsweek*, Dec. 5, 2008.

6. Lisa Rose, "Interview with Anne Rice," *The Star-Ledger*, Oct. 31, 2010.

7. Emre Oktem, "Balkan Vampires Before Ottoman Courts," *Cesnur: Centro Studi Sulle Nuove Religioni*, 2009. www.cesnur.org/2009/balkan_vampires.htm.

8. Sheridan Le Fanu, *Carmilla*, 1872, Chapter 15.

9. Ray Porter, "The Historical Dracula," 1992. www.eskimo.com/~mwirkk/vladhist.html.

10. Richard Pallady, "Vlad III: Ruler of Wallacha," *Encyclopædia Britannica*, www.britannica.com/biography/Vlad-III.

11. Marilee Hanson, "Lord Byron; the Life of George Noel Gordon—Facts & Information," http://englishhistory.net/byron/life-of-lord-byron/, accessed Feb.1, 2015.

12. Sigmund Freud, *Taboo and Totem*. London: Routledge and Kegan Paul, 1950.

13. Nancy Dougherty, "Vampires, Eroticism, and the Lure of the Unconscious," in Mary Lynn Kittelson, ed., *The Soul of Popular Culture: Looking at Contemporary Heroes, Myths, and Monsters*. Chicago: Carus Publishing, 1998.

14. Karl Marx, *Capital*, vol. 1, 1867. https://www.marxists.org/archive/marx/.../1867.

15. Maggie Koerth-Baker, "Why Rational People Buy into Conspiracy Theories," *New York Times*, May 26, 2013.

16. "What Is a Master Narrative?" The Harwood Institute for Public Innovation, 2007. www.coveringcommunities.org/PDFs/MasterNarrativeNEW.pdf

17. Jean-François Lyotard, *The Postmodern Condition*. Manchester: Manchester University Press, 1984.

18. www.bridgetochange.com/handbook/chapterthree.shtml.

19. Anne Rice, *Interview with the Vampire*. New York: Random House, 1976, 288.

20. www.the-numbers.com/movies/franchise/Twilight.

21. Pamela Madsen, "Three Unspeakable Truths About Female Sexuality," *Psychology Today*, Nov. 2, 2010.

22. Nina Bahadur, "Female Friendship: Women Less Likely to Befriend Promiscuous Peers Regardless of Their Own Sexual History, Study Finds." *The Huffington Post*, June 4, 2013.

23. Atara Stein, "Immortals and Ghosts, Oh My!: Byronic Heroes in Popular Culture," Romantic Circles, University of Maryland, 2002.

24. Phillip L. Hammack and Bertram J. Cohler, "Narrative, Identity, and the Politics of Exclusion: Social Change and the Gay and Lesbian Life Course," *Sexuality Research and Social Policy* 8, no. 3, Sept. 2011, 162–182.

25. Margaret Hartmann, "Feminist Reviewer Says *Lesbian Vampire Killers* Sucks," *Jezebel*, March 24, 2009.

26. Stephanie Coontz, "Why Gender Equality Stalled," *New York Times*, Feb. 16, 2013.

27. David Crary, "Gender Stereotypes Easing More for Girls than Boys," Associated Press, May 8, 2011.

28. "What's the Deal with All the Teen Vampire Movies and Books?" *Newswise*, June 9, 2010.

29. Kate Muir, "*Twilight*: How Bella Swan Became a Feminist Icon," *The Times*, Nov. 16, 2012. www.thetimes.co.uk/tto/arts/film/article3601424.ece.

30. Amanda Podonsky, "Bram Stoker's *Dracula*: A Reflection and Rebuke of Victorian Society," *Student Pulse* 2, no. 2, 2010.

31. Bram Stoker, *Dracula*, 1897, Chapter 3.

32. Stephen Marche, "What's Really Going On with All These Vampires," *Esquire*, Oct. 13, 2009.

33. "Gay Marriage: Key Data Points from Pew Research," *Pew Research Center*, June 11, 2011.

34. ttp://www.people-press.org/2013/03/20/growing-support-for-gay-marriage-changed-minds-and-changing-demographics/.

35. Dramadoll, "Vampires: The Remote Ideology Behind Them," http://www.fanpop.com/clubs/philosophy/articles/77404/title/vampires-romantic-ideology-behind.

36. Kevin J. Wetmore, *Post-9/11 Horror in American Cinema.* New York: Continuum, 2012, 164.

37. J. Gordon Mellon, *The Vampire Book: The Encyclopedia of the Undead.* Canton, MI: Visible Ink Press, 1999, 50–51.

38. Neela Banerjee, "Study Shows U.S. Religious Tolerance," *New York Times*, June 24, 2008.

39. Peter Beaumont, "Religious Intolerance on the Rise Worldwide, Says U.S. Report," *The Guardian*, Sept. 20, 2012.

40. Kenny Paul Smith, "Vampire Churches, Vampire Images, and Invented Religions," *Bulletin for the Study of Religion*, March 7, 2012.

41. Trudi Van Dyke, "At Midnight Drain the Stream of Life: Vampires and the New Woman." slayageonline.com/SCBtVS_Archive/Talks/Van_Dyke.pdf.

42. Daphne A. Lofquist, "Multigenerational Households: 2009–2012," *American Community Service Briefs*, U.S. Census Bureau, Oct. 2012.

43. Eric Kleinenberg, "One's a Crowd," *New York Times*, Feb. 4, 2012.

44. "Monster of the Week," *AXS Entertainment*, Feb. 11, 2011.

45. "Trust Issues: Only One-Third of Americans Feel They Can Trust Fellow Citizens," CBS News, Nov. 30, 2013. ap-gfkpoll.com/featured/our-latest-poll-findings-24.

46. *Department of Justice Statistics, Sourcebook of Crime and Justice*, table 2.61 (29th edition, 2001).

47. "Crime in the U.S. 2012," *FBI Uniform Crime Reports*. https://www.fbi.gov/.../crime.../preliminar...* https://www.fbi.gov/stats.../crimestats.

48. John L. Sloop, *The Cultural Prison: Discourse, Prisoners, and Punishment.* Tuscaloosa: University of Alabama Press, 2006, 142.

49. Scott LeBarge, "Heroism: Why Heroes Are Important," Markkula Center for Applied Ethics, Santa Clara University, 2005. www.scu.edu/ethics/publications/ethicsoutlook/2005/heroes.html.

50. Katherine Ramsland, "Vampire Personality Disorder," *Psychology Today*, Nov. 21, 2012.

51. "When a 'Vampire' Threat Hit Close to Home," *New York Times*, Dec. 1, 2014.

52. C. N. Trueman, "The Black Death of 1348 to 1350, " HistoryLearningSite.co.uk. www.historylearningsite.co.uk/medieval-england/the-black-death-of-1348-to-1350/.

53. www.archives.gov/exhibits/influenza-epidemic/.

54. Hanne Thommesen, "Master Narratives and Narratives as Told by People with Mental Health and Drug Problems," *Journal of Comparative Social Work* 5, no. 1, 2010.

55. Richard Corliss, "*Daybreakers*: And Now, Junkie Vampires!" *Time*, Jan. 11, 2010.

56. Joe H. Slate, *Psychic Vampires: Protection from Energy Predators and Parasites.* St. Paul, MN: Llewellyn Publications, 2002, 2.

57. Richard Webster, *The Complete Book of Auras*, Woodbury, MN: Llewellyn Worldwide, 2010.

58. Robert Todd Carroll, *The Skeptic's Dictionary: A Collection of Strange Beliefs, Amusing Deceptions, and Dangerous Delusions.* Hoboken, NJ: John Wiley and Sons, 2003.

59. David DiSalvo,"Vampires vs Zombies: Who's Winning the War for the Recession Psyche?" *Neuronarrative*, Oct. 28, 2010.

60. "Feature Interview: Charlaine Harris," www.fantasy-magazine.com/new/new.../feature-interview-charlaine-harris/.

61. Nicole Allan, "The Vampire Novelist Next Door: Anne Rice in Palm Desert," *The California Sunday Magazine*, Oct. 2014. https://stories.californiasunday.com/2014–10–05/anne-rice-in-palm-desert/.

62. Grady Hendrix, "Vampires Suck: Actually, They Don't. and That's the Problem," *Slate*, July 28, 2009.

63. Antonio Regalato, "Google to Try to Solve Death, LOL," *MIT Technology Review*, Sept. 18, 2013.

64. Carl Zimmer, "Young Blood May Hold Key to Reversing Aging," *New York Times*, May 4, 2014.

65. Jennifer Viegas, "Why Blood Tastes Good to Vampires ... Bats, That Is," Discovery News, June 24, 2014. news.discovery.com/animals/endangered-species/why-blood-tastes-good-to-vampire-bats-140624.htm.

66. www.jesus-is-savior.com/Evils%20 in%20America/goth.htm.

67. vampireunderworld.com/vampire-subculture/.

68. Jennifer J. Baker, "Natural Science and the Romanticisms," *ESQ: A Journal of the American Renaissance* 53, no. 4, 2007.

69. Jasper Hamill, "Why We've Fallen in Love with Twenty First Century Vampires," *the Herald Scotland*, Oct. 29, 2011.

70. Bram Stoker, *Dracula*, 1897, Chapter 14.

71. Michael Suk-Young Chwe. "Scientific Pride and Prejudice," *New York Times*, Feb. 2, 2014.

72. Herman Leberecht Strack, *The Jew and Human Sacrifice: Human Blood and Jewish Ritual, an Historical and Sociological Inquiry*. London: Cope and Fenwick, 1898, English edition 1909.

73. www.spiritsociety.org/ghost.php? page=articles&article=vampire1.html.

74. Daniela Deane, "Twilight Fans Flock to Forks,' *CNN*, Dec. 3, 2009.

75. www.Talkorigins.org/Faqs/Flood-Myths.Html#Hopi.

76. Wetmore, Page 165.

77. www.Academia.Edu/391983/True_Blood_The_Vampire_As_A_Multiracial_Critique_On_Multicultural_Pluralism.

78. Aviva Briefel and Sam J. Miller, Eds., *Horror After 9/11: World of Fear, Cinema of Terror*. Austin: University of Texas Press, 2011, 111.

79. Travis Sutton and Harry M. Benshoff, "Forever Family Values," in Aviva Briefel and Sam J. Miller, eds., *Horror After 9/11: World of Fear, Cinema of Terror*. Austin: University of Texas Press, 2011, 215–216.

80. Alan Abramowitz, "How Race and Religion Have Polarized American Voters," *The Washington Post*, Jan. 20, 2014.

81. Lindsay Bradshaw, "Blood Thirsty: Why Are Vampires Ruling Pop Culture?" *Texas Tech Today*, July 2012.

82. Maxine Shen, "Flesh & 'Blood,'" *New York Post*, June 23, 2009.

83. C.G. Jung, "On the Psychology of the Unconscious" (1912), in *Two Essays on Analytical Psychology*. Princeton: Princeton University Press, Second Edition, 1966.

84. Sigmund Freud, "The Ego and the Id," 1923.

85. Sigmund Freud, "Beyond the Pleasure Principle," 1920.

86. http://dictionary.reference.com/browse/we+have+met+the+enemy,+and+they+are+us.

Bibliography

Articles

Abramowitz, Alan. "How Race and Religion Have Polarized American Voters." *Washington Post*, January 20, 2014.

Adler, Margot. "For Love of Do-Good Vampires: A *Bloody* Booklist." National Public Radio, February 18, 2010.

Allan, Nicole. "The Vampire Novelist Next Door: Anne Rice in Palm Desert." *The California Sunday Magazine*, October 2014. https://stories.californiasunday.com/2014-10-05/anne-rice-in-palm-desert/.

Ani. "The Jewish Vampire: Gothic Anti-semitism." *Writinghood*, March 27, 2008.

"Are Energy Vampires Sucking You Dry?" *Energy.gov*, October 30, 2014. energy.gov/articles/are-energy-vampires-sucking-you-dry.

Badash, David. "Study Shows How Many Americans Are Gay, Lesbian, Bisexual, and Transgender." *Gay Agenda News*, April 7, 2011.

Bahadur, Nina. "Female Friendship: Women Less Likely to Befriend Promiscuous Peers Regardless of Their Own Sexual History, Study Finds." *The Huffington Post*, June 4, 2013.

Baker, Jennifer J. "Natural Science and the Romanticisms." *ESQ: A Journal of the American Renaissance* 53, no. 4, 2007.

Beaumont, Peter. "Religious Intolerance on the Rise Worldwide, says US Report." *The Guardian*, September 20, 2012.

Bem, Sandra Litsitz. "Gender Schema Theory: A Cognitive Account of Sex Typing." *Psychological Review* 88, no. 4, 1981.

Benefiel, Candace R. "Blood Relations: The Gothic Perversion of the Nuclear Family in Anne Rice's Interview with the Vampire." *The Journal of Popular Culture* 38, no. 2, 2004.

Berry, William. "How Recognizing Your Death Drive May Save Your Life." *Psychology Today*, October 26, 2011.

Billson, Anne. "Vampires: There Will Always Be Blood." *The Telegraph*, October 31, 2012.

Blair, Elaine. "I'll Have What She's Having—'What Do Women Want?' by Daniel Bergner." *New York Times*, June 13, 2013.

Boffey, Philip M. "Rare Disease Proposed as Cause for 'Vampires.'" *New York Times*, May 31, 1985.

Bradshaw, Lindsay. "Blood Thirsty: Why Are Vampires Ruling Pop Culture Today?" *Texas Today*, July 2, 2012.

Bruckner, D.J.R. "Stage: Vampire Lesbians of Sodom." *New York Times*, June 20, 1985.

Callaway, Ewen. "How Vampires Evolved to Live on Blood Alone." *New Scientist*, October 2008.

Cardos, Nancy. "Twilight Attracts Unexpected Audience." CBS News, November 22, 2009

Chwe, Michael Suk-Young. "Scientific Pride and Prejudice," *The New York Times*, February 2, 2014

Connolly, Angela, "Psychoanalytic Theory in Times of Terror." *Journal of Analytical Psychology* 48, no. 4, September 2003.

Coontz, Stephanie. "Why Gender Equality Stalled." *New York Times*, February 16, 2013.

Corliss, Richard. "*Daybreakers*: And Now, Junkie Vampires!" *Time*, January 11, 2010.

Crary, David. "Gender Stereotypes Easing More for Girls than Boys." Associated Press, May 8, 2011.

Deane, Daniela. "Twilight Fans Flock to Forks." *CNN*, December 3, 2009.

Delaney, Tim. "Pop Culture: An Overview." *Philosophy Now*, Issue 64, November/December 2007.

de Lazaro, Enrico. "Study Unveils Why Healers See Human Aura." Sci-New.com, May 7, 2012. http://www.sci-news.com/medicine/article00298.html.

DiSalvo, David." Vampires vs Zombies: Who's Winning the War for the Recession Psyche?" *Psychology Today*, October 28, 2010.

Dixon, Suzanne. "Dracula and the New Woman: The Underlying Threat in Bram Stoker's Classic." *Cross-Sections* 2, 2006.

Dougherty, Nancy. "Vampires, Eroticism, and the Lure of the Unconscious," in Mary Lynn Kittelson, ed., *The Soul of Popular Culture: Looking at Contemporary Heroes, Myths, and Monsters*. Chicago: Carus, 1998.

Ebert, Roger. "The Fearless Vampire Killers, or Pardon Me But Your Teeth Are in My Neck." RogerEbert.com, January 22, 1968.

Fallows, Tom. "More Sex and Violence Please, We're British: The Story of Hammer Horror." *What Culture*, November 6, 2009.

"Feature Interview: Charlaine Harris." www.fantasy-magazine.com/new/new.../feature-interview-charlaine-harris/.

Fenkl, Heinz Insu."The Literary Vampire." *Realms of Fantasy* 45, February 2002.

Ferraro, Susan. "Novels You Can Sink Your Teeth Into." *New York Times*, October 14, 1990.

Feuer, Alan. "The Preppers Next Door." *New York Times*, January 26, 2013.

Frohreich, Kimberly A. "Sullied Blood, Semen and Skin: Vampires and the Specter of Miscegenation." *Gothic Studies* 11, no. 1.

Gaines, Janet Howe. "Lilith, Seducer, Heroine, or Murderer?" *Bible History Daily*, August 11, 2014.

Gaul, Ilona. *Women's Sexual Liberation from Victorian Patriarchy in Sheridan Le Fanu's Carmilla*. Munich: GRIN Verlag, 2004

Goddu, Tersea A. "Vampire Gothic." *American Literary History* 11, no. 1, 1999.

Goodman, Peter S. "Economists Say Movie Violence Might Temper the Real Thing." *New York Times*, January 7, 2008.

Gordon, Joan, and Veronica Hollinger. "Introduction: The Shape of Vampires." *Blood Read: The Vampire as Metaphor in Contemporary Culture*. Ed. Joan Gordon and Veronica Hollinger. Philadelphia: University of Pennsylvaia Press, 1997.

Gray, Emma. "Vampires and Sexuality: What are 'Twilight' and 'True Blood' Saying About Sex?" *HuffPost*, October 28, 2011.

Greydanus, Steven D. "*Twilight* Appeal: The Cult of Edward Cullen and Vampire Love in Stephenie Meyer's Novels and the New Film." decentfilms.com/articles/twilight, 2008.

Haggerty, George E. "Anne Rice and the Queering of Culture." *NOVEL: A Forum on Fiction* 32, no. 1, Autumn 1998, pp. 5–18.

Hammack, Phillip L., and Bertram J. Cohler. "Narrative, Identity, and the Politics of Exclusion: Social Change and the Gay and Lesbian Life Course." *Sexuality Research and Social Policy* 8, no. 3, September 2011.

Hanson, Marilee. "Lord Byron; The Life of George Noel Gordon—Facts & Information." http://englishhistory.net/byron/life-of-lord-byron/. Accessed February 1, 2015.

Harland, Sophie. "Sex, Booze and 18th-Century Britain." smarthistory.khanacademy.org/hogarths-a-rakes-progress.html.

Hartmann, Margaret. "Feminist Reviewer Says *Lesbian Vampire Killers* Sucks," *Jezebel*, March 24, 2009.

Hazlewood, Robert R., Park Elliott Dietz, and Janet Warren. "The Criminal Sexual Sadist." *FBI Law Enforcement Bulletin* 61, no. 2, February 1992.

Hendrix, Grady. "Vampires Suck: Actually, They Don't. And That's the Problem." *Slate*, July 28, 2009.

Herman, Alison. "Why Do We Keep Coming Back to 'True Blood'?" *Flavorwire*, June 17, 2013.

Howe, Desson. "Quentin's 'Dusk': Hurry Up Dawn." *Washington Post*, January 19, 1996.

Howell, James C., and Scott H. Decker. "The Youth Gangs, Drugs, and Violence Connection." *Juvenile Justice Bulletin*, January 1999.

Jesep, Paul P. "Darwin's Lost Essay on Vampires." http://www.allvoices.com www.allvoices.com/article/15765711.

"John Polidori and the Vampyre." *Bloodstone: The Vampire Magazine* 1, 1998.

Johnson, Allan. "Modernity and Anxiety in Bram Stoker's *Dracula*." *Critical Insights: Dracula*. Hackensack, NJ: Salem Press, 2009.

Johnston, Claire. "Women's Cinema as Counter-Cinema," in *Sexual Stratagems: The World of Women in Film*, ed. Patricia Erens. New York: Horizon Press, 1979, 133–143.

Jonason, Peter K., and Gregory D. Webster. "The Dirty Dozen: A Concise Measure of the Dark Triad." *American Psychological Association* 22, no. 2, 2010, pp. 420–432.

Jordan, David Starr. "The Blood of the Nation: A Study of the Decay of Races." *Popular Science Monthly*, May 1901.

Jung, C.G. "On the Psychology of the Unconscious" (1912), in *Two Essays on Analytical Psychology*, ed. and trans. R.F.F. Hull et al. Princeton: Princeton University Press, second edition, 1966.

Karius, Megan. "Kicking Butt in a Mini-Skirt: The Complicated Feminism of Buffy the Vampire Slayer." *MK Feminist*, 2011 megankarius.com/academic-papers/feminism-in-buffy/.

Keenan, Mark. "Ireland: Poetic Justice at Home of Byron's Exiled Lover." *Sunday Times* Online, November 17, 2002.

Keyworth, David. "The Socio-Religious Beliefs and Nature of the Contemporary Vampire Subculture." *Journal of Contemporary Religion* 17, no. 3, October 2002, 355–370.

King, Stephen. "Why We Crave Horror Movies." *Playboy*, January 1982.

Klein, Simon Pascal. "A Critical Examination of Gender Roles within Goth Subculture." *Klepis*, August 11, 2009, http://klepas.org/a-critical-examination-of-gender-relations-within-goth-subculture/.

Koerth-Baker, Maggie. "Why Rational People Buy into Conspiracy Theories." *New York Times*, May 21, 2013.

Kramer, Peter D. "The Great Proselytizer of Orgasm." *Slate*, June 27, 2011.

Labrecque, Lauren I., and George R. Milne. "Exciting Red and Competent Blue: The Importance of Color in Marketing." *Journal of the Academy of Marketing Science* 40, no. 5, September 2012, 711–727.

Lahr, Angela. "Preaching Eugenics: Religious Leaders and the American Eugenics Movement." *Indiana Magazine of History* 102, no. 1, March 2006.

Lang, Nico. "Trampire: Why the Public Slut Shaming of Kristen Stewart Matters for Young Women." *HuffPost*, November 4, 2012.

LaRoche, Kaleah. "Cutting the Psychic Energy Chords." *Ezine Articles*, March 10, 2009.

LaRoche, Kaleah. "Spiritual Recovery from Emotional Abuse." *Ezine Articles*, March 22, 2007.

Lavender, Catherine. "The Cult of Domesticity and True Womanhood," 1998. https://csivc.csi.cuny.edu/history/files/lavender/386/truewoman.pdf

Laycock, Joseph. "Vampires, Gay Rights, and the Political Underpinnings of HBO's *True Blood*." *Religion & Politics*, August 27, 2012.

LeBarge, Scott. "Heroism: Why Heroes Are Important." Markkula Center for Applied Ethics, Santa Clara University, 2005. www.scu.edu/ethics/publications/ethicsoutlook/2005/heroes.html.

Lee, Chris. "*Abraham Lincoln: Vampire Hunter*, Seth Grahame Smith on its Real-Life Origins." *The Daily Beast*, June 22, 2012.

Levy, Ariel. "Lesbian Nation: When Gay Women Took to the Road," *The New Yorker*, March 2, 2009.

Lewis, Helen. "Feminism's Biggest Challenge for 2012: Justifying Its Existence," *New Statesman*, December 29, 2011.

Leiber, Fritz. "The Girl with the Hungry Eyes," in *Blood Thirst: 100 Years of Vampire Fiction*, ed. Leonard Wolf. Oxford: Oxford University Press, 1997.

Lindeman, Marjaana, and Marieke Saher. "Vitalism, Purpose and Superstition." *British Journal of Psychology* 98, no. 1, February 2007, 33–44.

Loo, Dennis D., and Ruth-Ellen Grimes. "Polls, Politicians, and Crime, the Law and Order Issue of the 1960s." *Western Criminology Review* 5, no. 1, 2004.

Lovecraft, H. P. "Supernatural Horror in Literature." *The Recluse*, 1927, *Supernatural Horror in Literature*, ed. E. F. Bleirer. New York: Dover, 1973, 11–106.

MacDermot, Hal. "Top Horror Movie Directors Discuss Art and Impact of Their Movies." *QuietEarth.us*, March 8, 2009. http://www.quietearth.us/articles/2009/03/08/Top-horror-movie-directors-discuss-art-and-impact-of-their-movies.

Madsen, Pamela. "Three Unspeakable Truths about Female Sexuality." *Psychology Today*, November 2, 2010.

Mann, Bonnie. "Vampire Love: The Second Sex Negotiates the Twenty-First Century," in *Twilight and Philosophy: Vampires, Vegetarians, and the Pursuit of Immortality*, ed. William Irwin, Rebecca Housel, and J. Jeremy Wisnewski. Hoboken, NJ: John Wiley & Sons, 2009.

Marche, Stephen. "What's Really Going on with All These Vampires." *Esquire*, October 13, 2009.

Mewald, Katharina. "The Emancipation of Mina? The Portrayal of Mina in Stoker's *Dracula* and Coppola's *Bram Stoker's Dracula*." *Journal of Dracula Studies* 10, 2008.

Mottram, James. "Director Neil Jordon and Actor Gemma Arterton Talk Vampire Feminism in Byzantium." The List, May 17, 2013. https://film.list.co.uk/article/51106.

Moyer, Justin Wm. "How 'Survivalists' in America are planning their escape from Ebola Apocalypse—Right Now." *Washington Post*, October 6, 2014.

Muir, Kate. "*Twilight*: How Bella Swan Became a Feminist Icon." *The Times*, November 16, 2012.

Nethercot, Arthur H. "Coleridge's 'Christabel' and Le Fanu's 'Carmilla.'" *Modern Philology* 47, no. 1, August 1949.

Newport, Frank. "Americans More Likely to Believe in God Than the Devil, Heaven More Than Hell." Gallup News Service, June 13, 2007.

Oktem, Emre. "Balkan Vampires before Ottoman Courts." *Cesnur: Centro Studi sulle Nuove Religioni*, 2009. www.cesnur.org/2009/balkan_vampires.htm.

Olcott, Henry. S. "The Vampire." *The Theosophist* XII, 1891. www.austheos.org.au/clibrary/bindex-olcott.html.

Ortega y Gasset, José. "Taboo and Metaphor," in *The Dehumanization of Art and Ideas about the Novel*. Princeton: Princeton University Press, 1925.

Pallady, Richard. "Vlad III: Ruler of Wallacha." *Encyclopædia Britannica*. www.britannica.com/biography/Vlad-III.

Parry, Graham. "Minds and Manners 1660–1688," in *Stuart England*, ed. Blair Worden. London: Guild, 1986, 176–178.

Perez, Andrew. "Horror as Metaphor: *Dracula's Daughter*: Homosexuality and Vampirism." *Sound on Sight*, August 19, 2013.

Peters, Sarah L. "Repulsive to Romantic: The Evolution of Bram Stoker's *Dracula*." *2003 Academic Forum/ Number 20*, Henderson State University.

Phillips, Denny. "Good Vampire, Bad Vampire." *Ezine Articles*, February 13, 2012.

Podonsky, Amanda. "Bram Stoker's *Dracula*: A Reflection and Rebuke of Victorian Society." *Student Pulse* 2, no. 2, 2010.

Pope, Alexander. "Epistle II: To a Lady, of the Characters of Women." 1743.

Porter, Ray. "The Historical Dracula." 1992. www.eskimo.com/~mwirkk/vladhist.html.

"Psychoanalytic Theory in Times of Terror." *Journal of Analytical Psychology* 4, no. 48, September 2003, 48.

"Public Trust in Government." *Pugh Research Center: 1958–2014*, November 13, 2014. www.people-press.org/2014/11/13/public-trust-in-government/.

Quinn, Meryl. "Borderline Personality Disorder: Breeding Psychic Vampires." *Yahoo Voices*, January 14, 2008.

Quirk, Michael. "Vampire Fangs Dentistry Is a Real Thing." *Dental Products Report*, July 30, 2013.

Radford, Benjamin. "The Real Science and History of Vampires." *Live Science*, November 30, 2009.

Radicallesbians. "The Woman Identified Woman." Pamphlet, 1970.

Ramsland, Katherine. "Lady of Blood: Countess Bathory." *Crime Library*.

"Red Cross to Use Blood of Negroes." *New York Times*, January 29, 1942.

Regalato, Antonio. "Google to Try to Solve Death, LOL." *MIT Technology Review*, September 18, 2013.

Roach, John. "Cannibalism Normal for

Early Humans?" *National Geographic News,* April 10, 2003.

Rose, Lisa. "Interview with Anne Rice." *The Star-Ledger,* October 31, 2010.

Rosen, Lisa. "R.I.P Buffy: You Drove a Stake through Convention." *Los Angeles Times,* May 20, 2003.

Rosman, Jonathan P., and Philip J. Resnick. "Sexual Attraction to Corpses: A Psychiatric Review of Necrophilia." *Bulletin of the American Academy of Psychiatry and Law* 17, no. 2, June 1989.

Schaeffer, Jamie. "Lincoln's Changing Views on Slavery." *Illinois History,* February 1997. http://www.lib.niu.edu/1997/ihy970 225.html.

Scott, A.O. "Film Review Shadow of the Vampire." *New York Times,* December 29, 2000.

Sellah, Anna. "Human Bite Stronger Than Thought," *ABC Science Online,* November 27, 2012.

Senf, Carol A. "Dracula: Stoker's Response to the New Woman," *Victorian Studies* 26, no. 1, Autumn 1982.

Shelley, Percy. "A Defence of Poetry." 1821, first published 1840; Charles W. Eliot, *The Harvard Classics.* New York: P.F. Collier & Son, 1909–1914.

Shen, Maxine. "Flesh & 'Blood.'" *New York Post,* June 23, 2009.

Signorotti, Elizabeth. "Repossessing the Body: Transgressive Desire in Carmilla and Dracula." *Criticism* 38, no. 4, September 1996, 607.

Slate, Joe H. "Psychic Vampires." *The Llewellyn Journal,* October 10, 2003. www.llewellyn.com/journal/article/513.

Smith, Kenny Paul. "Vampire Churches, Vampire Images, and Invented Religions." *Bulletin for the Study of Religion,* March 7, 2012.

Snyder, Scott. "Personality Disorders and the Film Noir Femme Fatale." *Journal of Criminal Justice and Popular Culture* 8, no. 3, 2001.

Stein, Atara. "Immortals and Ghosts, Oh My! Byronic Heroes in Popular Culture." Romantic Circles, University of Maryland, 2002.

Stewart, Andrew. "Number of Frequent Young Moviegoers Plummets in 2013." *Variety,* March 25, 2014.

Stuart, Anne. "Legends of Seductive Elegance," in *Dangerous Men and Adventurous Women,* ed. Jayne Ann Krentz. Philadelphia: University of Pennsylvania Press, 1992.

Sutton, Travis, and Harry M. Benshoff. "Forever Family Values," in *Horror After 9/11: World of Fear, Cinema of Terror,* ed. Aviva Briefel and Sam J. Miller. Austin: University of Texas Press, 2011.

"Take a Stake to Energy Vampires." Duke Energy, October 22, 2013. http://www. duke-energy.com/news/releases/201 3102202.asp.

Tamborini, Ronald, and James Weaver. "Frightening Entertainment: A Historical Perspective of Fictional Horror," in *Horror Films: Current Research on Audience Preferences and Reactions.* Mahwah, NJ: Lawrence Erlbaum, 1996.

Thommesen, Hanne. "Master Narratives and Narratives as Told by People with Mental Health and Drug Problems." *Journal of Comparative Social Work* 5, no. 1, 2010.

"Top Horror Movie Directors Discuss Art and Impact of Their Movies." *EarthQuiet. com,* March 8, 2009.

"*True Blood*—100% Anti-White Propaganda." Stormfront.org, January 6, 2011.

Trueman, C. N. "The Black Death of 1348 to 1350." www.historylearningsite.co.uk/ medieval-england/the-black-death-of-1348-to-1350/.

"Vampire Fan Base Runs Thicker Than Blood Online." Nielson.com, July 22, 2009.

Van Dyke, Trudi. "At Midnight Drain the Stream of Life: Vampires and the New Woman." slayageonline.com/SCBtVS_ Archive/Talks/Van_Dyke.pdf.

Varvoglis, Mario. "What Is Psi, What Isn't?" *Parapsychological Association.*

Viviano, Joanne. "Vampires and Religion in Popular Culture." *Columbus Dispatch,* October 28, 2012.

Weaver, James, and Ronald Tamborini. "Frightening Entertainment: A Historical Perspective of Fictional Horror," in *Horror Films: Current Research on Audience Preferences and Reactions.* Mahwah, NJ: Lawrence Erlbaum, 1996, 1–13.

Weisburd, David. "Vigilantism as Community Social Control: Developing a Quantitative Criminological Model." *Journal of Quantitative Criminology* 4, no. 2, June 1988.

"What's the Deal with All the Teen Vampire Movies and Books?" *Newswise*, June 9, 2010.

"When a 'Vampire' Threat Hit Close to Home." *New York Times*, December 1, 2014.

Viegas, Jennifer. "Why Blood Tastes Good to Vampires ... Bats, That Is." Discovery News, June 24, 2014. news.discovery.com/animals/endangered-species/why-blood-tastes-good-to-vampire-bats-140624.htm.

Williams, Carol J. "Column One: Dracula Is No Villain in Romania." *Los Angeles Times*, October 25, 1994.

Wilson, Natalie. "On Seduction: Seducers, Seductresses, Angels in the House, and Vampires in Shining Armor...." https://seducedbytwilight.wordpress.com/2009/08/14/.

Winnail, Douglas S. "How the Media Mold the World." *Tomorrow's World* 5, no. 1, January-February 2003.

Winnubst, Shannon. "Vampires, Anxieties, and Dreams: Race and Sex in the Contemporary United States." *Hypatia* 18, no. 3, Autumn 2003.

Wolf, Leonard. "The Transfer," in *Blood Thirst: 100 Years of Vampire Fiction*. Oxford: Oxford University Press, 1997.

Yabroff, Jennie. "A Bit Long in the Tooth." *Newsweek*, December 5, 2008.

Yabroff, Jennie. "Vampires Everywhere." *Newsweek*, December 5, 2008. http://www.newsweek.com/vampires-everywhere-83275.

Zimmer, Carl. "Young Blood May Hold Key to Reversing Aging." *New York Times*, May 4, 2014.

Books

The American Heritage Dictionary of the English Language, Fourth Edition. Boston: Houghton Mifflin, 2009

Aristotle. *The Basic Works of Aristotle*. Ed. R. McKeon. New York: Modern Library, 2001.

Aristotle. *The Rhetoric*, III. Trans. George

A. Kennedy. Cedar Lake, MI: ReadaClassic, 2010.

Asma, Stephen T. *On Monsters: An Unnatural History of Our Worst Fears*. Oxford: Oxford University Press, 2009.

Auerbach, Nina. *Our Vampires: Ourselves*. Chicago: University of Chicago Press, 1997.

Auerbach, Nina, and David Skal, eds. *Dracula*, Norton Critical Editions. New York: W. W. Norton, 1996, Preface.

Baumgardner, Jennifer, and Amy Richards. *Manifesta: Young Women, Feminism, and the Future*. New York: Farrar, Straus and Giroux, 2000.

Bender, Albert J. *Emotional Vampires: Dealing with People Who Drain You Dry*. New York: McGraw-Hill, 2009

Beresford, Matthew. *From Demons to Dracula: The Creation of the Modern Vampire Myth*. London: Reaktion, 2008.

Belanger, Michelle. *The Psychic Vampire Codex*. New York: Weiser Books, 2004.

Bernstein, Albert J. *Emotional Vampires: Dealing with People Who Drain You Dry*. New York: McGraw-Hill, 2000.

Bloomfield, Morton W. *The Seven Deadly Sins: An Introduction to the History of a Religious Concept*. East Lansing: Michigan State College Press, 1952.

Boggs, Carl, and Tom Pollard. *A World in Chaos: Social Crisis and the Rise of Postmodern Cinema*. Lanham, MD: Rowman & Littlefield, 2003.

Briefel, Aviva, and Sam J. Miller, eds. *Horror After 9/11: World of Fear, Cinema of Terror*. Austin: University of Texas Press, 2011.

Carroll, Robert Todd. *The Skeptic's Dictionary: A Collection of Strange Beliefs, Amusing Deceptions, and Dangerous Delusions*. Hoboken, NJ: John Wiley & Sons, 2003.

Carter, Margaret L., ed. *Dracula: The Vampire and the Critic*. Ann Arbor: UMI Press, 1956.

Chillicoathe Encyclopedia of Arcane Knowledge, First Edition, 1884.

Christensen, Jerome. *Lord Byron's Strength: Romantic Writing and Commercial Society*. Baltimore: John Hopkins University Press, 1993

Coleridge, Samuel Taylor. *Christabel*, first published in *Christabel; Kubla Khan, a Vision; The Pains of Sleep*, London, 1816.

Day, Peter, ed. *Vampires: Myths and Metaphors of Enduring Evil.* Amsterdam: Rodopi, 2006.

Dorey, Dawn. *From Evil to Love: As Channeled by my Spirit Guides.* Bloomington: AuthorHouse, 2014.

Douglass, Paul. *Lady Caroline Lamb: A Biography.* New York: Palgrave Macmillan, 2004

Dugdale, David C., M.D. *Medline Plus—U.S. National Library of Medicine and National Institutes of Health,* February 28, 2012.

Ehrenreich, Barbara. *Blood Rites: Origins and History of the Passions of War.* New York: Henry Holt, 1997

Faludi, Susan. *The Terror Dream: Fear and Fantasy in Post-9/11 America.* New York: Henry Holt, 2007.

Flynn, John L. *Cinematic Vampires: The Living Dead on Film and Television, from The Devil's Castle (1896) to Bram Stoker's Dracula (1992).* Jefferson, NC: McFarland, 1993.

Freud, Sigmund. *Beyond the Pleasure Principle and Other Writings.* Trans. John Reddick. London: Penguin, 2003.

Freud, Sigmund. *The Ego and the Id,* London: Hogarth Press, 1962.

Freud, Sigmund. *The Interpretation of Dreams,* 1900.

Freud, Sigmund. *Taboo and Totem.* London: Routledge and Kegan Paul, 1950.

Gordon, Joan, and Veronica Hollinger, eds. *Blood Read: The Vampire as Metaphor in Contemporary Culture.* Philadelphia: University of Pennsylvania Press, 1997.

Keats, John. *La Belle Dam Sans Merci.* London: *The Indicator,* May 10, 1820.

Lakoff, George, and Mark Johnson. *Metaphors We Live By.* Chicago: University of Chicago Press, 2003

LaVey, Anton. *The Satanic Bible.* New York: Avon, 1969.

Le Fanu, Sheridan. *Carmilla.* 1872.

Linnane, Fergus. *The Lives of the English Rakes.* London: Portrait, 2006

Lyotard, Jean-François. *The Postmodern Condition.* Manchester: Manchester University Press, 1984.

Ma, Roger. *The Vampire Combat Manual.* New York: Berkley, 2012.

Marchand, Leslie A. *Byron: A Biography.* New York: Alfred A. Knopf, 1957

Marx, Karl. *Das Kapital, Vol. 1,* 1867. www.philosophyparadise.com/quotes/marx.html.

McClelland, Bruce A. *Slayers and Their Vampires: A Cultural History of Killing the Dead.* Ann Arbor: University of Michigan Press, 2006

Mcdonald, D. L. *Poor Polidori: A Critical Biography of the Author of The Vampire.* Toronto: University of Toronto Press, 1991.

Melton, Gordon. *The Vampire Book: The Encyclopedia of the Undead.* Detroit: Visible Ink Press, 1999.

Morrison, Robert, and Chris Baldick, eds. *The Vampyre and Other Tales of the Macabre.* Oxford: Oxford University Press, 2001.

Muller, Eddie. *The Art of Noir: The Posters and Graphics from the Classic Era of Film Noir.* New York: The Overlook Press, 2004.

Nietzsche, Friedrich. *Beyond Good and Evil.* 1886.

Nietzsche, Friedrich. *Thus Spake Zarathustra,* 1885. Project Guttenberg translation by Thomas Common, 1998, University of Adelaide, *ebooks@adelaide,* Dec. 12, 2014.

Orloff, Judith. *Positive Energy.* New York: Harmony Books, 2004.

Piatti-Farnell, Laura. *The Vampire in Contemporary Popular Literature.* New York: Routledge, 2014

Pollard, Tom. *Hollywood 9/11: Superheroes, Supervillains, and Super Disasters.* Boulder: Paradigm, 2011.

Pollard, Tom. *Sex and Violence: The Hollywood Censorship Wars.* Boulder: Paradigm, 2009.

Regardie, Israel. *The Complete Golden Dawn System of Magic.* Tempe: New Falcon Publications, 1984.

Rice, Anne. *Interview with the Vampire.* New York: Random House, 1976.

Rice, Anne. *Queen of the Damned.* New York: Alfred A. Knopf, 1988.

Rice, Anne. *The Vampire Lestat.* New York: Alfred A. Knopf, 1985.

Robinson, Sara Libby. *Blood Will Tell: Vampires as Political Metaphors Before World War I.* Brighton, MA: Academic Studies Press, 2011.

Rolls, Albert. *Stephen King: A Biography.* Westport, CT: Greenwood Press, 2008.

Rossetti, William Michael, ed. *The Diary of Dr. John William Polidori, 1816.* Ithaca: Cornell University Press, 2009.

Seal, Graham. *Outlaw Heroes in Myth and History.* London: Anthem Press, 2011.

Sharaf, Myron R. *Fury on Earth: A Biography of Wilhelm Reich.* New York: St. Martin's Press, 1983.

Silver, Alain, and James Ursini, *The Vampire Film: From Nosferatu to Bram Stoker's Dracula.* New York: Limelight Editions, 1993

Slate, Joe H. *Psychic Vampires: Protection from Energy Predators and Parasites,* Saint Paul: Llewellyn, 2002.

Sloop, John L. *The Cultural Prison: Discourse, Prisoners, and Punishment.* Tuscaloosa: University of Alabama Press, 2006.

Stoker, Bram. *Dracula.* 1897.

Strack, Herman Leberecht. *The Jew and Human Sacrifice: Human Blood and Jewish Ritual, an Historical and Sociological Inquiry.* London: Cope and Fenwick, 1898, English edition, 1909.

Thorne, Tony. *Countess Dracula: The Life and Times of Elizabeth Bathory, the Blood Countess.* London: Bloomsbury, 1997.

Varma, Devendra. *The Gothic Flame: Being a History of the Gothic Novel in England: Its Origins, Efflorescence, Disintegration, and Residuary Influences.* London: Arthur Barker, 1957.

Webster, Richard. *The Complete Book of Auras,* Woodbury, MN: Lewellyn Worldwide, 2010.

Wetmore, Kevin J, Jr. *Post-9/11 Horror in American Cinema.* New York: Continuum, 2012.

Wise, Jeff. *Extreme Fear: The Science of Your Mind in Danger.* Basingstoke: Palgrave Macmillan, 2009.

Zieger, Susan. *Inventing the Addict: Drugs, Race, and Sexuality in Nineteenth Century British and American Literature.* Amherst: University of Massachusetts Press, 2008.

Index